ROGER CASEMENT

CASEMENT IN HIS THIRTIES

Roger Casement

A New Judgment

BY

RENÉ MacCOLL

W · W · NORTON & COMPANY · INC · New York

Memorandum, written by Casement when he was in Brixton Prison, awaiting his trial for Treason in May 1916, copies of which were sent to several of his close friends:

I was always an Irish separatist in heart and thought.

FOREWORD

ROGER David Casement I believe to be one of the most extraordinary men who lived in the first part of this century. Books have already been written about him; but because he was an Irishman, hanged by the British for Treason, I think that these earlier books, of which I have read most, are written for patriotic reasons, and in consequence lack objectivity.

I have tried to establish the truth about Casement. This has presented many difficulties. On one hand the biographer encounters the fanaticism of the Irish Nationalists and hero-worshippers. On the other, he comes up against the stonewall unhelpfulness of much British officialdom. The Irish, or so I think, overstate their case. The British Government, and again, this is only my opinion, have put themselves in a false position.

Roger Casement is variously regarded as a saint, a traitor, a patriot, a windbag, and an egotist who took all the wrong turnings. I am constantly asked why I chose to write my book, and in view of the above, it seems to me that the venture could scarcely be resisted.

Casement's was a highly unlikely progress over fifty years. The world applauded him as a gifted British Civil Servant. He righted wrongs. He exposed evil. His life ended in 1916, when he was hanged.

While the controversy over his guilt on the capital charge still continues with sporadic intensity, there remains also a subplot to the Casement story: was he a homosexual?

The point has to be examined by all students of the history of that time. After Casement's arrest, and soon after he had been brought to London for questioning as a suspected traitor, the British intelligence authorities came into possession of a number of Casement's diaries and account books, covering the period 1903–1911. These books revealed that Casement was a habitual pederast. They gave chapter and verse, the dates tallying exactly with his known travels and sojourns. The record was appalling.

Although the British Crown had an unanswerable case against Casement on the treason charge, and was sure that it could hang him, it decided to do two things with the seized documents: (1) It caused photographs to be made of some of the more repulsive entries in the diaries. These were then shown by British agents, on both sides of the Atlantic, to influential persons who might otherwise have been tempted to sign the various petitions for Casement's reprieve which were then in preparation. (2) The chief prosecution officer for the Crown, Sir F. E. Smith (later the first Earl of Birkenhead), the British Attorney-General, suggested to counsel defending Casement that if the defence would introduce the diaries into evidence and then plead guilty but insane, the prosecution would cooperate with that plea and would not press for the death sentence. (Casement's counsel refused this.)

Casement's Irish followers have contended to this day that the diaries were not those of Roger Casement, but were probably forged by the British, in order to denigrate their prisoner. The question has been rendered difficult of solution because the British Home Office—the government directly concerned—has, through a succession of Home Secretaries, consistently refused to make any statement confirming or denying the existence and genuineness of the diaries. Since the British edition of this book appeared in the spring of 1956, a number of questions have been addressed in the House of Commons to the spokesmen of the Home Office there; but the replies, in spite of a rather derisive atmosphere evident among members of Parliament, have remained noncommittal.

There exists in Britain an act of Parliament called the Official Secrets Act, and in writing the British version of this book I had to be most circumspect. I have seen and studied what I am perfectly satisfied is an official copy of Casement's homosexual diaries and account books—a copy of the kind which was circulated in Europe and the United States in 1916. There is no question in my own mind but that Casement was an habitual pervert. The documents which I saw were voluminous, covered a period of nearly a decade, and were completely in character with Casement's other writings, in every sort of small detail.

In addition, since the British edition of the book appeared, I have the following evidence to submit: The official (Irish Government) photostat of a document written and signed by E. Duggan, one of the signatories of the Anglo-Irish Peace Treaty of 1922. The late Mr. Duggan, made aware during the nineteen-thirties that an attempt was to be made to whitewash Casement on the homosexual issue, wrote down in his own hand the following unequivocal statement (original in the archives of the National Library of Ireland, Dublin): "Michael Collins and I saw the Casement Diary by arrangement with Lord Birkenhead. We read it. I did not know Casement's handwriting. Collins did. He said it was his. . . . The Diary was in two parts—bound volumes—repeating ad nauseum details of sex perversions—of the personal appearance and beauties of native boys—with special reference to a certain portion of their anatomies.

"It was disgusting.

"There was nothing to suggest that it was a copy of another man's diary. Collins was satisfied that it was Casement's. So was Birkenhead.

"At a later date someone who had surreptitious recourse

to the diary wrote a book—a life of Casement, I think—making public the diary. At the request of certain people here (Dublin) who didn't wish the memory of Casement or anyone associated with 1916 reviled, Birkenhead went to the publishers (who happened to be, because of his posi-tion, amenable to the suggestion that he made to them) with the result that the book was not published.

"I think unless your friend can definitely prove that the diary was a copy, to suggest, without proof, that it was, will merely advertise a thing that very few people know.

"I believe it was *his* diary, Collins and Birkenhead were satisfied it was, and remember Birkenhead was his prose-cutor and must have known.

"I should like to think it wasn't, but if our friend's theory is put forward without definite proof, he will be doing a very poor service to the memory of Casement and his associates, many of whom are in their graves, and were very dear personal friends and comrades of mine.

"E.D.

"If he is sure of his ground—certainly. If not, don't.

"E."

This is annotated by the National Library of Ireland, "E. Duggan's manuscript."

This document was prepared by Duggan when he heard that a man named William Maloney was writing a book, to be called *The Forged Casement Diaries,* which set out the proposition that the diaries were the work of British Intelligence. Maloney produced his book anyway.

In the wake of the British edition of my book, which stirred a considerable controversy in the press of Ireland, Professor Denis Gwynn, Professor of History at the Uni-versity of Cork, and himself the author of a biography of Casement, wrote in an article for an Irish newspaper: "[In 1931] I was invited to meet another of Casement's Eng-lish friends, Mr. Sidney Parry, who married Casement's cousin, Miss Gertrude Bannister. . . . Mr. Parry spoke to me about the diaries, and he gave me one piece of information which I now disclose. . . . He told me that after the war, he and his wife received information that extracts from the photographed diaries were to be published in a forthcoming book. They were naturally anxious to prevent publication of such unauthorized documents, which it would be impossible to refute adequately.

"Mr. Parry decided to approach Mr. Baldwin personally [Stanley Baldwin, then Conservative Prime Minister of Britain] and he obtained an interview. Baldwin, he told me, had been really helpful. He decided at once that, as Prime Minister, he would assume personal control of the diaries and have them registered as documents of State. They could not thenceforward even be inspected without permission in writing from the Prime Minister of the day.

"I have no reason to doubt the accuracy of what Mr. Parry told me. His intervention had, he believed, been successful, and he was genuinely grateful to Baldwin for having thus assumed personal responsibility."

The inference from this, although Professor Gwynn does not say so, is that Mr. Parry feared that the diaries were indeed genuine. At all events, he went to considerable lengths to ensure that they did not receive publication.

If the story is accurate, and Baldwin did have the diaries registered as State documents, accessible only to those who might manage to secure the Prime Minister's written authorization, it would explain why the Home Office and successive British Home Secretaries have been coy to the point of absurdity in saying that they can reveal nothing about them.

I believe that the book in which excerpts from Casement's diaries were planned to be published was one which my friend Major G. R. Singleton-Gates was engaged on, about 1926.

Word got out about the book and about what it would contain. Singleton-Gates was summoned by the Home Secretary of the day, the late Sir William Joynson Hicks, and told in no uncertain terms that if he dared go ahead with his work he would be prosecuted and almost certainly be sent to jail. Not unnaturally, Singleton-Gates dropped his project.

One last point. A microfilm has now been made of these Casement diaries and account books. It is at present resting in a safe place. In nine years' time—in 1966—the microfilm will be made available to all serious students of the Casement affair.

It saddens me that some of my findings about this man, notably his moral divagations, will cause pain not only to his surviving friends and admirers, but also to those in Ireland who know him only as a symbol and a legend.

The last thing which I want to do is to upset my Irish friends. But if they will read through to the end, they will find that the picture which I give is honest. What I have written is the truth as I see it.

The documents about Casement form a vast dossier. His own writings provide a formidable fund of material. But there is much else besides. For over two years I have been examining the record. Some of it has been scrutinised previously. Much of what appears in this book is derived from sources which were either not available to the earlier biographers, or were ignored by them. I cite particularly the documents in the Public Record Office, which provide hitherto unpublished details of Casement's early career; the valuable collection of material in the National Library of Ireland, including the moving and hitherto unpublished journal of Gertrude Bannister; the German Foreign Office documents now in St. Antony's College, Oxford; and the invaluable interviews which I have secured with those who knew Casement intimately and who still survive.

I have, of course, been to Ireland. It was thanks to the courtesy of Doctor R. J. Hayes, the Director of the National Library of Ireland, and of his able staff, that I had the opportunity of looking at the extensive Casement files which exist in the library. I am most grateful to Mr. James Joll, of St. Antony's College, Oxford, for permission to examine the microfilm copies of the documents obtained from Berlin at the end of the last war—documents which help greatly to establish some of the facts about Casement's strange visit to Germany.

My gratitude also to Mr. Robert J. Stopford, C.M.G., the nephew and executor of Mrs. Alice Green. He has given me permission to quote from the letters of Casement to his aunt. Thanks also to Mr. G. Woledge, head of the Library of Political and Economic Science at the London School of Economics (the Morel letters).

I must especially mention Mr. and Mrs. George Cadbury, of Wast Hills, Birmingham. The Cadburys, who were close friends of Casement, and who knew that I was writing a completely objective book about their old friend, made me welcome at their home and frankly discussed Casement as they remembered him. Mr. Cadbury placed at my disposal a valuable file of correspondence.

I would also like to acknowledge the help given me, in interviews, by the following: Serjeant A. M. Sullivan, Q.C., Casement's Counsel; Mr. John J. Horgan, the Cork Coroner; Mr. Bulmer Hobson, former intimate of Casement; Princess (Evelyn) Blücher; the Dowager Countess of Birkenhead; Sir Gerald Campbell, G.C.M.G.; Mr. Alfred Noyes and Dr. Michael Shanahan, of Tralee.

I owe a great debt of gratitude to Roger Machell, who spent much time and effort on the re-orchestration of the MS, and who on at least one occasion sat up all night in order to do so.

Above all I want to acknowledge the part played in the completion of this book by my wife. She has not only done a great deal of the research and provided much of the encouragement to get it written, but has by her advice and practical help made it a readable proposition.

Finally, my name is not Irish but Scotch. I hold no brief. I plead no cause. I grind no axe. I simply set out to try to establish the truth about the late Roger Casement.

RENÉ MACCOLL

I

ROGER David Casement's ancestors came from the Isle of Man to settle in Antrim, which is the county at the extreme north-eastern corner of Ireland, and which contains Belfast, to-day the capital of Northern Ireland. Although he happened to be born in a cottage at Sandycove, near Dublin, he spent most of his early years in Antrim, and went to school at the Academy of Bally-mena, a substantial town, north of Belfast and almost exactly in the middle of the county. His father, also named Roger, served in the 3rd Light Dragoons, The father was a fervent Protestant, and young Roger's mother, née Anne Jephson, quietly renounced Catholicism soon after her marriage. Casement Senior seems to have developed mild eccentricities towards the end of his life.

Young Roger was the youngest of three sons. Tom emigrated to South Africa. Charles went to Australia. The daughter, the 'Nina' of so many entries in Roger's diaries, the recipient of so many of his letters, lived on for a long time in Antrim, and eventually went to the United States. Both the parents died when the children were still small, and Roger was sent to live with relatives. It seems possible that whether they were kindly or indifferently treated by their foster parents, the children may have suffered from the sense of insecurity which nowadays we assume to be the lot of most orphans. I do not know whether young Roger's childhood was happy. If it was, then it was probably the only really happy period of his life.

After Ballymena, Casement dickered with the notion of enter-ing the Civil Service; but after a brief period of tutoring, he dropped the idea, went to Liverpool and got a clerkship in a ship-ping firm. About a year later he was appointed assistant purser in one of the Elder Dempster Line's ships and sailed for West Africa. This was in 1884, and he was twenty.

Casement at this time was in the full flush of what the Dictionary of National Biography calls his 'dark beauty'. Tall, romantic looking, full of words and charm, he was bound to create favourable attention. He had energy and muscular strength; but he was fundamentally delicate, and all his life he was dogged by various kinds of ill-health.

West Central Africa in the 'eighties was popularly—and indeed, with every reason—known as the White Man's Grave. Casement succeeded in avoiding the more lethal forms of disease which lurked there so plentifully, and it seemed certain that with any luck, he would soon be earning golden opinions.

His advent on the equatorial scene took place within only a few years of the start of the 'opening up' process, to which the formerly inaccessible African continent was to be subjected with increasing avidity and tempo, following the then recent explorations of Livingstone and Stanley; and the general realisation of the astonishing natural wealth, notably rubber, only waiting to be collected.

By a coincidence, the year in which Casement first scanned this exciting and in many ways tempting region, saw the European powers meeting at a conference in Berlin, at which all eyes were turned speculatively on Central Africa. The scramble among the Europeans to come by chunks of Africa was reaching its climax, and all concerned felt that it was necessary to formalise matters by treaties and agreed borders. But it was borne in on the larger interested powers, notably Britain, France and Germany, that one of the greatest prizes had fallen not into any of their own capacious laps, but into that of little Belgium.

This vexatious circumstance was largely due to Leopold, King of the Belgians. Leopold was a man who would have been completely at home in Threadneedle or Wall Street, but found himself sitting, not on a swivel-chair, but a throne. Undeterred by this circumstance, the King addressed himself to the world of international big business with a combination of shrewdness, foresight and ruthlessness which remains to this day a model to be followed by all businessmen, big or little.

14

Leopold had smartly possessed himself of one of the greatest prizes which even Africa had to offer. It not only included an abundance of natural treasure, but had in addition one of the world's cheapest means of communication, the enormous Congo River, for getting the treasure easily out to the markets of the world.

There it all lay, stretching from the sea at Boma and Banana in the west, over to the vast lakes—Tanganyika, Albert Edward, Kivu, Mweru—far to the east. From French Equatorial Africa in the distant northern hinterland, across to the Sudan, Rhodesia, Barotseland, German South-West Africa and Portuguese Angola far down in the south-east, south and south-west, there lay nearly one million square miles of huge mountains, huge plateaux, huge forests, and plenty of people—about 20 million Bantu—to do the wageless work. Annual mean temperatures were 79 degrees on the coast, 82 degrees in the interior, and a delightful 73 on the lower slopes of the mountains. Not at all bad, especially if you were manipulating it all from the Palace of Waelcheren, near Brussels. And the spoils! Not only rubber, but ivory, palm-nuts, palm-oil, coffee, cocoa, tobacco, copper and sulphur.

Leopold had first got on to this ultra-good thing in 1877, when Stanley[1], fresh from his explorations, had drawn so glowing a picture of the possibilities of the region, that the next year the King founded the International Association of the Congo, to develop, explore and exploit. Leopold, ready to gamble on what looked like a certainty, was generous in supplying funds from his personal resources. Stanley helpfully returned to Africa to tidy up, and all went with a swing.

Leopold rarely made a mistake. He was shrewd enough not to annex the Congo on behalf of Belgium, for that would have resulted only in unworthy jealousies on the part of the other—and stronger—nations. Instead he got the other nations, at that 1884 Berlin conference, to guarantee the Congo Free State, as the territory was now to be called, including special guarantees for such matters as the freedom of navigation on the river, and free

[1] See Appendix I.

trade and equal opportunities for the commerce of all nations. The next year the Belgian Parliament agreeably recognised Leopold as the head of the new state, and at the same time declared that any union which there might be with Belgium itself was a purely personal affair, vested in the person of the King.

Nowadays it is a commonplace for persons of substance to form themselves into one-man companies, mainly with an eye to tax problems, but there cannot be many instances of self-transformation into a one-man State. Angry protests were not long in coming; complaints that the Berlin agreements were being flouted; and that the attempts at trading by others than the Belgians anywhere in the vast Congo basin were, as one account put it, being 'vexatiously hampered'. Leopold's withers remained totally unwrung, but in 1889 the King announced that he proposed to leave the Congo to the Belgian people in his Will.

For Casement, Africa seems to have provided love at first sight. He returned to England after his first glimpse of the place, but one surmises that already he was fascinated and could scarcely wait to go back. His chance came when he obtained a place on an exploration expedition, organised by General Henry Sanford (U.S. Army, retired). In the wake of Livingstone and Stanley, African exploration was rather the done thing, and Sanford, who had money of his own, was able to join the current fashion without having to concern himself with sponsors or tiresome budget considerations.

The pattern in the Congo Free State was becoming unmistakable. Not only were there the increasingly angry complaints from the non-Belgian traders that they were the victims of discrimination in violation of the Berlin Treaty, but rumours of awful treatment of the native rubber workers were starting to seep out. Leopold prevaricated with great success for some time. While elbowing away the foreign traders, he also played the rôle of champion of native rights. He thundered against the slave trade and pointed an indignant finger against the Arab raiders from the north. For some years this policy worked. Even if outsiders suspected anything, they hesitated to say so. Meanwhile Leopold was seeing to it that his unhappy blacks were maintaining or exceeding what in a later jargon would be termed their 'norms', by resort to torture and mutilation. With a million square miles—leafy miles, at that—there was plenty of room for latitude.

Whitehall was preparing to take a long, hard look at what was afoot, but was moving with caution. In the meantime good men in the tropics were hard to find, and at this point his first public employment was proffered to the promising young man, Roger Casement. Fast preferment, it may seem, and yet even to-day, in most of the African colonies, where the white population is not only modestly numbered but sharply assessed, men of real talent and flair emerge quickly. How much more so seventy years ago, when the place was just starting to shake off savagery. As late as 1910 the white population of the entire Belgian Congo (as it had by then become) amounted to only 3,361. On July 31st, 1892, when Casement was given his first Foreign Office appointment, the white population of such a spot as the Oil Rivers Protectorate, to which he was posted, was minute.

As long as you contrived to stay alive, behaved with moderate decorum, and showed a certain amount of energy and efficiency, you were pretty sure to get along in the government service. And Casement, although his decorum may already have been suspect in private, behaved well in public, and was soon to display initiative and drive well above the average.

Casement's chief at Old Calabar, on the innermost corner of the Gulf of Guinea, was fleetingly Major Sir Claude MacDonald, a formidable soldier-intelligence-agent-diplomat, later to command the Pekin Legation Quarter during the Boxer Rebellion, and finish as Ambassador to Tokyo. MacDonald returned to London that September, and his successor, R. Moor, who took over as Acting High Commissioner of the Niger (Oil Rivers) Protectorate on September 6th, found Casement down on his staff list as a member of the Survey Department. Although this sounds a humble position, there was rather more to it than merely

17

mapping the terrain, and there is reason to suppose that from the start Casement, in those days of swift African development, was in fact a British intelligence agent, whose task was to keep an eye on the moves of the Germans, whose Cameroons Colony border was not far off, and on the French, who were alongside, in their own coastal colony at Dahomey, and north in the Sudan and their part of Nigeria. Casement also had to watch closely what was going on in the Nigerian ports, for gun-running was always a probability.

By October 1892 Casement was signing himself on official documents as 'Roger Casement, Acting Director-General of Customs'. Among the documents which he signed in this capacity were those 'constituting Ida on the Orasi River, a port of entry for the Oil Rivers Protectorate on or after September 21st, 1892', and a similar notice in regard to New Calabar, 'the Customs House for the latter being at Bakana. It has been considered advisable to establish Customs Houses in these two places, so that vessels having cargo for them may not have to go into Bonny to enter their vessels before discharging.'

So there was Casement, operating in a fairly responsible position, for his was the decision as to what should be discharged from the sea and where. He was operating, moreover, in a brand-new country, for it was only ten years earlier that Britain had acquired, through the National African Company, her first territorial rights in Nigeria; and its borders were not established by treaty until 1893 (with Germany) and 1898 (with France).

Surveyor-Customs-Officer Casement performed his duties with diligence, and two years later (September 13th, 1894) Sir Claude MacDonald distributed from the London offices of the Niger Coast Protectorate, at 14 Suffolk Street, what he termed 'a very interesting report written by Mr. Roger Casement, of the Protectorate Service, describing a journey he made in the company of the late Captain Lalor[1] from Oron, on the Cross River, in the direction of Eket, at the Kwo Ibo River. . . . Mr. Casement

[1] He died from wounds received in the BENIN disturbances of September 3rd, 1894.

also made a journey from Opoko and the Kwo Ibo River. . . . I also forward a sketch map to illustrate the attempted journey Mr. Casement made into the Inokum country. . . .' The Foreign Office copy of this report was marked for distribution to the Admiralty, War Office Intelligence Division, and 'add to general report for Parliament'.

The main object of this journey of Casement's seems to have been to find the best route for a road from Oron to Eket, a distance of about thirty-four miles. The area in which he was working was near the upper reaches of the Cross River, which flows down from near the border of the Cameroons in a scythe-like pattern and reaches the sea at Calabar. Casement wrote: 'No white man has, up to the present, ever penetrated a mile from Oron or Eket. The people of the latter district fear our coming, and to overcome this distrust and suspicion, and disinclination to admit the white man, particularly the "consul", will be the work of time and require persistent effort.' These notes form a prologue to the report which runs to ten foolscap pages, but are as nothing compared with the gargantuan documents which Casement was consistently to produce later in his career. Casement regrets his 'non-success from both Oron and Jamestown', but 'Our journey has not been altogether barren of result. We have laid the first stone in the path that I trust will ere long unite the Kwo Ibo river to Calabar . . .'

On September 22nd, 1894, MacDonald distributed another despatch with a report of Casement's journey from Okoyou to Okurike, together with another sketch map. The Foreign Office indicated the same distribution as for the earlier reports, adding 'Thank him for interesting report'.

Casement again went with a Mr. Bourchier (who had replaced Captain Lalor as his companion on these exploratory journeys). His report mentioned heavy rain. He said that the people were very friendly and 'brought presents, implored us to remain with them for the night, rolled over on their backs, addressed us as "father". We had literally to run away to prevent delay.'

He suggested that a road could be made from Uwet to the

Upper Cross River, as a 'first step towards obtaining knowledge of the country'.

On December 6th, 1894, Sir Claude MacDonald, who was revisiting the Protectorate, wrote from Old Calabar to the Under Secretary for Foreign Affairs: 'I have the honour to report as follows for the information of Lord Kimberley. On my arrival at Opobo on the 19th November, I was informed by Mr. Casement, acting Vice-Consul,[1] that the people of Ohumble, a large town, some thirty miles up the Opobo River, had for some time been inclined to give trouble, notably with regard to the practice of human sacrifice, to which they were supposed to be addicted. I myself had spoken on two occasions in the past to the chief of this town, and had pointed out to him that this practice would not be tolerated by the Protectorate Government, and that if a case occurred, the town would suffer for it.

'Mr. Casement informed me that one of the principal chiefs of the town had recently died and it would be not improbable that some of his servants and slaves would be sacrificed. From what Mr. Casement told me and from what I had ascertained from Mr. Tanner, who has been in charge of the Opobo District for the past year, I saw that the time for friendly advice had come to an end, and force or the display of it was immediately necessary.

'On the following day I left for Old Calabar, and by the first opportunity from there despatched a force of 100 men and 3 officers of the Protectorate Troops. Before leaving Opobo, I wrote Mr. Casement a despatch giving him the necessary instructions. The day before the troops left Old Calabar, I received a letter from Mr. Casement informing me that 3 persons had already been sacrificed. I regret exceedingly that this should have occurred, but everything was done that could be to hurry up the departure of the troops.

'Yesterday evening I received a letter from Mr. Casement informing me of the complete success of the operations. . . .'

This despatch, together with a report from Casement himself,

[1] In that far-off time, the Foreign Office code word for a vice-consul was 'Sidesman'.

were duly annotated (in red ink) by Lord Kimberley. Another feather in young Casement's cap.[1]

On June 30th, 1895, by now well esteemed in both London and Africa, Casement, a vigorous and sun-tanned thirty-two, a young veteran of African travel and native administration, was transferred from West to East Africa. His new post was Her Britannic Majesty's Consulate at Lourenço Marques, the primary seaport of Portuguese East Africa, on Delagoa Bay.

The transfer was significant, for the portents were of approaching trouble in South Africa. In 1881 the British had been defeated by the Boers at Majuba Hill. An uneasy truce still held, but it looked certain that war would again break out, and probably soon. In fact it was only six months after Casement had taken up his new post in Lourenço Marques that Dr. Jameson made, in December 1895, his ill-fated raid on the Transvaal. War with the Boers lay just over the horizon.

Casement's new post was of great importance. Nowadays we would, I suppose, describe Lourenço Marques as a listening-post. For the Foreign Office to appoint Casement to it was striking evidence of their confidence in him. With war against the Boers coming, Lourenço Marques assumed first-class significance as a neutral port through which Germany, and other pro-Boer powers, would be likely to send arms and thence, by the 300-mile long railway, to Pretoria, Paul Kruger's Transvaal capital; and via Lourenço Marques, Johannesburg, with all its wealth, was eighty miles closer by rail than it was from Durban. Yet another railway ran from Lourenço Marques to the border of the native protectorate of Swaziland, and this offered further interesting possibilities as a back-door to the Transvaal.

So Casement, in this tense and turbulent period, was obviously in Lourenço Marques, not merely to stamp passports, but to try to discover what might be moving in by ship and out by rail. He carefully examined the local topography, noted that the border of

[1] Lord Kimberley was then (1894-95) holding the post of Foreign Secretary for the third time in a career which had also included the Colonial Secretaryship.

friendly Natal was barely fifty miles to the south, and presently hatched a plan to be kept in reserve for the outbreak of war.

But before war actually came he was switched back again, in July 1898, to the other coast. His post this time was that of Consul for the Portuguese Possessions of West Africa, based on St. Paul de Loanda, up on the northern coast of the considerable colony of Angola. Here he was quite near to familiar territory, for the narrow neck of land connecting the Congo Free State with the Atlantic Ocean, and the mouth of the Congo itself, were only about 200 miles to the north.

Seemingly unable to resist the lure of the Congo, Casement wrote to the Foreign Office, on January 3rd, 1899, suggesting that he should revisit the Upper Congo region, which he had got to know well in 1887, chiefly with the idea that—so he urged—more trade could be achieved there, especially now that travel was notably easier than before. But the Foreign Office replied that he must wait until a certain Major Pulteney got back from a similar voyage on which he was then engaged, and it was remarked, in a rather tart minute at the Foreign Office, 'It would be better at all events that they should not both be roaming up and down the river at once.'

However, Casement did now and again get north to Boma, the capital, first of the Congo Free State and then, until the 1920's, of the Belgian Congo. His despatches of that period both from Boma and from Loanda, all written in longhand, reveal him as a man in love with the scratch of his own pen, for they habitually run to an average of twenty foolscap pages. In one of them (February 20th, 1899) he wrote: 'From my observation of the resources of civilisation in the Congo Free State, I should say it will not exhaust them (the Belgians) to provide that wherever Major Pulteney travels, he shall have occasion to see only their milder aspects: and the Lothaires[1] of varying notoriety will have

[1] Lothaire was a Belgian with a reputation for reckless cruelty. He had hanged a British trader named Stokes and gone unscathed. So much so, that Casement in the following month (March 1899) was coming to the view that Lothaire must be a Belgian Government agent, and a powerful one at that, to get away with all that he did.

22

been given the word to assume an air of almost missionary for-bearance, tempered by military fortitude.'

On March 3rd Casement concluded another of his voluminous reports with 'I make mention of these remarks by my French colleague—trivial as they may seem—as evidence that others besides Englishmen resident on the Congo have arrived at con-clusions hostile to the Congo State in its profession of disin-terested devotion to the cause of civilisation in Africa'. So Case-ment was already starting the campaign against Leopold which was to culminate a few years later in world-wide uproar.

II

CASEMENT's preoccupation with the Congo was again inter-
rupted when, in October 1899, the head of steam which had been
steadily building up in South Africa, finally blew out, and the
Boer War began.

Obviously Casement was the man for Lourenço Marques, and
he was instantly posted back there. He went ostensibly on holiday,
visiting his former post on a 'pleasure trip'. In reality his cyphered
instructions from the Foreign Office were that he was on 'a special
mission to discover if munitions of war are passing through
Lourenço Marques to the Transvaal'. Casement evidently knew
the local form, for he started off, realistically enough, by handing
over a £500 bribe to the chief of the Lourenço Marques customs
bureau, in exchange for a promise to tip him off on any ship's
manifests which seemed to hint at weapons. The official was complaisant enough, but the ultimate finding seemed to be that not
very much in the way of arms was coming in that way. Casement
sent a cypher cable to London (February 5th, 1900) from Capetown: 'Secret. My conviction is that the best course for H.M.G.
to ensure stoppage of German route for contraband of war for
the Transvaal, is for the military authorities at Natal to send
expedition through British territory and Swaziland, and seize and
hold or destroy Netherlands Railway' (the one connecting
Lourenço Marques with Pretoria). 'I am prepared to give personal
assistance and to bring several useful helpers from Lourenço
Marques.'

This was the plan that Casement had had in mind since his
original tour of duty at Lourenço Marques.

That Casement was planning to sabotage the efforts of Imperial
Germany to aid an enemy of Britain was sufficiently ironic a
circumstance, in view of later events; but it was as nothing to the

fact that Casement (March 5th, 1900) indignantly reported to the Foreign Office that the Boer Government was attempting to seduce Irish prisoners of war, whom they had captured, to fight against England.

1,078 Irish soldiers, he explained, were then in prison camps near Pretoria, most of them taken in the action at Nicholson's Nek, during the disaster of Lombard's Kop, early in the war.

'The attempts' (at suborning the men) went on Casement, 'were, of course, futile. . . . Only another proof of the methods of those in power at Pretoria to leave no weapon untried to induce men loyal to their Queen to be false to their own allegiance, and to be false to themselves, and to dishonour their Oaths.' In the same message he referred to the attempted formation by the Boers of an 'Irish Brigade' and to a Major MacBride who was supposed to lead it.

This was from Roger Casement who, sixteen years later, was to be hanged in London for High Treason—the charges concerning which were mainly based on the fact that he had been found guilty of trying to do, among the Irish prisoners of war in the German prison camps of the 1914–18 war, precisely that which apparently evoked such indignant contempt in him during the Boer War. It even seems possible that he may have got the notion of forming a turncoat 'Irish Brigade' from the very Boers towards whom he professed such contemptuous scorn in 1900.

Before going down to Capetown, Casement had written to Whitehall saying that he felt he could do no further good in Lourenço Marques. There not only seemed to be little contraband passing through, but the purpose of his mission had now become quite clear to everyone in the place and even if arms shipments were to turn up, it was unlikely that he would any longer be in a position to get to know about them. Someone wrote across the bottom of this letter: 'He might just as well be at Capetown. Tell him he may go.'

So Casement did go, aboard H.M.S. *Racoon*.

Six months later Casement sent in his expenses account for the period December 29th, 1899, to May 7th, 1900, covering his stay in Lourenço Marques, Durban and Capetown. He charged £2 a day for Lourenço Marques. This was presently queried by the Foreign Office, which reminded Casement that £1 only was the normal consular allowance. Casement came back with the classic plea of 'exceptionally expensive conditions', and he seems to have got away with it.

Casement, whose activities in Capetown for the rest of the war were discreetly cloaked under the nondescript official phrase of 'special duties', now gave a foretaste of the kind of fiasco with which his path was to be littered as the years wore on. He was forever sketching wonderful plans. While the mood was on him, and while the particular plan still appeared to retain some chance of success, Casement was in it heart and soul, bubbling with energy and enthusiasm; but almost always something would go wrong, and then his hopes and drive would fade.

A case in point was his scheme for blowing up the railway connecting Lourenço Marques with Pretoria. In April 1900, Casement wrote to Sir Martin Gosselin at the Foreign Office, giving his opinion that the natives of the Congo were being cruelly exploited by the callous whites, and quoting the testimony of missionaries and non-Belgian traders to this effect.

Then he went on: 'I am still kept here [Capetown] in connection with the Delagoa Bay question, which I think might have been solved long ago, and may still be settled by the military. Sir Alfred Milner [later Lord Milner, High Commissioner in South Africa] has asked me to stay on until a final decision has been come to, and it is possible I may take a more active part than by mere assisting in discussions. I hope so, and I conclude there would be no objection on the part of the Foreign Office to my giving the matter any personal help I could—even if by doing so I must remain still longer absent from Loanda and the Congo. I feel it somewhat on my conscience being so long away from my post; but then the question to be settled here is so urgent and of such transcendent importance that any help that can be given here is of greater moment than anything I could possibly do to help British coloured people on the Congo.'

The Foreign Office comment on this was, 'Interesting. Put with other papers . . . and inform him that there is no objection to his remaining on in South Africa as long as his services are required by Sir A. Milner.'

Alas, on July 5th Casement ruefully reported to Lord Salisbury, by then Foreign Secretary, on the failure of his expedition to blow up the railway bridge and wreck the line. 'The fact that the expedition in question has entirely failed to act its part does not, I think, reflect upon the feasibility or wisdom of the plan proposed. . . . The failure I attribute first to the delay in sending the force from Capetown, and in the second place to what seems to have been a series of misunderstandings among the military men in authority, which resulted in the recall of the expedition from Eshowe in Zululand. . . . Other minor causes of possible non-success no doubt existed, such as insufficient knowledge of the country. . . . When I first proposed that a force should be sent to the neighbourhood of Komatipoort to seize and hold the military line and bridge at that place, and if necessary destroy the latter, there was only a very small Boer commando there. . . . On March 31st I drew up at Capetown a memorandum embodying my views . . . which was despatched to Lord Kitchener. In April I gathered that steps were being taken under the direct orders of Lord Roberts to put into execution the project . . . practically as I had proposed it.

'The memorandum suggested that a force of 500 men (mounted), with cannon, should be despatched through Zululand to Komatipoort. . . . A copy of the memorandum was subsequently handed at his request to Lord Milner, whose personal efforts to ensure the attainment of the end in view, I should like to say, were entitled to a successful issue.

'Early in May the matter had been approved; Strathcona's Horse, 540 strong, had been selected . . . 340 were embarked for Durban at the end of May . . . Colonel Steele, with two squadrons, their horses, pack animals, rifles, rifle ammunition and blasting materials, embarked at Capetown on May 28th for Kosi Bay, but ostensibly for Durban. I accompanied this force at the wish of both the High Commissioner and the Commanding Officer....'

The painstaking account continued to the tune of another eleven foolscap pages, and concluded, 'If worth doing at all, it was worth doing well; and the fact that it was not done well should be attributed to others than those who made the recent attempt.'

The Foreign Office comment on this was: 'If the bridge had been blown up, it would have been repaired in a fortnight. Smuggling by road would not have been stopped. There was another question from the very beginning. The small destroying force could not have held Komatipoort had the Boers sent a large force there. The utility of the destruction would then have been measured by the time it would have taken to rebuild the bridge.'[1]

For Casement the war was ending and he was awarded the first of several well-merited tokens of official gratitude which he was to accept from time to time at the hands of the government which employed him. He got the Queen's South African Medal. Then he said good-bye to Capetown, and on August 20th, 1900, was transferred to Kinchassa, up`the Congo. That was more like it—he was back again on the Congo, and able at last to get down to a close investigation of what was going on behind the mask of forest and mountain and distance.

As early as that year, 1900, rumours must have been reaching King Leopold, whose intelligence services, as might be expected,

[1] The expedition, even before its two parts had effected a junction, was recalled by Sir Alfred Milner, and never got within striking distance of the objective. Casement, a civilian, was presumably asked to accompany the expedition because it was assumed that he had a good working knowledge of the terrain. Some time after this little failure, there came an epilogue in the shape of a letter to Casement from the adjutant of Strathcona's Horse, asking him to return or account for the sum of £100 which Casement had apparently been lent in connection with the expedition. Annoyingly, Casement's reply to this demand was forwarded by the Foreign Office to the War Office, and I have not been able to see it.

were efficient, that young Mr. Casement was not the sort of consul who would be content to sit out his two or three years in Kinchassa, contemplating the jungle through the bottom of a whisky glass. Casement travelled, made notes, talked to people, sent reports. The Belgians, some of whom greeted him with surly hostility and others with cultivated charm, became increasingly aware that something was in the wind. In any event, when Casement was on his way back to London on leave that autumn, he broke his journey in Brussels at the request of Leopold.

Casement was invited by His Majesty to what he called 'breakfast at one o'clock', although I suspect here some slight misunderstanding of French which may have caused him to confuse '*déjeuner*' and '*petit déjeuner*'. Those present at the meal included the Queen, Princess Clementine, the Duke of Aosta, Prince Victor Napoleon and various court dignitaries, to all of whom the King spoke before arriving at Casement. During this first meeting the King sounded rather on the defensive about the Congo; but he asked Casement to come back and see him the next day.

On October 11th the two really got down to business, and had a discussion about the Congo, *tête-à-tête*, lasting an hour and a half. Casement, in his subsequent report to the Foreign Office, said that the King did most of the talking—a state of affairs never greatly to Casement's liking.

'His Majesty referred to the reported outrages on the Congo, which had provoked in England, as also in Belgium, hostile comment, sometimes well-founded, upon the Congo Administration, since it was impossible to have always the best men in Africa, and indeed the African climate seemed frequently to cause deterioration in the character.'

Finally the King expressed the hope that in administering the Congo he would not tread on other toes, notably British, in trying to do his best for his own subjects. And Casement ended by saying: 'I trusted I should always be found trying to facilitate good relations between my countrymen and His Majesty's people,' and added that he felt 'sincerely grateful for the gracious manner in which His Majesty had received me in Brussels'.

Foreign Office comment on this report: 'We might thank Mr. Casement for what seems a very good account of his conversations.'[1]

In January 1901, when Casement returned to the Congo after his home leave (and it cost him only £11 to travel from London to Lisbon, including *wagon-lit* accommodation from Paris onwards), he was approaching the first great climax of his professional career.

The Congo was in a rushing boom. The territory was being developed, and to some extent modernised, everywhere. Trading posts were multiplying for hundreds of miles up the banks of the river, and for other hundreds of miles inside the bush of the remote hinterland. But the prospect of quick millions in a hitherto unexploited part of the world produced, as has usually been the case, an exhibition of the least attractive side of human nature.

The brawling, boozing, whoring, free-for-alls that marked the nineteenth century gold rushes of Australia and California involved only members of the white race. If a couple of hundred avaricious and unscrupulous fortune-seekers got frozen or drowned or shot, it was the luck of the game. But in the Congo, while the motives were the same, the possibilities for cold-blooded cruelty, against luckless blacks who had no one to speak for them or defend them, were vastly greater. There, in that huge, hidden dungeon, the torturers could go about their activities, happy in the knowledge that the cries of the victims were unlikely to be heard by passers-by. The monstrous assembly-line which spewed out the rubber was very simply worked. The only machinery required was a supply of guns, knives and whips. Labour presented no problem. Possibly the treatment of the Incas by the silver-

[1] Mr. Bulmer Hobson tells me that at one of Casement's meetings with King Leopold, either then or subsequently, the King produced a blank cheque, signed by himself, and offered it to Casement, the implication of course being that Casement should fill it in for whatever he liked in return for keeping silence about the Congo. Hobson says that Casement indignantly spurned the bare-faced bribe. I have not so far come across any other reference to this episode.

seeking Spaniards provides some sort of historical parallel to what was going on in the Congo when Casement returned there. But at least the Spaniards were operating several hundred years before the enlightened and liberal era which was supposed to usher in the present century.

But word of what might be afoot among the rubber plantations was leaking out. E. D. Morel[1] was getting into full stride back in England, with a rip-roaring campaign against abuses of the African natives. He brought to the task all of his journalistic flair, and was beginning to obtain a respectful hearing with a stream of pamphlets on the subject. Later on, in 1904, he was to found the Congo Reform Association, which played a leading part in the later stages of the battle. Morel also stimulated a similar movement in the United States. He based many of his more telling allegations on evidence which he obtained from missionaries and traders.

Parliament was also taking notice; and one way and another the climate in England was to be highly receptive for Casement's own devastating report. The motives of some of those who attacked Leopold's Congo Administration may well have been based on other than strictly humanitarian grounds. If it is felt that a man is hogging all the business opportunities, and won't listen to conventional protests, then the fact that he is highly vulnerable on the score of his bad treatment of the native labour force may prove a heaven-sent chance to get him on ethical grounds.

But no such considerations seem to have entered Casement's mind. There is no reason to suppose that his uncomfortable and sometimes hazardous jungle journeys, and his build-up of the case against Leopold were ever actuated by anything but moral indignation and an admirable determination to right the wrongs of unfortunates who had no means of helping themselves.

Of course Casement was duty-bound to concern himself with the trading situation. He was, after all, a consular official; and Whitehall would undoubtedly have taken a poor view of one of their representatives in so sensitive an area who neglected to send

[1] See Appendix I.

31

reports regarding harm that might be done to British commercial interests. That stood to reason.

But while Casement performed his duty as required in regard to the commercial aspects of the matter, it seems sure that his energies and enthusiasm were primarily enlisted on behalf of the plight of the blacks. It was the fact that some of these blacks were British subjects which gave the Foreign Office the excuse of having Casement there at all. Some ill-advised natives had found their way to the Congo from various British West African possessions, and it was while investigating complaints of false imprisonment, starvation and beating of these men, that Casement was able to travel freely and at the same time to get an overall picture of what was going on.

There have been allegations that Casement's examination of the Congo situation was far too brief and cursory for so important a matter, and that the whole tone and tenor of his subsequent report was wildly exaggerated and based on highly debatable evidence. I am speaking now not of the heated and immediate self-defence which was naturally forthcoming from the Belgians, but of comments made to me in these last two or three years by reputable British officials who were discussing the whole affair in the calm and dispassionate atmosphere of half a century later.

In any case, by the beginning of February 1901, he was moving up-country. He had to make difficult river crossings, was frequently drenched in tropical peltings of rain, and, worn out as evening came, sought sleep in often wretched conditions, after a meal of sopping biscuits and rum.

He made his way—sometimes having rows with his carriers—through places with names such as Nzungi, Luasi, Kimfuma and Mdadisi, and eventually came to Matadi, an important town on the right bank of the Congo, about 100 miles from the sea, on the border of Portuguese Angola.

Through the spring and summer of 1901 Casement was hard at work, travelling almost incessantly, afoot, by donkey and sometimes by Congo steamer. He visited Brazzaville, Philippeville and Boma, the capital, as well as the smaller places. As he went he sent back reports, and far off in Whitehall, the Foreign Office files were thickening as the long-hand letters of 'Mr. Casement' came in. Curiosity started to quicken, and the name of 'Mr. Casement' appeared with increasing frequency in the In and Out trays.

On went Mr. Casement, his carriers lugging in his wake long boxes, demi-johns, despatch boxes, bags, bedding, cooking pots, cutlery, teaspoons, tablespoons and teapots. That August his sphere of influence was considerably widened when he was notified of his appointment as Consul for a part of the French Congo, in addition to his other duties.

Early in September Casement left for England again, this time on sick leave. He stayed at the Wellington Club in Grosvenor Place from November 3rd until early December, having consultations with the Foreign Office.

It was probably on this visit that Casement first met Edmund D. Morel, with whom he became fast friends and a fellow crusader. Conan Doyle described their meeting, with a touch of hyperbole, as 'the most dramatic scene in modern history'. Morel, like Casement, had started out as a clerk in a Liverpool shipping office. By the age of twenty-four he was constantly being sent by his firm on business missions to Belgium, because being half-French, he spoke that language fluently. On these missions he gradually found out what was happening in the Congo. In his indignation he threatened an exposure, whereupon his firm, not unnaturally, dismissed him.

Undaunted, Morel started his crusade in a paper called *The West African Mail*. This soon attracted Casement's attention, and from Africa he wrote to Morel, 'Chuck up everything, and devote your life to it. It is the most monstrous thing that has been done in the world!'

Their meeting followed soon afterwards, and the two took to each other immediately.

Now Casement went over to Dublin, stayed at the famous Shelbourne Hotel on St. Stephen's Green, and was back in London for Christmas. He completed his leave in Ballycastle, County

Antrim, in February 1902, and by May was back in Boma. Apparently the Foreign Office had agreed to an increase in his local establishment, for his reports were now written—the final drafts, at all events—by a clerk.

A pleasant instance of the necessity for maintaining the diplomatic niceties, however difficult the general situation, was afforded by a minor, and in any other circumstances, routine, event, in the summer of 1902. On July 5th, Monsieur E. Wangermée, Vice Governor-General of the Congo Free State, wrote officially from his office in Boma, to inform 'M. le Consul R. Casement'—'I have the honour to thank you very warmly for your presence at the Te Deum and the celebrations held on the occasion of the seventeenth anniversary of the proclamation of the founding of the Congo Free State.

'I take this opportunity to underline to you how much I appreciate the excellent relations which exist between the Local Government of the Congo Free State and the Representative in Africa of the Government of Her Britannic Majesty.

'Please accept, M. le Consul, the assurance of my very high regard.'

That Casement, almost ready to stagger and confound the Congo Administration with his revelations, should attend a solemn thanksgiving service to celebrate the anniversary of the founding of that administration, is high comedy. And that Monsieur Wangermée, the Vice Governor-General, who by this time could have had few illusions as to what Casement was about, should talk of the excellent relations which existed between them, was at least a tribute to his irreproachable diplomatic training.

That August, Casement was back in Sao Paulo do Loanda, and from there he telegraphed to the Foreign Office, asking for sanction to close the Boma Consulate, and then to visit Matadi and Leopoldville, before making another journey to the most distant reaches of the Upper Congo. The Foreign Office duly agreed to all this, but on September 5th Casement, still in Loanda, telegraphed, 'I have abandoned journey to Upper Congo, propose return Europe, leave Loanda by mail packet of 10th September for Lisbon. Existing consular accommodation Boma most uncomfortable, rendering difficult work there. I think it better to hasten plan for house than go journey interior. Consulate at Boma closed. No local representative. Nightingale will attend to correspondence forwarded here. Please sanction.'

This, to say the least, was odd. Casement was (1) asking his superiors in London for permission to close a consulate, after he had already done so, (2) telling them he did not intend to carry out an important mission which he had himself suggested, and (3) telling them that he proposed to leave for Europe in a few days, although he had been back at his post from his last European leave for only six months.

On top of all that, he seemed to prefer covering the Congo from a neighbouring colony, because he found the working conditions in Portuguese Loanda more comfortable than those in Boma. Finally he said that he thought that personal details about his housing accommodation were more important than the Upper Congo journey—which would, presumably, have yielded significant new material concerning the main task for which he had returned to Africa.

Not surprisingly, one of those who read this message when it reached the Foreign Office, wrote across it: 'I really think the poor man must have gone off his head. There is nothing, I presume, to do but sanction his return. A.N.C. 10 September.'

Another wrote: 'As Mr. Casement's application was pressing, we have telegraphed that he can leave. He is a good man, has had fever, and he would not telegraph like this unless it was really necessary. F.A.C. Sept. 6th.'

Lord Lansdowne himself, who had by then succeeded Lord Salisbury as Foreign Secretary, initialled the papers. Whether he felt that fever or dementia was at work is not disclosed.

Pressing or not, something must have happened to change the mind of the always unpredictable Casement, and far from catching the Lisbon packet on September 10th as he was now free to do, he stayed on for another month, during which he weighed in first with an enormous despatch about trade in the Chiloango River region, and next (October 4th) with another, of equally dismaying proportions, concerning the Kasai Syndicate.

Once those were out of the way—possibly as a sop to his conscience for having played the gad-fly—he actually embarked on October 8th, and by December of 1902 he was again back in London.

It was soon February 1903, and time to go back to the Congo. This was to be the last round. Well briefed by the Foreign Office, and seen off at Euston by a party of well-wishers, he sailed in the *Jebba*. The weather was bad and the ship rolled; but Funchal was reached, and there Casement gambled gently in the casino. On March 18th he resumed his onward journey to the Canaries. He was in a bad state and had some poor nights due to what he described as 'semi-dysentery'. He was also most vexed at the aspect and behaviour of some German fellow-passengers, whom he described as 'vile'. Late in March he sailed from the Canaries. The ship encountered what Casement thought were tornadoes. He lay on his bunk reading Marie Corelli's *The Soul of Lilith*.

At last, in mid-April, he reached Kabinda, a seaport in a little pocket of Portuguese territory just north of the mouth of the Congo (the great mass of Angola lies south of this river). Casement was greatly shocked at the reports, which he had just read, of the death, in a Paris hotel, of Sir Hector MacDonald[1]—not to be confused with his former chief Sir Claude. Sir Hector had committed suicide by shooting himself. Casement was sleeping badly, he was troubled by mosquitoes and centipedes and heat. He went to Boma, and there was a miserable interlude during which he played billiards, lay gasping on his bed in the heat, and waited for instructions.

In the middle of May, he moved up-river from Boma to Matadi, and started his final investigation. Through June, July and August he was in a frenzy of work, interviewing witnesses, writing notes, drafting his reports for London. Occasionally he stayed up until 4 a.m. talking to the men who came in to tell him

[1] See Appendix I.

of the atrocities, but they were sometimes, as he complained, a 'rotten, bad lot'.

In June he moved into the uplands; drenching mists and cool winds replaced the enervating coastal heat. By this time Casement was writing thousands of words every day, and his reports were being sent off regularly to London; Nos. 11, 12, 13, all of them weighty.

We have before us now a portrait of Casement in the time of his greatness. He was caught up in his task and absorbed and fascinated by everything about him. 'What I am writing now would make a big book, if published,' he wrote; and besides travelling, interviewing, observing, note-taking, talking and sifting, with his energy and stamina at their best, he was aware of the irrelevant things—the hippo, the elephant, the antelope, the buffalo and pelican. He saw an ibis flying above him—'a lovely fellow in full flight'. But he was appalled by the terrible human de-population which had taken place, for he had been to these same regions many years before and could make comparisons.

In July he was at Chumbiri, near the border of the French Congo, and the monotonous diet of chicken and custard was not to his liking. He suffered headaches, stomach upsets and other minor ills. He flew into a rage when his safari could not be resumed on time one morning, because one of his chief carriers was dallying with a local charmer. He was, he complained, delayed in starting by the infallible cause of all delay and every miscarriage since Eve upset Adam's apple—'Curst Woman!'

Exhausted and often taking large doses of quinine to keep himself going, Casement plugged on. He was horrified by the tales the natives brought him, cast down by·their mutilations and their fear of the white man. The people ran away as he approached, and he spent much time assuring them that he came as a friend.

Meanwhile Lord Lansdowne, in response to growing restiveness in and out of Parliament about the rumoured misdeeds in Africa, sent off a note to Brussels which, while written with due regard to diplomatic protocol, spoke of reports that systematic cruelty and oppression were being condoned by the Congo

Administration. The Note added that it was not yet known to what extent these reports were true.

This drew a reply which presumably gave someone in Brussels, conceivably Leopold himself, a good deal of pleasure in drafting. It reminded the British, in effect, of the biblical remark about beams and motes, drew attention to blots on the British record of colonial administration, and ended up by jeeringly asking to be shown the proof of the allegations against the Congo Administration.

That was where Casement came in and, stung, doubtless, by the sardonic rejoinder from Brussels, Whitehall must have turned with renewed and lively anticipation to see when his final report, containing all the proof that anyone could need, would be ready.

By then Casement was on his last lap. In the middle of August he was at Ikenge, and again he was horrified at the extent to which the population had been decimated since he was there in 1887. The villages had collapsed in ruin, the jungle was encroaching, and where once there had been a community of several hundred people, now only eighty survived.

He found a land laid bare, a people terrorised and banished. Casement was beside himself. 'Poor wretched souls!' he wrote. It seems beyond dispute that during much of this expedition Casement was displaying great courage. For he was making his way about Belgian-dominated territory, much of it very isolated. He was alone, except for some native carriers. With large stakes to be played for, there was always the possibility that the Belgians would try to arrange a regrettable incident. The tipped canoe; the strange disappearance off a river steamer; the tree that fell suddenly in a tropical storm; such hazards of the trail were entirely feasible. But Casement, it seems, accepted these occupational threats without fuss.

On August 29th Casement arrived at Bongandanga, where he was horrified anew by the sight of the remnants of the local population, guarded by armed men as if they were convicts, and kept at forced labour in the rubber plantations. Men, women and children were kept in chains when they staggered back from their work. Casement described it as 'infamous and shameful'. To cap all, the local commissioner, a Monsieur Lejeim, saw fit to organise some native dancing in honour of Casement's visit. That, as Casement later remarked, 'took the cake'.

Three days later it was Casement's thirty-ninth birthday. His mood was bitter. He was near exhaustion and he was feeling ill. His nerves were on edge and he was in a fury of indignation over the callous treatment of the blacks by the Belgians. After the fine start of his career he might have felt that the impetus had been lost and that he was perhaps in danger of becoming a forgotten man.

He had an intense conviction that he was doing important work—but did others share his views? There he was, stuck away in the heart of Africa, sending off his reports, hoping for the best; he was on the threshold of middle-age; all might be for nothing; miserably he noted, 'Poor old woman died on the way back from work....' A bitter birthday.

By September 5th he was headed downstream, his dossier fairly bursting with information. His mercurial mood changed. He met a river steamer, which stopped and gave him a batch of his London mail. His morale soared and he jauntily hoisted his consular pennant. London was displaying by now the keenest interest, and all doubts as to the usefulness of his labours could be banished.

Next day at Boginda a boy was brought in to see him; his hands had been amputated by black soldiers at the direction of the Belgians. Casement, infuriated, sat down and wrote a letter to the Vice Governor-General (the sophisticated M. Wangermée had by now been succeeded by a M. Fuchs). The latter was strongly worded.

Casement said that the letter would give pain to M. Fuchs— and it gave him pain to write it. But there could be no cure, he pointed out, without pain.

At the start of October he reached Loanda, where he struck up a sudden friendship with the German Consul, a Herr Doeberitz. For the next few weeks he saw Doeberitz almost every evening, and had long talks with him about the lot of the African native and other matters; Casement was feeling seedy most of the time, but continued to produce his usual formidable output of writing. Reports on Africa, 40, 41, 42, 43 went off; still he kept at it.

On November 4th Casement received a long telegram from the Foreign Office, telling him to go home and complete his report in London. On the 6th he sailed.

Casement reached London on December 1st, 1903. He went immediately to the Foreign Office, but was apparently ruffled by his reception. He had a cold coming on, and he referred darkly to his official superiors, in a letter he wrote at the time, as 'a gang of stupidities'.

However, things improved. Lord Percy saw him and was kind. Then Lord Lansdowne, at Lansdowne House, was, reported Casement later, 'very nice', and, having listened to his description of the Congo situation, commented 'proof of the most painful kind, Mr. Casement'.

It was now a case of getting his reports into readable shape. The Foreign Office provided him with a team of assistants for this formidable task. Casement started to dictate his report to what he described as 'typers', and was soon dashing off between 4,000 and 5,000 words a day. On December 3rd, Casement received a letter from a Foreign Office official, informing him that a number of people had been asking if they could have talks with Casement about the Congo. The important name among these information-seekers was Mr. Fox-Bourne, a well-known righter of wrongs. 'I have naturally always replied,' the writer said, 'that we should not keep you in a tower of brass, and that anybody could write to you. But I have never said that there was no objection to anyone discussing with you the situation in the Congo. That is entirely a matter for you to settle. There are many ways of discussing the situation in the Congo. It is quite obvious, as I have said to some of the inquirers, that you are not at all likely to give them by way of interviews, the substance of the Report you are about to write for H.M.'s G.'

This was presumably intended as a tactful reminder to Casement that he was not supposed to let anyone know what was in his report before the Foreign Office chose to release it. It may have come to the ears of his colleagues in Whitehall that Reuters had been badgering Casement for interviews.

On the same date, Casement received another letter, signed by the same official, which rather' obviously struck the note of scepticism about Casement's Congo findings, which was to recur later on. In this Casement was requested to clear up 'a few conundrums' and, rather peremptorily, was asked 'How did it come about that so many cases of ill-treatment of British subjects came to your notice in the eight weeks or so before you wrote your despatch No. 10 of 1902, and that, practically, none came before or after?'

Finally the writer says, flatly, 'There constantly occurs in the MS of your despatches the name of a Belgian official which looks like COCU. Is it possible that this is really his name?'

Casement worked on at his report, and Lord Lansdowne may have permitted himself a slight smile as he pondered his coming rejoinder to the taunting Belgian Note, which had remained for so long unanswered. In the evenings Casement relaxed, dining either at the houses of friends or alone at some restaurant, such as the Comedy. By December 10th, the report was nearing completion. E. D. Morel came to call. Casement found him as 'honest as the day'. They dined together at the Comedy, talked until two o'clock the next morning, and then Morel went to sleep on a sofa in the study.

By December 12th the report was finished. Casement took it round to the Foreign Office. On the 16th he was again there with some further footnotes and he took umbrage at the official with whom he dealt. 'An abject piffler,' he describes him. The Foreign Office showed signs of indecision and even 'despondency', and Casement was gloomy. He dined with Sir Lionel Cust at a club.

Just before Christmas when he was staying at The Savoy, Denham, Bucks, the home of one of his greatest friends, Richard Morton, and where he was a constant visitor, the *Daily Mirror* carried a flattering piece about Casement. On December 22nd Casement went over to Dublin, and then north to Belfast. He reached Ballycastle on Christmas Eve, but the return of the wanderer proved a sore disappointment. His train was late, there was nobody at the station to meet him, all was cold and dark. The Christmas gathering of surviving relatives and friends was not at all to his taste. Christmas Day itself was miserable. He worked moodily at revisions of his report—but next day there came a cheering letter from the Foreign Office. They said his report was admirable in style and in substance, so Casement took heart. He got his revisions finished, but the weather was biting, he had a cold, and stayed in bed. By New Year's Eve he was back in London.

The New Year opened well. Casement went to the Foreign Office and was well complimented on his report by several officials, among them the 'abject piffler'. Later the same day Casement met the famous adventurer-romantic Cunninghame Graham, perhaps to try to enlist his support.

On January 2nd all was bustle and expectation. Casement was all over the place, discussing the Congo, dashing off memoranda, and urging that Britain should resume her extra-territorial jurisdiction in the Free State Territory. There was lunch and animated conversation at the Carlton Grill. Casement went down to spend the next day with Joseph Conrad and his wife on their farm at Hythe; and on the 6th, on his way to Liverpool, he encountered Lloyd George in the train. They had a long talk about the Congo.

At the end of that January Casement wrote to Morel saying that he was anxious to press ahead with the formation of a Congo Reform Association, since they were then merely an ill-organised band of individuals all trying to attack 'one powerful, wealthy league, with a Sovereign State for execution and a King as chairman', and that their efforts necessarily tended to be dissipated.

Until then Casement had received fairly enthusiastic but haphazard support from such existing bodies as the African Society, with headquarters in Albemarle Street, W., and Grattan Guiness' Regions Beyond Mission.

The response to his idea for a brand-new organisation was on the whole good, although there were one or two faint-hearts.

Sir Charles Dilke,[1] for example, proved a disappointment. His answer, complained Casement, was 'feeble and illogical', and Casement suspected that Dilke and the other objectors were not anxious to see their influence with the anti-slavery bodies usurped. W. T. Stead was assured that the sole aim of the C.R.A. was to enlighten systematically and continuously public opinion in England and abroad on the condition of the Congo people—'wretched people, panic-stricken people'.

Soon Casement and Morel were busy collecting big names for the C.R.A. and joyfully egging each other on ('The Bishop of Liverpool! Lord Aberdeen as President! Good, good, good!' crowed Casement). The C.R.A. had its public birth (Casement's phrase) on March 23rd and the prospects looked encouraging.

Casement's moment of triumph and acclaim arrived when, on February 15th, 1904, 'The Congo State' was issued as the 'Report of a Parliamentary Paper'. After a brief introduction in the shape of a letter from Lord Cromer to Lord Lansdowne, the bulk of the document consisted of 'the Report by Mr. Casement, British Consul at Boma, giving an account of his journey, June 5th—September 15th, 1903'. A brief and automatic Belgian denial came the next day, but made little impression. Lord Lansdowne saw to it that the most was made of Casement's report. Not only was it sent at once to Brussels, together with a cool covering memorandum, and splashed in the British press, but copies were also despatched to His Majesty's diplomatic missions in twelve European countries, with instructions that nothing should be left undone in obtaining for it the utmost publicity.

The report spoke of indiscriminate and callous shooting of natives by the black soldiery of the Congo Free State; there were instances of mutilation (principally the cutting off of the hands of natives adjudged to have committed some misdemeanour); mass conscription for the Army; forced labour; gross underpayment of the natives for their arduous services—and sometimes no payment at all.

[1]See Appendix I.

Casement also complained of women and children being seized as hostages in order to force the men of the various districts to work still harder, and of groups of women being kept prisoner, manacled together, in squalid prison sheds. Prisoners were systematically starved and, if they survived their terms, emerged terribly emaciated. Hippopotamus-hide whips were constantly resorted to, and the resultant weals on the bodies of the surviving recipients were a common sight.

It was admitted by Casement in the report that some of the worst instances which he cited were hearsay—but hearsay which he himself believed implicitly. And he pointed out that nearly all of the excesses which he listed were performed not by the whites but by the black troops (Casement always referred to them as 'sentries') under their control. But this point, alleged Casement, was no excuse whatever for the Congo Free State authorities. They were well aware of what was going on, and it was their policy and their thirst for profits from the rubber which led directly to the atrocities.

In sum: here was a thoroughly callous organisation which was so obsessed by the need for swift riches that its members were prepared to condone and wink at the most dreadful neglect of the ordinary human rights of the natives, and to accept killings, torture and general brutalisation of the blacks as a necessary and everyday concomitant of their commercial activities.

The effect was tremendous. The details of the report caused an international shock of horror, the totality of which we may find it hard to grasp to-day.

III

OUR world to-day is unfortunately scarred by so many recent and contemporary evidences of man's inhumanity to his fellows, that the uproar over what was done to the Congo blacks, caused by Casement's report, may nowadays strike us as a vast to-do about something which, while bad, could have been much worse. With Buchenwald and Belsen on the record, Brazzaville could seem in comparison not so black as it was painted.

However, there was no question but that in 1904 Casement had stirred up consciences all over the world. Nobody had then heard of gas ovens, and in the meantime the whips and knives of the Congo were quite enough to disturb public imagination. In England, Sir Charles Dilke, M.P., led the hunt, and he was ably supported by such talented whippers-in as Dr. Grattan Guiness,[1] an old Congo hand, who rapidly started off on a nationwide speaking tour; W. T. Stead, ever the crusader; Mr. Fox-Bourne, who had been so eager to question Casement on his return; and of course E. D. Morel, who, at a monster meeting in Liverpool, started his Congo Reform Association, of which the first president was to be the respected Lord Beauchamp.

Over in Brussels, Leopold, as was to be expected, counter-attacked. Casement was represented as the tool of British Big Business; and described as a typically hypocritical and sanctimonious puppet of Imperialism hiding behind a mask of humanitarianism. The Church abroad took its cue. The Belgian bishops complained that the whole thing was a shabby trick by which the English Protestants sought to smear the Continental Catholics. And in the United States, by another of those strokes of irony which crop up plentifully in Casement's story, he was denounced with rage and hatred in the Irish-American press, which like the

[1] See Appendix I.

45

Belgians, came to the conclusion that he could be only a renegade Irishman who had sold out to John Bull in return for English gold.

In spite of the hubbub from abroad, the Foreign Office was sure—or fairly sure—that it was on firm ground. The very intensity of the indignation in Brussels seemed reassuring, but there were some men in high places in London who still reserved judgment about Casement and his report.

In any event, and whatever the private doubts, Casement was squarely in the middle of the limelight. Not yet forty, he had arrived. It was a remarkable jump into international fame. This young orphan, without influence, friends or money, starting from scratch, locally recruited as a surveyor and customs functionary in a distant hole of an African possession, had crashed on to the world scene, enormously embarrassing as he did so one of Europe's most famous monarchs, catching the eye and ear of diplomats, press and public; and causing, so it was to turn out, the eventual disappearance of the Congo Free State. Here was an achievement of which his friends and surviving family, to say nothing of the ageing masters at Ballymena Academy, might well feel proud.

To another than a man of Casement's unusual character, with its disastrous failings as well as its great virtues, the future at this point must have looked full of promise. What now was to stop him? Were there limits to his continued successful march upwards in the British Foreign Service, at a time when the United Kingdom stood second to none in the counsels of the world, with her wealth, prestige, possessions and great sea-power? Surely it was not presumptuous to think that in another fifteen years or so the poor boy from Antrim might find himself very near the top of the tree. A Minister—an Ambassador? Why not?

Even if the future failed to provide quite so splendid an apotheosis, there could be no gainsaying that the present was a time for personal rejoicing. Could there be anything but smiles and congratulations for this dashing Irishman who had played so bold and brilliant a rôle in the revelation of evil and the imperious direction of world attention upon that evil? Casement had but to play his professional cards with normal care, and all would be well. But that was what Casement was incapable of doing.

What a strange man he was. It would be difficult to imagine a more rootless, more sadly homeless man than Casement remained throughout his life. When he was in London, he drifted about in various 'digs'—Aubrey Walk, in Kensington; Philbeach Gardens, in Earls Court; and in Ebury Street; or else he stayed with friends such as Morton at Denham, or the Cadburys in Birmingham. Although he returned often to Antrim and to other places in his native Ireland, he never had a home there, and as far as I know, never contemplated buying one against his eventual retirement. His belongings in Ireland were dumped at the home of his friend, F. J. Biggar, in Belfast. When he crossed the Irish Channel he would put up in hotels, such as the Shelbourne in Dublin, or at the homes of friends. His interests, apart, of course, from whatever contemporary crusade or project was engaging his fierce energies, seem to have been strangely limited. He very rarely went to the theatre; never, so far as I know, to a concert. He was not interested in the arts. He read little. Fairs, or such public attractions as the Earls Court Exhibition, which he constantly visited and re-visited in 1910, seem to have been to his taste.

On the whole he seems to have been a man of narrow intellectual horizons. He had an obsessive and bafflingly trivial preoccupation with money and how he spent it. He rarely had time to see or at least recall anything of beauty in the world about him. His own accounts of his life show only an embarrassingly pedestrian interest in what he had to eat and drink, where he dined, what were his creature comforts and discomforts. There was nothing exciting in what he wrote, nothing to uplift or fire the imagination. Professor Denis Gwynn writes in his book, *The Life and Death of Roger Casement* (Jonathan Cape, 1930) of Casement returning at this period to 'Antrim, with its remote and lovely countryside, under its dreamy skies, with its gentle and soft rains'.

Unfortunately Casement himself almost never wrote in that vein. Only once, in his letters, have I come across a remark which shows that he was perceptive about his surroundings. He was out

47

for a walk in Antrim and noted 'the glorious light on Cantyre in the sunshine'; banal perhaps—but in such welcome contrast to the sort of thing with which Casement normally concerned himself that I could not but accept it with gratitude.

Whatever the gifts or the shortcomings of his character, however, it seems clear that Casement was doomed, in spite of his *tour-de-force* in the Congo, to be at loggerheads with his superiors in Whitehall. There was nearly always something amiss, a sense of unease, a grating note. Was it that Casement suffered from an inferiority complex, knowing that in spite of his astonishing triumphs, he was only a poor boy from Antrim who had gone to the wrong sort of school? Was he snubbed by the elegant professionals of the Foreign Office? Or—which would be as bad—did he imagine that he was? Casement really was a walking fluke. The Foreign Office men must have sometimes wondered among themselves what strange prank of fate had landed them with this all too colourful gypsy. And while it was perfectly all right for an Old Wykehamist, say, to develop congenial eccentricities in the course of his career in the Foreign Service, it was perhaps not the same thing if an Old Ballymenian did so. Even to-day, a half century later, the strenuous efforts which the Foreign Office has been making since the end of the last war to democratise itself may or may not be a success; but try to imagine the climate in 1904, with Victoria not long in her grave; and cultured elegance the order of the day. Casement in a salon, as the darling of the hostesses, might be all very well; but this fellow with the beard who keeps coming into the office and talking interminably when one's busy—bit of a nuisance, really.

So I picture Casement very much on the defensive, even in this moment of triumph; quick to take offence; on the look-out for slights and sneers. If the Foreign Office men went out of their way to be nice to him, all was well. But if they gave the impression of being off-hand or seemed not to take Casement at quite his own valuation, then they at once became 'abject pifflers' or even 'fierce cads'. For their part, even if the Foreign Office men did not go so far as to label Casement privately as whatever was

48

the 1904 equivalent of 'oick*, they were probably far from feeling that he was even remotely one of them.

Although it cannot be proved, my feeling is that Casement could rather easily have been steered away from the path of the treason which he finally chose, by the simple expedient of some-one having been a bit nicer to him. All he really needed was to be flattered, made much of, jollied along. He was vain—far vainer than most. He was an egocentric. He could be easily cast down; quickly be put into a rage of resentment. It is altogether possible that some cutting little remark uttered in a languid voice in a corridor of the Foreign Office one morning in 1904 may well have started Casement on the road which led to the noose. I do not believe that Casement would ever have turned to Irish Nationalism, let alone treason, unless he had been hurt by White-hall and was furiously seeking some way of 'getting back at them'. I do not believe that patriotism was his primary motive in joining the Nationalist Movement. I consider that it was due to wounded vanity, a sense of slight. The English manner can often have the most disastrous effect on quick-tempered foreigners; to a warm and oncoming Irishman, as to members of other foreign nations, the superior English manner, which we take for granted and do not regard as being ill-bred, can be at the least daunting and at the worst infuriating. Casement must have felt himself to be under unbearable pressure in his dealings with Whitehall. He thought that he was being shabbily treated, that they were all laughing up their sleeves at him. Very well—that was England for you. They would always let you down, you, the Irishman who had been trying to serve them loyally. So where to turn? Why to your own country, of course—to Ireland.

So, in my opinion, Casement was at this time particularly receptive to the sort of eager propaganda which he was just start-ing to hear from an able woman of outstanding personality, a woman passionately dedicated to the cause of Irish Nationalism, a woman of intensely anti-English and anti-Imperialist persua-sion. Mrs. Alice Sophie Amelia Green, then, in 1904, aged fifty-seven, and at the height of her intellectual attainments and personal magnetism, was to play a great part in Casement's life from then on.

Alice Green was a mordant, well-educated, civilised woman of startling will-power and dazzling wit. She was the seventh child of a Protestant Archdeacon of Meath, and her parents provided her with a home and an upbringing almost Calvinist in its austerity. In her 'teens this remarkable child taught herself Greek—and then fell almost blind, and so continued for seven years more, during which she was able to read for only a quarter of an hour each day. In 1871, when she was twenty-four, her full sight was restored by an operation. By this time her original gifts of courage and daunt-lessness had been reinforced by an extraordinary faculty of total recall, first hinted at, and then deliberately fostered during the blindness through which she never lost hope nor stopped trying. Three years later (1874) the Archdeacon died, and the family emigrated to London, where young Alice met, fell in love with and married J. R. Green, the historian, who had achieved fame overnight with his *Short History of the English People*.

The flame of Green's genius and that of his life expectancy were in inverse proportion. Beside working at his side with almost masculine drive, and helping him at his work with energy and intelligence, Alice Green nursed her ailing husband devotedly. To no avail, for Green died in 1883, whereupon Alice Green completed, with insight and competence, the work, *Conquest of England*, on which he had been engaged at his death; and then, in her own right, wrote a biography of Henry II, the favourable comment on which had scarcely subsided before she followed it with a work, *Town Life in the Fifteenth Century*, which made her name in the literary circles of the day. Mrs. Green was by then living in Kensington Square, and almost inevitably a 'salon' spread its sofas about her. The witty, disputatious, attractive woman magnetised to her hearth such people as Florence Nightingale, Mary Kingsley, Bishop Creighton, H. A. L. Fisher, the Humphry Wards, and—although one feels that this must have been at a time when Mrs. Green was keeping to herself her anti-Imperialist sentiments—the youthful Winston Churchill.

By 1900 the widow, immensely active, and—in an age of servants and ease—still with much spare time on her hands, began to think of Home Rule for her native Ireland. Just about that time she fell under the compelling influence of an Irish journalist, John Francis Taylor, who was to swing her into a mood to take an aggressive rôle in the Independence movement. From then on Mrs. Green stood in the forefront of the battle, exhorting, intriguing, financing, challenging.[1]

Casement's first contact with Mrs. Green was by a long letter dated April 24th, 1904, on behalf of the Congo Reform Association, appealing in passionate and dramatic terms for her support.

So this incisive, knowledgeable and competent woman of the world met the romantic, impractical and probably by now resentful, Congo consul. Both were Irish. Both had got mixed up with the English. Neither relished the fact, although from time to time the English, in their own fumbling way, tried to make the visitors feel at home. But it didn't work. Alice Green's determination to free Ireland from this complacent band of prosperous and pretentious thugs—for that was how she and eventually Casement saw them—struck a chord with Casement. If only we might have heard some of the early conversations between this vinegar-sharp woman and the dreamy romantic from Africa. But the result of

[1] In 1908 Mrs. Green's book, *The Making of Ireland and its Undoing*, intended to prove that the English conquerors of Ireland destroyed a civilisation instead of implanting one, caused a literary uproar. Mrs. Green continued to write books, agitate for Home Rule, charm other people, talk to the young, and be altogether captivating until the end of her days. The Dublin Rising of 1916, followed immediately by Casement's execution, hit her hard; and she soon afterwards gave up her London home and went back to Dublin. There, in St. Stephen's Green, she went on, philosophically accepting the periodic searches of her house during the 'troubles'. In 1921, when the peace and independence treaty at last brought the promise of a relaxed and mature nationhood to Ireland, the dauntless woman was herself able to relax. The following year, President Cosgrave made the pleasant gesture of nominating Alice Green for the office of Senator. Just two days before her 82nd birthday in 1929, she died.

the talks over the coffee cups, first in Kensington Square and later in Grosvenor Road, made itself clear enough in the long run.

In the month following the publication of the Congo report something, for whatever reason, caused Casement to misplay his hand in his relations with the Foreign Office. There must have been some surprising emergency, for on March 27th Eric Barrington[1]—who was to become the object of Casement's special detestation—was writing: 'My dear Casement, Nobody wants you to resign. I never heard of such a thing. As to your temporary return to the Congo, I think it very unlikely, but it has always been intended to appoint you to Lisbon when the time came. The present incumbent will go, I am assured, at any moment.'

One can but guess at the reason for this unlooked-for turn of events, just when Casement should have been the hero of the hour. Casement went to Lisbon (in November 1904) but his tenure of the post lasted a very short time, probably only a month or so. His thoughts were all on the Congo controversy and he was aching to get back to the centre of things in London, there to help Morel and the others. Accordingly he asked to be seconded for sick leave, without pay. This greatly upset the Foreign Office, and some of its officials—important ones—never really seem to have forgotten this wayward conduct. Nor can they have relished the opinion held by Casement, of which he made no secret, that the Foreign Office was making a sad mess of things in its dealings with Leopold, and was, in particular, squandering the excellent ammunition with which his Congo report should have furnished them.

The Foreign Office, although outwardly backing Casement to the limit, was getting some advice from its own representatives which was not favourable to him. On April 17th Sir Constantine Phipps, who, as British Minister to Belgium, was squarely in the middle of the row (and conceivably wishing that Casement had never been heard of) wrote to Lansdowne: My Lord, I have twice recently received in the Legation Baron Nisco, the Senior Judge of the Congo Court of Appeal who, each year, passes a few days

[1]See Appendix I.

in Brussels, before taking his annual leave in Italy. He has several years' experience in the Congo. He is a reserved Italian, rather of the quiet, unenthusiastic type, and appears to take a very impartial view of events there. Of systematic atrocities he had heard nothing, nor has he ever had "tales of wrong" imparted to him by Italians from the interior. . . . Whilst entertaining the most friendly feelings towards Mr. Casement, with whom he had lived on terms of intimacy, Baron Nisco appears to have arrived at entirely opposite conclusions as regards the results of Belgian rule in the Congo. . . .'

Lord Lansdowne wrote back to Phipps, discussing the question of the notes prepared by the Congo Government and handed to Phipps on March 13th as 'a preliminary reply to Mr. Casement's Report', saying that these notes contained statements which must be carefully studied. Lansdowne also remarked that the request made by the Congo Government for the full text of Casement's report 'raises questions of considerable difficulty'.

He went on: 'With regard to the application, renewed in the notes, for previous reports from the British Consular offices, it is necessary to explain that these reports, though forwarding testimony upon which reliance could apparently be placed, were found to be hearsay and lacked the authority of personal observation, without which His Majesty's Government were unwilling to come to any definite conclusion unfavourable to the Administration of the Congo State. Moreover, some of the reports are of very old date; the Congo State have admittedly been very active in pushing forward occupation of the country, and it would be unjust to bring forward statements regarding a condition of affairs which may have entirely passed away. In the Note of 8th August, 1903, H.M.G. explicitly declared that they were unaware to what extent the allegations made against the Congo State might be true, and it was in order to obtain direct and personal information as to the state of affairs actually existing that Mr. Casement undertook the journey of which the results are recorded in his report. . . .'

At the point in this letter where Lansdowne talked about the reports being hearsay and lacking the authority of personal observation, Casement, in the margin of the copy sent him, scrawled in an obviously furious hand, 'A deliberate lie!' He did not, however, return his copy to the Foreign Office with this unstatesmanlike notation on it.

It looks, therefore, as though part at least of the trouble which had so swiftly developed between Casement and Whitehall lay in the fact that Casement thought they were doubting his word.

He presumably thought that Lansdowne, in talking of hearsay and so on, was referring to some of Casement's own earlier reports, made on what he was satisfied was reliable enough firsthand testimony, but which were not actually based on personal observation because they were made before Casement embarked on his final fact-finding trek.

Casement was in a rage. He was under attack outside the Foreign Office and he knew that he also had his enemies and detractors within it, chief among them Phipps. He wrote a tremendous draft letter for general distribution to the press (June 12th, 1904) in which he said that his accusers were snobs, and explained—to the extent of many foolscap pages—that many men who had originally been 'traders' later held positions of high public importance.

He also wrote to Morel, full of dark forebodings about the Belgian Commission of Inquiry which was in its turn going out to the Congo. 'Whilst Lansdowne and Leopold "kiss again with tears" after their recent disagreement—the man-in-the-street and his journals, known to have the briefest of memories, will be induced to believe that the lot of the Congo native was an ideal one, and that Mr. Casement's report was that of an incompetent, or at any rate, a too enthusiastic observer.

'Our sweet friend Phipps will chortle with delight—he has made himself the complacent mouthpiece' [of the Belgians] 'in every insinuation and sneer affecting me which they wished passed on to the Foreign Office. I don't think there is another Minister in His Majesty's service who would have played quite so low-down a game as Phipps, and I don't think the Foreign

Office think any more highly of him. . . . Letting oneself go does not pay. Phipps' cheap sneers at me are on the score of my "unrestrained condemnation" of everything Congolese—the "un-diplomatic language I employed in some of my despatches".'

Later: 'The Foreign Office has certainly *not* played the game with me—for they have lifted no finger to show that they trust me. Since the storm of abuse began in June last—the whole action has been—without *saying* anything, to give the impression that they did not themselves accept my report. They conveyed the impression privately particularly through such starvelings as Villiers, Percy, etc., and that they "would keep an open mind" This attitude leaked out—as it was meant to leak out—and I have gathered from many quarters since that it was thought "Mr. C. has deceived the Foreign Office". That is what I resent. It is so cowardly and mean. They shove me into the forefront, bitterly against my will—promising that they will do the needful to stick up for me—and then they shirk off and leave me exposed to vulgar abuse and openly expressed contempt. . . . It is a dirty, mean trick and I have an overmastering contempt for them—and yet I shall be compelled to swallow my scorn and creep back to serve such effigies of men! . . . If I could only see my way to earning £150 a year I'd shake the dust of Government office off my feet forever. . . . If I went round begging for a job the very fact would turn them against me and induce them to exploit me, just as that cad Jones did when I was a boy of sixteen, or Strauch three years later. All men are snobs—and they worship assurance and position. The men I have scorn for are not these—the jackals —but the King of Beasts and his pimps. . . . Mrs. Green is quite right—England sacrificed her *moral* position in the councils of the world when she strangled those two little free states in South Africa.'

In April 1905, he was still seething. 'I wonder what that black-guard Phipps will do? He will certainly try to keep the Commis-sioners quiet too. He is playing all the time for his own hand, and indeed I should not put it past Phipps to take a cash *douceur* from Leopold. They might call it a "service of plate", such as he got from the French Government once. He is a thorough-going blackleg, and it will be a question of *amour propre* with him to get the Commission to water down their report with a nice vagueness and trash of diplomacy. Please goodness I shall go for Phipps some day. I am biding my time but when I get an opening I shall not spare the cur.'

Later (lumbago-racked) he wrote that 'every effort will be brought to bear on the Commissioners—promises of reform, sweeping enactments, etc., and there is no chance, I think, of the truth being published by the Commission. But I may be wrong, at any rate we can but wait and see. I hope Balfour & Co. will be out in darkness before then!'

Later he was saying that 'I think perhaps [his enemies] *will* have to be attacked. I am told privately that H. has an arrangement with Leopold that he shall have *okapi* hunting galore if he sticks up for Congodom.'

In May there is a good word for 'Herbert Samuel who is something of a kindred spirit, I fancy, and subscribed £5. Not bad.' And there is a conspiratorial note when he writes that 'Emmott, Col. Stopford, G.G. [this was Grattan Guiness] Samuel and I will meet in secret conclave to-morrow. G.G. will help *subterraneously* to organise. . . .' This was to be the public meeting which eventually took place at the Holborn Town Hall, but before that there was an immense amount of rather fussy planning by Casement. He told Morel that 500 seats should be specially reserved for 'the Smart Folk, who want to be sure of getting their seats after dinner'. He wanted to hold the meeting at the Mansion House, but was dissuaded on the ground that the Lord Mayor would object to his house being the scene of an attack on King Leopold. There was a brief haggle over the charge for using the Town Hall organ, but it was finally secured for a guinea. Casement's co-adjutors were clearly nervous lest his propensity for long-windedness might spoil things, and one wrote urging him to stream-line the projected programme 'as otherwise people will be fleeing for the exit before even the Resolution can be put'. Morel required reassurance at one point—'Of *course* you shall have a table to yourself—you can put your notes on it and stand by it. . . .' John Burns, the famous labour leader, also counselled compression ('two hours at the very outside') and, told that Morel planned to speak for forty-five minutes, Burns commented to Casement: 'He could say a lot in thirty-five.'

So, with the Foreign Office exacerbated, Casement felt an immense weariness. The Foreign Office thought that in Lisbon they were giving him a plum—a lovely climate, not too much to do in friendly Portugal, not too far from London and Ireland. What could be better? Lisbon, thought Whitehall not unreasonably, would form the ideal contrast to the rigours and sordid scenes of which Casement had had so much in the past few years. There, in the civilised and enjoyable surroundings of the Portuguese capital, Casement would have ample opportunity to re-knit his raddled nerves and restore his vitality and health.

But Casement did not see it that way. He was on his dignity. He was also a sick and exhausted man—although my own view is that often (not always) when Casement complained of illness it was what we should nowadays term psychosomatic trouble. He determined to apply for, and was granted, his sick-leave, and he retreated to the hills of Antrim there to convalesce after his own fashion. And there he had plenty of time and opportunity to harken to other siren voices of Nationalism besides that of Mrs. Green. Casement vastly enjoyed the burning enthusiasm of the Bulmer Hobsons and P. S. O'Hegertys and the rest of the talented and restless young men who felt (rightly, as it proved in the up-shot) that the dawning twentieth century must surely put paid to England's long domination of her sister island. There must have been marathon conversations among all these easy, amusing, quick-witted and talkative Irishmen and women, gay times when Casement, beginning now to feel a bit better, was able to take a less unhappy view of matters, to flex his muscles again, and even to contemplate a further tour of overseas duty for the Foreign Office. (More than once, in the course of his life, Casement was asked the obvious question: why, feeling as strongly as he did, did he not sever his connection with the British Government—sever it, that is to say, in a less drastic manner than the method he eventually chose? To which he replied prosaically and frankly that he needed the money. Much as he disliked it, the Foreign Office provided him with his bread and butter, and although there were occasional attempts to secure different employment, these never came to anything.)

Casement was later to take up the cause of Irish Nationalism fully and completely; from the most innocuous, almost old-maidish sort of manifestations, such as the stimulation of Gaelic singing and dancing and cottage industries—the weaving of tartans and the like; to the revival of the Irish language (there came a moment when Casement's bank manager wrote a letter imploring him to cease making out his cheques in Irish as it was making things so very confusing); and lastly to the sinister and extreme forms of active plotting and conniving, and the writing of straight and violent anti-British propaganda under various pseudonyms. But that was not yet. This was only the start. Perhaps at first, in those convalescent days in the spring of 1904, when the last decade of 'respectability' lay before him, Casement did not quite let himself think of going all the way. But the conversion, when it came, was quick and total: and the conversion included active participation in the attempt, which the Sinn Feiners[1] were then starting to push as hard as they could, to discourage young Irishmen from recruiting in the 'Imperialist' British Army. It would no doubt have caused Lord Lansdowne and his colleagues the utmost surprise to learn that the so gifted Mr. Casement had collaborated in a pamphlet, with Mrs. Green and Bulmer Hobson, to discourage recruiting.

There seems little reason, therefore, to doubt Casement when he wrote in prison that he became an all-out Separatist in 1905–1906. That period which he spent in Ireland after his return from the Congo, re-indoctrinated him, so to say. When he returned to

[1] The closest translation of the words 'Sinn Fein' is the French 'Nous-mêmes.' The party was founded in 1905 by a Dublin journalist named Arthur Griffith. It advocated, inter alia, the building-up of Ireland into a great manufacturing country by means of a tariff system.

active consular duties in the service of the Crown, he was, to all intents, a fifth-columnist for Sinn Fein.

But while he was immersing himself increasingly in the seductive waters of Nationalism, Casement, always energetic, found plenty of time to support in a score of different ways the Congo Reform Association, which his friend Morel had founded, and of which Casement was an obvious and highly esteemed adornment. There is a massive correspondence concerning the C.R.A., for Casement was full of schemes for money-raising, getting a move on, flaying the malefactor, organising public meetings and generally sweeping the crusade forward.

'Names always count,' wrote Casement sapiently, in announcing 'the capture of a Baronet', in a letter to Mrs. Green. 'And I have a few more pounds, and a promise from Lord Listowel (d.v.) when he returns. Don't doubt all will go well—truth and justice and honour and mercy and kindliness prompt us—to help the oppressed. The end is with mercy and kindness, never doubt. Dear old Lord Listowel! It really was good of him to come out—and I heard to-day from a friend he was delighted with my report. He is a straight, honest gentleman and when I think of that Belgian gang of blackguards—I laugh!'

Still in search not only for names but titles too, he enlisted Lord Ennismore ('Dear Roddie') and his Lordship writes with raillery, 'Thanks for your long letter. You are a wonder—do you know you covered twelve sheets?'

In a letter to Morel, Casement quoted Lord Ennismore as saying, 'Personally I shall be glad to subscribe to the C.R.A. if you can give me some idea what the money is wanted for and how they intend spending it?' Casement adds eagerly: 'I am getting typed copies of C.R.A. programme, so shall send one to Lord Ennismore—with a personal appeal for funds. By the way, in my letter to Lord Ennismore, asking him to join, and begging him to get his Lordship, his father, to do so too—I mentioned that I understood that Lords Northbourne and Beauchamp had joined in as supporters. Their names do not appear, however, on your list of "supporters". How is that? You must enter these two recruits as follows among the supporters—"the Earl of Listowel, K.P. Viscount Ennismore".' 'The Earl of Listowel is a Knight of Saint Patrick,' explains Casement a mite gratuitously, 'Viscount Ennismore is his son and heir, and an old friend of mine. Lord Listowel's name will carry a lot of social influence—and he is personally a charming, kind-hearted, excellent Irish nobleman, whose name is a guarantee of honourable worth. Do not, later, write to him or anything of that—send any Congo news of the C.R.A. to Lord Ennismore. . . .'

There came further hints of trouble with the Foreign Office. 'Your lawyer's letter is splendid' (continues Casement to Morel). 'If only my Report had come out with all the names and dates and places, as I wrote it, you need not have feared much libel—but I feel, knowing what *was*, that it is a poor production, with so much obscurity imported into it—and it is shorn of half its power to be convincing. However, this is a strictly private wail to you alone.'[1]

The fervour of Casement's denunciations is equalled only by that of his commendations. To Morel it was always 'My dear old chap.' 'You are a brick!' 'My own Morel!' 'Good, good, good!!!' In March 1904, he wrote to him, from Ballycastle, 'Got back to-night after a week away, and found your letters. . . . I *am* delighted about John Morley—the truest of the true, the Champion of the Weak—brave, good John Morley! May God bless him!' Drawing breath, Casement then turns to more mundane matters. 'I am trying to get two more Peers—English ones—for the C.R.A. . . .'

The Times on June 8th, 1904, reported a conference held at the Westminster Palace Hotel, organised by the Aborigines Protection Society, to 'consider Consul Casement's report'. The Bishop of Hereford was in the chair, and among those present was the respected young Liberal M.P., Mr. Herbert Samuel, full of

[1] This seems fair comment. In the printed Report almost no place names are mentioned, merely 'AA' or 'QQ'. Initials are substituted for the names of men interrogated—'KK', 'JJ', etc.; and even dates, when Casement was at known localities, are left blank.

admiration, of course, for the efforts of Consul Casement. Indeed it fell to Mr. Samuel, seconded by the Rev. Silas Hocking, to propose a tongue-bending resolution urging the Government to 'persevere in its proposal that as a means of obtaining international agreement as regards the assumed rights of concessionaire companies and State appropriation of lands previously at the disposal of the natives, this important part of the matter be referred to the Hague Tribunal' (carried nem. con.)

So 1904 went its way, and there was rarely a dull moment on the two-front war which Casement waged. By the beginning of 1905 relations with the Foreign Office, far from mending themselves, had become even more dislocated, to judge from this letter to Morel (February 2nd):

'. . . It is the dirty, cowardly, knock-kneed game the Foreign Office has played that puts me out of action. They *know* the truth, and yet deliberately, for the sake of paltry ease, prepare to throw over an honest and fearless official whom they deliberately thrust forward last year when it suited their book. They are not worth serving—and what sickens me is that I must go back to them, hat in hand, despising them as I do—simply to be able to live. I know what the Foreign Office tactics are—simply to "save their face". If, as is certain, the Commission Report[1] whitewashes Leopold

[1] The Commission to which Casement refers was set up by Leopold in July 1904, to investigate the truth or otherwise of his allegations. It consisted of three men: Edmond Janssens, a Belgian Court of Appeals Judge, who was its president; Baron Nisco, President of the Boma Court of Appeal; and Dr. E. de Schumacher, a Swiss jurist. Baron Nisco was, of course, the same man who had told Sir Constantine Phipps, the British Ambassador to Belgium, that he had heard nothing of atrocities in the Congo.

But when, in November 1905, the Commission presented its report, it is hard to know who can have been the most surprised by its contents—King Leopold, Phipps or Casement. It fell to Phipps to pass the gist of the report to Lord Lansdowne, and he could not do otherwise than state that 'it contains the most scathing criticisms of the policy pursued in the Congo State'. 'Strong criticism', 'severe condemnation', 'coercion' . . . 'In short, the entire report proves the administration of (while possibly damning the Albi and Anversoise, which is what Leopold wants!) the Foreign Office will accept it and say that as they had a "Representative" there no one can call its *bona fides* in re the question final. If the Commission takes a strong view in support of the charges against the Congo State—the Foreign Office will equally claim that their diplomacy has been successful and justified from the first, and they will invite admiration for their far-sightedness in having *asked* for the Commission. You see, they felt after some months that it would be a little too bare-faced to allow the Commission to carry out its work without the *show* of keeping an eye on it—hence the insistence on pretending to find a "representative". But this "representative", as they well know, is even a bigger blind than the Commission itself.'

Casement was in fiery mood at this time. A month or so later, he wrote: 'Balfour is a dirty soap-bubble, and please God, we Irishmen will blow him into suds'—scarcely, perhaps, the phrase to be expected from a senior official awaiting further employment from the British Crown.

But as far as the worthies on the Congo Reform Association, the Aborigines Protection Association, the Anti-Slavery League and the rest were concerned, this side of Casement remained unknown and unsuspected. To them his Fenian hatred of Britain was as dark a mystery as the furtive little errands of self-gratification upon which he slid off under cover of night into the streets of any town in which he found himself. If anyone had at that time tried to reveal the full truth about Casement to his colleagues in the great humanitarian movements, it is difficult to know which they would have found it the more impossible to believe—his political or his sexual eccentricities. The latter are more fully gone into in a later chapter.

Now and again there was a fleeting hint—about the political

the company to be a system of hardly restricted savagery.' Finally Phipps said that 'proof is here afforded of how drastic and sweeping must be the changes. . . .'

Casement could scarcely have received more complete and dramatic a vindication—and from the appointees of his great enemy.

side of things. Among the men with whom Casement's work in the Congo brought him into contact, ripening into warm friendship, was William Cadbury, one of the great Birmingham Quaker family. Cadbury's large business interests in West Africa had caused him to take a natural interest in the region; his religious convictions and natural compassion for the ill-treated and the wronged made him eager to help in the campaign to set matters right. He became a supporter of the C.R.A., and from his considerable resources he made generous financial contributions to the Association.

On July 7th, 1905, Casement wrote to Cadbury from Ballycastle. '. . . Morel has sent me your generous offer and told me of his answer. He must be backed up through thick and thin. I am only a broken reed to lean on—and just at present I am up to my eyes in the Irish question, which is causing me grave anxiety on behalf of others.

'The Congo question is very near my heart—but the Irish question is nearer—and I have a fight on hand so near home here, that for some time I shall not be free to help or advise Morel.' After a reference to 'those wretched fellow-creatures of ours out in the Congo', Casement adds, 'I hope I may meet you before long, but until I get this Irish trouble settled, I am not sure of my movements. I don't know if you have any sympathy for Ireland or her people, and you may not understand how deeply moved an Irishman can be at things here. But it was only because I was an Irishman that I could understand *fully*, I think, the whole scheme of wrong-doing at work on the Congo.

'Again, thank you from the bottom of my heart for all you are doing to aid and sustain Morel in his splendid fight for truth and decency and humanity, and may God bless the work.'

Just before this, in the Honours List of June 30th, it was announced that Casement had been made a Companion of the Order of St. Michael and St. George, the order to which those who outstandingly distinguish themselves in the foreign service are traditionally admitted. This was very good going for the forty-year-old Irishman, and he was entitled to warm congratulations on a richly deserved award. But, characteristically, the news brought nothing but heartsearching and uneasiness to Casement himself. Mr. Bulmer Hobson was staying with Casement at the time, in Cushendall, on Red Bay in Northern Antrim. A distant cousin of Casement's, a Vice-Admiral in the Royal Navy, was also of the party. Hobson says that Casement 'was all for turning it down', and a long argument ensued before he would consent to change his mind.

'He simply didn't want it,' Mr. Hobson recalls. 'But I reminded him that it was a mistake to make a hasty decision. I pointed out that if he refused it, that would be tantamount to sending in his papers and resigning from the foreign service. Did he really want that, I asked him. Casement paced up and down the sands in agitation for over an hour, before he sighed and reluctantly agreed to accept the honour.'

But Casement continued to feel that he had done the wrong thing in accepting, and went to some lengths to ensure that at least he should not have to go through the physical acceptance of the insignia at the hands of his Sovereign, King Edward VII. He pleaded ill-health, and was on that account excused from making the journey to London for the investiture at Buckingham Palace.

Accordingly we find William Tyrrell[1] writing from the Foreign Office: 'I am *very* glad that you got off your attendance for the investiture. . . .' Tyrrell had earlier written to Casement suggesting that he should write to Lord Baillie Hamilton, explaining that he had had an operation (this was true—for piles), that a further one might be necessary, and pleading that in these special circumstances he hoped that Lord Baillie Hamilton might see his way to submit to the King that his presence at the investiture be dispensed with, and the decoration sent to him by post instead. 'I *am* sorry you are not mending,' went on Tyrrell. 'Please don't run a wholly unnecessary risk in coming over if you are not fit. . . .' (In his death cell at Pentonville, Casement was asked to return the insignia of the C.M.G. He wrote to Mrs. Green, asking

[1] See Appendix I.

her to try to find it among his effects, and he also asked her to look out his Coronation Medal of 1911 and return that too.)

Just before being awarded his decoration, Casement had visited London at the beginning of June to attend the C.R.A. meeting at the Holborn Town Hall. The cost of the meeting was £40 5s. 2d., including £6 6s. od. for the hire of the hall itself, postage and telegrams £8 1s. 4½d.; £12 8s. 9d. to Grattan Guiness for the printing expenses; stationery £2 6s. 7d.; and typing £3 4s. 9d. These expenses were covered by means of a whip-round, and some of those who helped included Mr. Herbert Samuel (£2 10s. od.), Lord Norbury (£5), Mr. Richard Morton (£5) and Mrs. Green (£5).

By October Casement was writing to Cadbury, urging that everything should be done to needle Members of Parliament, 'in season and out, Liberals—and Unionists, too, for that matter,' to get Congo reform considered by the House when it reassembled. He thought that to make the Congo a Belgian Colony—which, in fact, was what happened—would be a shocking betrayal of the natives. He also thought that but for the C.R.A., little or nothing would have been done, and the whole thing allowed to slide. He may well have been right in that estimate.

He felt (he went on) that he had better not attend a scheduled meeting because he was not to be the main speaker, 'and the temptation is always very strong on me when I hear someone speaking on this subject' [the Congo] 'to get up and join him and add my verbal testimony to my written judgment as expressed in my Official Report. But I have already seriously compromised my career in the public service by my attitude on this subject, and the additional help I could now give the cause by speaking publicly would not materially forward its propaganda, while seriously injuring myself.'

At a dinner given by Mrs. Green about this time Casement had toyed with the idea of becoming consul in the French islands of St. Pierre-et-Miquelon, off the Newfoundland coast. This was at the suggestion of Lord MacDonnell, a fellow diner. But since he had already relinquished Lisbon, in spite of all its attractions, such a post as St. Pierre could have seemed nothing but an even sadder sort of exile.

1906 got under way with the breach between Casement and the Foreign Office still far from healed. Tyrrell, the peace-maker, sent Casement, still over in Ireland, a succession of letters trying to calm him down. One of these letters of Tyrrell's contained the remarkable passage, 'I must assure you that Barrington is not your enemy. There must be some misundertanding.' I do not know what Sir Eric Barrington had done, so to ruffle Casement all over again, other than to offer him the Stockholm Consulship at another dinner party, but matters finally reached such a pitch that the pacifying Tyrrell arranged for Casement to come to London to see Lord Fitzmaurice. This was a good move, the meeting went off amicably, and the difficulty, whatever it was, was temporarily ironed out.

But on April 4th, Barrington angered Casement afresh by writing to him, 'I am afraid that the Secretary of State will not be able to offer you one of the present vacancies in the Consular Service, although he recognises your claim to re-employment when a suitable opportunity presents itself. It is in my opinion most unfortunate that you should have so hastily resigned Lisbon, which is one of the nicest posts in the Service, and was given you in recognition of your work in Africa.'

By now Casement was convinced that he had enemies in high places and was irrevocably on the defensive professionally, besides being increasingly anti-British emotionally, and he seems to have been incapable of realising that the Foreign Office, in giving him Lisbon had acted with kindness and, as they thought, sympathetic consideration for a man who had had a tough time of it.

Although obdurate about Lisbon, Casement had at least signified that he was fit again and ready to resume work; and Louis Mallet wrote at the end of July 'Sir Edward (Grey) is glad to hear that you have decided to return to the fold, and that the Foreign Office will have the benefit of your assistance. I suppose that you would not prefer Santos, which is also vacant? It has occurred to us that your knowledge of' (word indecipherable) 'might tempt you to go there.'

Casement wrote at the bottom of this letter, 'Bilbao is £600, and £350 office allowance, although Whitaker 1905 shows it £700. Santos is shown in Whitaker 1905 as £850. All Consulates seem to have been reduced in salary this last year, so Santos may now be only £700 or £750. Cowper told me it was a hideous hole and very expensive.'

But he resolved his financial doubts, and Tyrrell from his Sussex home on August 3rd sent a typically charming note saying how glad he was that Casement had decided to 'close with Sir Edward's offer' and that he was 'actively one of us again'.

Perhaps Casement's decision, after so long a pause, to get going again with the Foreign Office may have been influenced by an interchange which he had with Morel in July.

IV

CASEMENT had been tempted by the prospect of a non-government job. In a memorandum to Morel, he noted that a suggestion about some non-official employment in the Congo had now (July 13th, 1906) been made three times, twice by Morel himself and once by John Harris of the Anti-Slavery Society. 'While *then* I refused to consider the offers,' wrote Casement, 'now I am quite prepared and decided to remain idle no longer.'

To this Morel replied that if Casement were really set on it, he would try to clinch the African post on his behalf. But he felt bound to point out the disadvantages, especially the lack of security or promise of a pension, as compared with the Foreign Office. This appreciation of the situation from his greatly esteemed comrade-in-arms may have been the factor which decided Casement that a 'return to the fold' was after all the advisable as well as the correct course.

In August Casement wrote to Mrs. Green from 110 Philbeach Gardens: ' . . . the place I go to, D.V., is Santos, Brazil . . . I simply go there because it is better paid than Bilbao—at latter I should have no money to spare for Ireland—at Santos I hope to be able to finance one or two small Irishisms of my own! . . . I don't find Ireland depressing as you do; indeed I find it a tonic after this abominable place' [London] 'with its abominable people. The English beat the Irish solely because they had no music in their souls and were capable of any cold-blooded crime—and they are just the same race to-day. . . .'

That August the engaging Tyrrell and the prickly Casement were still having a to-and-fro about whether it was to be Bilbao in Spain, or Santos in Brazil. Finally the die, after any number of false throws, was cast, and (August 26th) Tyrrell wrote to say that Sir Edward Grey would be glad to see Casement the following

Monday. That interview too went off well, and Casement reported to Mrs. Green '. . . Sir E. Grey was charming. We talked about the Congo—and about myself too. . . '

So off he sailed to Santos; but he was still disgruntled, not to say disaffected. He wrote again to Mrs. Green, aboard the R.M.S. *Nile*, on his way to his new post, '. . . Remember, my address is "Consulate of Great Britain and *Ireland*, Santos", NOT "British Consulate". . . All one's thoughts are really with Ireland—if only I could see daylight. . . .'

The Santos assignment started badly. In a letter (October 2nd, 1906) to his cousin Gertrude Bannister, Casement complained about how he hated it in Santos, where 'I am badgered to death with sailors and ship's captains, and ship's deserters and drunkards and beachcombers and others—an awful gang. I shall not stay long in Santos—that I am convinced of.' In this letter he again underlined the word 'Ireland' where it appeared at the head of the notepaper which he had presumably had specially printed—'Consulate of Great Britain and Ireland'.

In point of fact, Casement had been appointed Consul for the entire Brazilian state of São Paulo, and Santos was only his base. The town was then Brazil's second most important seaport, with a population of 75,000. It was the sort of post where a young and eager aspirant in the consular service would have gained plenty of experience in the run-of-the-mill activities of his profession; for not only was there an immense trade going on—coffee, of course, and bran, bananas, rubber and hides, with the place full of ships and seamen, but it was also becoming one of the largest points of entry for Brazil's swarming immigrants.

Casement was neither young nor eager when he reached the place. He was now forty-one, mature, experienced and resentful. After the tense excitements of the Congo, and the sense of being at the centre of important events in London for so long, his feeling of 'being badgered to death' by tiresome bores off the ships must have been acute. Nor was it easy to see what he had to look forward to.

Santos got him down, and the mood steadily darkened.

In April 1907 he was writing to Mrs. Green—on Consulate notepaper—a tremendous diatribe against the misdeeds of 'Perfidious Albion'. 'What a delightful book the *English in Ireland* would be if written by someone who knew the subject. I wish we had a Max O'Rell who knew his ground properly and could write. I get too angry to write about these things and this abominable people in their dealings with Ireland. . . . Here is a skit à propos the Shamrock Ball you might send on to "Sinn Fein" or "The Peasant"—am I not a horrid nuisance? I expect Major Berry here soon from Buenos Aires and we shall talk of *nothing but Ireland*.'

An eleven-pager to Mrs. Green followed on April 20th, '. . . I have been reading Charles Lever's life and it makes one shudder to think that we call him an Irishman. He knew nothing of his country's past and like all the rest, thought Ireland owed all to England, and although he disliked England personally and had indeed an Irishman's contempt for them morally and intellectually, yet he never dreamed but that they were in the right in Ireland, and mere Irishmen hopelessly in the wrong.

'He, like myself, was a Consul! But he was a "loyal" one and hobnobbed with Ambassadors and Cabinet Ministers—I, worse luck to it, am a Consul *malgré moi* . . . I have no belief in Englishmen. Do you know what Michael Davitt wrote of them? "The idea of being ruled by Englishmen is to me the chief agony of existence. They are a nation without faith, truth or conscience, enveloped in a panoplied pharisaicism and an incurable hypocrisy. Their normal appetite is fed on falsehood. They profess Christianity and believe only in Mammon. They talk of Liberty while ruling India and Ireland against the principles of a Constitution professed as a political faith but prostituted to the interests of class and landlord rule". . . . It is a mistake for an Irishman to mix himself up with the English. He is bound to do one of two things —either go to the wall, if he remains Irish, or become an Englishman himself. You see, I very nearly did become one once! At the Boer War time. I had been away from Ireland for years; out of touch with everything native to my heart and mind, trying hard to do my duty and every fresh act of duty made me appreciably nearer to the ideal of the Englishman. . . .[1] I had accepted Imperialism. British rule was to be extended at all costs, because it was the best for everyone under the sun, and those who opposed that extension ought rightly to be "smashed". I was on the high road to being a regular Imperialist Jingo. . . . Well, the war gave me qualms at the end, and finally when up in those lonely Congo forests where I found Leopold, I found also myself, the incorrigible Irishman . . . I knew that the Foreign Office wouldn't understand the thing, or if they did they would take no action, for I realised then that I was looking at this tragedy with the eyes of another race of a people once hunted themselves, whose hearts were based on affection as the root principle of contact with their fellow men and whose estimate of life was not of something eternally to be appraised at its market "price".

'And I said to myself then, far up the Sulanga River, that I would do my part as an Irishman and just because I was an Irishman, wherever it might lead me to. Since that, each year has confirmed me in my faith in that point of view. I got back to Ireland early in 1904—and all the old hopes and longings of my boyhood have sprung to life again. . . .

'You remember Charles Peace[2]; how he went to church and "prayed" —eminently respectable. Well, the English are a race of Charles Peaces—he is the national type—a race of successful criminals—Charles Peace, well-armed and ready to shoot at sight any of his hapless victims. The most successful are made Peers in order that the national succession of ideas may be preserved and their booty remain intact. . . .

'P.S. April 21st. Do you know, I am rather glad to hear of your threatened burst-up in the African Society! Why not leave it?

[1] Five years later, on the same subject, Casement was more precise. He wrote that in 1901 he was 'much more of an Imperialist than to-day, I should not to-day—nor for years now—have expressed the opinion' about the efficiency of a punitive expedition which he had carried out. The years 1901–05 were crucial in Casement's life.

[2] See Appendix I.

Africa has heaps of people interested in her future—Ireland so few. . . . I remember Hugh Law saying to me when I went to see Charles Russell about that case in 1905 that I was to keep myself out of it at all costs "on account of the Congo". I pointed out that Ireland had some claim too, and he said "Yes, but the Congo cause is *urgent*; the case of Ireland is different; urgency doesn't matter so much there". Now when you come to think of it, how entirely and dreadfully wrong Hugh Law was. Africa can wait for centuries and centuries. She will still be Africa. The black man will still be the black man. Leopold might murder millions but nothing could destroy or efface the ineffaceable negro—his ways, his colour, his mind, his stature and all that make him the negro. . . . And Africa could *always* be reconstituted by her own sons—and the waves of European misgovernment ebbed back leaving no trace upon her shores or native character. In the case of Ireland— how different. . . . It is now or never indeed. Ireland can wait less than any country in the world. If she is not helped now all the help of Christendom a few years hence cannot restore her as Ireland. . . .'

Doubtless Sir Edward Grey, to say nothing of the Admiralty and War Office intelligence services, which still presumably regarded Casement as a potentially skilful and reliable agent, as in the past, might have been non-plussed at the revelation of Casement's thinking in 1907. And it should be made clear that the letters just quoted were by no means isolated examples of this kind of thing. It was not just a matter of Casement blowing off steam, perhaps in a moment of fatigue or dejection, or after a glass too many. The vein was constant—a bitter, raging antagonism towards England, and all things and men English.

In June 1907, Casement wrote to Mrs. Green's brother, Colonel Stopford, one of his characteristic eleven-pagers in which he said, 'I *don't* believe in the English national character at all; individually there are lots of decent Englishmen—collectively they are a poisonous compound—and we Irishmen should realise that as long as we go on "appealing" to and supporting Englishmen in the hope that they'll do "something" for Ireland we shall be sold.

Hopelessly sold. Their one view of life is to make—to get—to have—to possess. Ireland is a bit of real estate. We belong to them; that is their view of it. . . .'

During the previous month, Casement had been discussing what sounded like a promising post with The Mozambique Company. A representative of the company whose signature, despite my best efforts, remains indecipherable, wrote to Casement a letter from his home in St. John's Wood, London, offering him the post of Inspector of Finances of the company; pointing out that it did not carry the security of the Foreign Service and finally suggesting that Casement should get leave to discuss the matter in London before actually resigning from the Foreign Office.

But however far these negotiations went, nothing ever came of the project. In July, Casement returned to London on leave, and it was again touch and go whether he would stay on in the Consular Service.[1] He was offered Haiti as his next post, and in due course the offer was to lead to yet another violent explosion. On August 23rd one D. Alston wrote from the Foreign Office, confirming that Casement would get Haiti in succession to Vansittart, and advising him to apply for an extension of his leave, so that he

[1] On Casement's voyage home, his ship called at Rio de Janeiro. The vice-consul at Rio was Mr. (now Sir Gerald) Campbell, and since Campbell was on the point of being transferred to the Congo, the two men arranged a meeting in order that Casement might brief Campbell concerning his new post. Sir Gerald recollects (London, March 1954) 'Casement came ashore and we talked for a time before going back to his liner for lunch. Half-way out to the ship, the villainous Brazilian boatmen who were rowing us out, suddenly rested on their oars and, as was often their wont, tried to hold us up for more money than the price already agreed on. But by then Casement was launched on a tremendous monologue about Irish Home Rule and nothing could stem the flood. For a while the boatmen tried to shout him down, but it was impossible. Finally they gave up in disgust and we continued on our way, with Casement still going strong on Ireland.' And Sir Gerald recalls that Casement 'continued to talk of nothing else all through lunch. The rest of us grew very bored.'

would be able to avoid a return to Santos for the remaining two months of his posting there.

Casement presumably felt an even greater longing to quit Whitehall after what happened next. He describes the event much later, in a letter written the following March to Miss Gertrude Bannister, and after he had returned in high dudgeon to Brazil.

'. . . suffice it to say that life is penance, I probably deserve it— although not from the Foreign Office. They have behaved to me in an unimaginably imbecile and inconsiderate way. I came home from Santos last July, intending to leave the Consular Service for good and all. I had been offered an excellent post in E. Africa by a big undertaking' [obviously the Mozambique Financial Inspectorship] 'good pay and *most interesting* duties—far more useful than a consul's. Well, the Foreign Office on my landing promoted me to be Consul-General in Haiti and San Domingo—one of the six first-class, top rank posts in the Consular Service. I accepted this, after some hesitation, and declined the good African offer.

'Well, when I went over from Ireland to London in November to get final instructions to go out to Haiti and be gazetted, they had the audacity to appeal to me and to my good nature to make room for another man—to resign Haiti and wait for another Consulate-General some time next year, when a certain post (Rio de Janeiro) would be vacated. . . . I gave up Haiti, and when this had been accomplished I told them that nothing should induce me to go to Rio or live in Brazil. . . . I also told them that if they made me Ambassador I should not live in Brazil. They offered me Pará!!!. . . The duties are puerile and fictitious. They represent no value received to the British tax-payer—the post should be abolished. Here am I, after thirteen years of service as a consul, sent to this idiotic place. . . . Now I have spoken very plainly, and told them that I come to Pará solely for *my own* convenience, to treat it as a jumping-off place for my own private ends. I have told them I shall leave the service at a moment's notice—go by telegraph when it suits me. . . . Fortunately, I had kept my mouth close shut about Haiti, so that when they came to me with their bare-faced proposal I was able to do the kindly act they forced on

74

me without any outsiders knowing anything about it. *That* was a blessing. If I had said when I got home that I was to be a 1st Class Consul-General and then four months later announced my approaching departure for Pará, how Ballycastle would have "rung with it"! . . . Those idiots would have thought I was in disgrace, etc., etc., whereas it was in reality a high compliment to me in one way that they should have dared to approach me with such a proposal. . . . I don't care what place they offer me now—I burn only with a desire to get clear of them for good and all and to be free to write a despatch to the Secretary of State that should make the whole office remember Roger Casement. . . .'

That he was in fact offered Haiti is clinched by a letter from A. G. Vansittart, who wrote from the Westminster Palace Hotel, London, on October 22nd, 1907, saying that he would be glad to give Casement any hints he could about Haiti and San Domingo. 'I was informed by Lord Dufferin at the Foreign Office yesterday that you are to succeed me at Port-au-Prince. I presume you will be officially gazetted on my fate being finally decided.'

But it also appears that when Casement first heard about the possibility of Haiti, he was far from enthusiastic. On August 24th, 1907, Alfred Emmott, M.P. (a great figure in the C.R.A. and kindred activities) wrote saying, 'I am going to make a very shabby return for your letter; but I must send a line, because it interested me so much. I am glad you are to have promotion, even if Haiti is "a devilish place". You can't hate it any more than you did Santos. . . .'

This episode seems to epitomise Casement's dealings with the Foreign Office. First they offered Casement a plum—only to withdraw it almost as soon as he had accepted it. That would have been calculated to cause umbrage in someone with a far more placid temperament than Casement's. As for Casement, he thought that the proffered post was 'devilish'—but flew into a paroxysm of fury on finding that he was not to go there after all.

But in any event the Foreign Office handling of Casement over this matter was cavalier, to say the least. One suspects that in Whitehall memories still lingered on—and rankled on—of Casement's rejection of the earlier Lisbon plum. Be that as it may, Casement—despite his protestations that the one place he would never return to was Brazil—duly returned there. In what must have been one of the blackest moods into which even the temperamental Casement ever sank, he went out to Pará at the beginning of December, 1907.

V

PARÁ, or Belem as the Brazilians themselves prefer to call it, had at the time a population of about 100,000, and was another of the bustling, sweaty ports, full of commerce and drunken sailors, which Casement so abhorred, possibly because they reminded him of his own unhappy struggling days as a youth in Liverpool.

It sits on a bay overlooking the great southern mouth of the Amazon, which is there called the Tocatins River. For a town mainly devoted to commerce, it has fine and stately buildings, but Casement probably was in no mood to go sightseeing at the Parliament House, the cathedral or the rest of it. But if he had known, the return to Brazil was a stroke of luck for him. Instead of burying him in dismal obscurity, as seemed all too evidently the case, the Foreign Office was sending him back to fresh adventure and vast new acclaim. His career, which had already reached a glittering climax on the banks of one of the world's great rivers, would mount to a second climax now that he was perched beside another.

However, as 1908 dawned, Casement sulked and fumed in Pará. In March he drafted a letter to Tyrrell, sending him his resignation. It was a tremendous affair—one of those letters in the course of which the writer gets steadily more angry as he progresses, whipping himself into a final frenzy of indignation. In the course of it he informed Tyrrell that he saw no reason for maintaining any of the Brazilian consulates, since they were just so much waste of time and money. But the letter was never sent.

He wrote to Morel complaining of the cost of living, bad health, bad food, insomnia. 'I must give up my servant, hair-cuts, laundry, even a cauliflower occasionally—or Pará! The only satisfaction I shall have is to think that I *must* be buried at the public expense—there'll be no estate to fall back on—and so the Government which swindled me into coming here, shall, please God, have to foot the bill for my funeral. It is a poor little comfort—but I intend that farewell to be as expensive as my dying behests can make it.' As it turned out, Casement was indeed buried at Government expense.

On April 15th he wrote to Gertrude Bannister: 'Dear Gee, Thank you for your cutting from the *Morning Post*. It is that form of smug, ignorant, satisfaction which makes the English Press so repulsive . . . I find Pará *hideously expensive*. It's perfectly awful. My pay, etc. (£900 a year, including all allowances) does not nearly cover the expenses of the post' [Casement also got £500 a year special allowance 'for office expenses'] . . . 'My house rent is £307 a year. My clerk £362, and an office boy (a darkie) £60 a year, and so it goes on all the time—and I find I am, so far, heavily out of pocket by coming to this delicious consulate. It is a much nicer place than Santos, that is all I can say for it. . . .'

In a letter from Rio, dated September 1st (he was on holiday), Casement wrote to Miss Bannister, enclosing the six-page outline of a novel with which he was toying, some of it perhaps significant; as are some earlier remarks about South America and Germany.

'. . . S. America needs European immigration and European Government too—but because the U.S.A. wants to keep it as a sub-continent under their "tutelage" until they are ready (200–300 years hence) to overflow into and swamp these Barbarian hordes dressed to look like Parisians, so the whole world must be kept back from realising its rights over this vast, unoccupied misused earthly Paradise. Someday Europe will challenge this pretence of the U.S.A. and put it to the arbitrament of battle, and I sincerely hope Germany will win and erect a great German state with honest, clean laws and institutions here under the Southern Cross. You must not quote your cousin! Heavens, if these people knew I said this, my Consulate would be stoned and I torn out and expelled the country with a howling mob of these piebald half-castes pelting me from the quays. . . .'

Next comes the outline of the novel, ending thus: '. . . Two days later the terrible truth became known. The Germans had landed in very strong force—advanced rapidly on Dublin, received everywhere as deliverers and friends—and had proclaimed a provisional National Government under the joint protection of Germany, Austro-Hungary and Italy.

'Lord Aberdeen had been taken on board the German Flagship. The Irish Flag had been hoisted on Dublin Castle, and in all the cities of the land. The terrified Unionists everywhere accepted the inevitable and a stable Government had been ably got together under German direction, while the R.I.C. took the Oath of Allegiance to Ireland to a man. Within a week the recognition of the U.S.A. was announced, and Ireland, like Norway, was organising a plebiscite to decide on her future form of Government.

'Joint friendly squadrons of German, Irish and American warships patrolled the coast, and Lord Charles Beresford and Sir Percy Scott slanged each other by flag signal, while the *Daily Mail* went into deep mourning, the British Government resigned and appealed to the country.

'I need not further pursue the theme.

'England in the end face to face with the intervention of Nature, no less than of the whole civilised world, recognised the inevitable and recognised the new "Kingdom of Ireland" as a friendly state. *The Times* alone protested to the last—and John Redmond & Co. became naturalised British citizens, prepared to live and die in the glorious land in which they were left behind.

'This is a very nice way to spend my 45th birthday, Miss Gee, isn't it? Sketching out an Impossible Novel. It could become *awfully* funny—an Irish H. G. Wells could do it.

'Well, my dear wee girl, I am starving and must fly to breakfast. My love to Lizzie, the dear old girl—and all hearty greetings to you and ever so many happy returns of the day.

'Always your very own loving
'Scrodgie.'

On December 1st, 1908, Casement was appointed Consul-General in Rio de Janeiro. At least the promotion in rank, now publicly announced, was some balm to his wounded feelings. But there was usually something to have a row about with the Foreign Office, and this time it was the office furniture. He wrote to Whitehall, angrily complaining that his predecessor, Sir A. Chapman, 'is holding me to ransom', to the tune of £50 or so, for 'old, worn-out, office furniture', for which Chapman himself had paid only £60 seven years earlier.

From the Foreign Office, Lord Dufferin rejoined that he was advised that the question of furniture 'is always being brought up', but that it had been frequently decided that the furniture of Consular offices could not be regarded as Government property, even if it had been bought out of savings from the office allowance. The system, went on his Lordship, was that on transfer, the Consul sold to his successor and bought from his predecessor at the new post. 'In the present case Sir A. Chapman certainly asks a good deal, but it is a matter for settlement between the two officers. . . .'

Through 1909 a situation was building up which was soon to banish all thought of office chairs from Casement's mind and put him again into the foremost calculations of the world's chancelleries.

The River Putumayo is one of the most remote and earliest tributaries of the Amazon. Its headwaters rise in the western part of South America, not very far away from the Pacific, and the Putumayo then runs south-east for 500 miles before it joins the Amazon. In 1909 the Putumayo basin was a wild and very little-known part of the world, where the ill-defined frontiers of Peru, Colombia, Brazil and Ecuador lunged carelessly through dense and inaccessible jungle.

To an extraordinary degree what was going on along the Putumayo at this time paralleled the conditions in the Congo seven years before. There was first of all the same lure: rubber. There was next the same sort of local population handy to serve as a free labour force, this time the pitiful copper-coloured South American Indians instead of negroes. Finally, there was the same sort of exploiter to do his brutal and callous worst.

The main difference was that whereas in the Congo wrong-doing had been cloaked for a time behind an apparently respectable and internationally supervised administration which appeared to busy itself in bringing the amenities of modern civilisation to the area under its control, the Putumayo was a tropical wilderness where ran no writ of law—least of all that of the governments under whose jurisdiction the Putumayo nominally lay. In Lima, the remote and sophisticated Peruvian capital, any interest in what might be afoot in the soggy, smelly jungle of the far north was scarcely to be expected.

But the Foreign Office began to take an interest, and they were technically justified in so doing by the fact that—as in the Congo —there appeared to be some British subjects, this time Caribbean negroes, at work on the rubber plantations; and by the additional fact that while Peruvian in origin, the firm against the methods of whose representatives on the Putumayo the worst of the allegations were being levelled, had set up its main office in London.

The allegations, of torture, mutilation, murder and terror—all made dreadfully familiar on the Congo—grew fast, and were starting to find their way into the weekly papers and magazines of Britain and the U.S.A.

A British Consul was appointed to Iquitos, a 'lost' spot on the Putumayo, and his presence was ostensibly explained by the necessity of seeing to the Barbadians and other West Indian negroes who had found their way to the neighbourhood.

That was the situation at the beginning of 1910. In mid-January Casement was at Petropolis, the lavish summer capital of Brazil, twenty-eight miles north of Rio. Once again he was ill and confined to his bed. Recovering, he went on to São Paulo, and at Santos he saw his old friend Parminter, on whose behalf he had succeeded in finding a job with a coffee firm there. Then he continued his holiday at Buenos Aires and Mar del Plata, and on April 4th he sailed for home, to consult with the Foreign Office and receive instructions about the mission to the Putumayo to which he had been, as was almost a foregone conclusion after his Congo record, appointed.

A month later he was back in London and was being warmly greeted by Miss Cox, the landlady at 110 Philbeach Gardens. On May 6th he saw Tyrrell at the Foreign Office. There were happy reunions with his old friends—Morton at Denham, 'Gee', his sister Nina, E. D. Morel, Robert Lynd and many others. He went several evenings running to the Earls Court Exhibition, by which he was much taken, and then sailed for Dublin, finding John Redmond aboard the same packet.

In Dublin he put up at the Gresham and visited a performance of the Irish opera *Eithne*, which was sadly disappointing. On May 20th there was a service of commemoration for Edward VII, who had just died, but Casement cut it and visited the Dublin Zoo instead. That day he wrote to William Cadbury, commiserating with him about 'an insensate campaign against the "Cocoa Press"', and complaining that the Foreign Office had been 'miserably weak' about following up his Congo revelations.

He then went north to Belfast, Ballymena, Cushenden and Portrush, all of them well-remembered spots. Casement was still feeling intermittently seedy, but was in fair spirits. By the end of the month he was back in London, and at the House of Commons he addressed a group of influential M.P.s which included Sir Charles Dilke, on the anti-slavery movement. On the night of the 24th there was a dinner with Conan Doyle and E. D. Morel, and afterwards they went to see *The Speckled Band*, a dramatisation of Conan Doyle's famous Sherlock Holmes story involving the snake, which had opened a few nights earlier at the Adelphi.

Casement now wrote to Cadbury full of a project for launching a national subscription for a public testimonial to Morel. Conan Doyle was in on it, so were Lord Cromer, the Earl Beauchamp and the Bishop of Southwark. Casement had between £15,000 and £20,000 as his target; the money was to be used mainly for setting up a trust fund for Mrs. Morel and the children, leaving Morel's 'whole personality to be released for greater good and more work for Africa—wherever such a fearless soul as his is needed. . . .'

The days flew by—lunch with Lady Caledon at Prince's

Restaurant, lunch with Mrs. Green, tea with Lord Listowel, dinner with the Count and Countess Blücher. The Count had married an Englishwoman, the former Evelyn Stapleton-Bretherton, and lived in London. He was co-treasurer of the C.R.A. He was to turn up again at a later stage of Casement's life.

On July 11th Casement wrote to Tyrrell saying he was all ready for the Putumayo venture, and Sir Edward Grey had but to say the word. Next day Tyrrell answered him by telegram, confirming that he was definitely appointed. There followed a whirl of briefing, consultation and preparation. Casement dashed off a note to Cadbury, explaining that now he was unfortunately no longer in a position to help the Morel testimonial scheme, at any rate for the present. He spent much of his remaining time at the Foreign Office, and had another long and gratifying talk there with Sir Edward Grey. But in spite of all the excitement and apparently cheerful atmosphere, he still characterised London as 'a beastly hole'.

By July 24th he was once more at sea, this time on the *Edinburgh Castle*. He reached Pará on August 8th, and was much incensed at not meeting the local governor, owing to a misunderstanding brought about by the British consul. The *gaffe* was compounded when the same luckless consul arrived at the wharf too late to see Casement off. 'What an ass!' Casement remarked in a letter.

Casement was joined by the other members of the Commission of Inquiry which had been sent out from London by the company itself to make a full investigation of the Putumayo situation and report back. The Commission consisted of Colonel the Hon. R. N. Bertie, L. H. Barnes, an expert on tropical husbandry, W. Fox, a rubber expert, E. S. Bell, a businessman, and H. K. Gielgud, the general secretary of the company.

Casement's relations with Gielgud, like his relations with many others, went through a number of phases, and while to begin with, he had a poor opinion of him, after the difficult and unpleasant safari through the jungle together they seem to have ended up on terms of something like friendship, and afterwards they corresponded for some time.

After four days of steaming up the Amazon, the Commission reached Otacoatiarra, where there was a lively tiff with the local Customs officials, who were difficult about allowing some of their baggage to be landed and sent on by train. Casement, himself an old Customs hand, decided they were 'Utter rotters!'

On the 16th they reached Manaos, a considerable place—its population was then about 50,000—standing close to the confluence of the Amazon and the Rio Negro. Here Colonel Bertie collapsed and had to return at once to England. Barnes took his place as leader of the expedition and they pushed on by steamer, over 1,000 miles more, across the shadowy Peruvian border, to Iquitos. Conditions were unpleasant; the ship was uncomfortable, the river smelled bad and members of the expedition could not have any baths.

There were rumours of whirlpools, and their ship passed another vessel hard aground. The mosquitoes and flies became troublesome. Huge logs and pieces of driftwood floated past them. At last, on August 31st, they made Iquitos, where they put up at a dismally bad hotel, unconvincingly entitled 'Le Cosmopolite'. Casement called on the Prefect, Dr. Paz Soldan, and had a talk lasting nearly two hours. Dr. Paz dismissed the atrocity stories as so many fables, but Casement thought that he let slip a good deal which tended to confirm them.

The heat was oppressive, the mosquitoes still bad, and as the members of the Commission walked about the town they found themselves picking their way through dirty streets, through which thronged hundreds of blue-uniformed soldiers and Indians.

The following day they met Lazardo Arana, a manager of the firm whose operations they had come to investigate. He blandly told them that the region was one of boundless prosperity, and expressed the hope that as a result of their findings there would be a large introduction of fresh capital. A note of cynical realism was struck by a former French consul, who called on Casement at the hotel and informed him that while the state of affairs in the Putumayo constituted virtual mass-slavery, yet that was only to be expected in a country like Peru and there was little that anyone could do about it.

Next day the interrogations of the coloured Barbadians started. In a letter Casement describes their evidence as 'dreadful—perfectly awful'. To take their minds off these painful matters, the members of the Commission played bridge most evenings. Casement was a keen player, and enjoyed gambling, both at cards and in casinos.

They stayed in Iquitos nearly a fortnight, amid heavy rain and thunderstorms, and mosquitoes, which worried Casement—he described them as 'drops of fiery poison'. More Barbadians turned up and were questioned, and Casement got off their preliminary depositions by steamer on the long voyage back to Whitehall.

Stocking up with whisky against the rigours of the jungle, the Commission resumed their own journey, but the start was inauspicious. Two of the Barbadians, having secured an advance on their wages, deserted, and the ship's cook was rolling drunk. By September 17th Casement was again feeling very seedy. In a letter to Mrs. Green he noted down an unexpected aphorism. 'The man who gives up his family, his nation, his language, is worse than the woman who abandons her virtue. What chastity is to her, the essentials of self-respect and self-knowledge are to his manhood. Men are conquered not by invasion but by their own moral turpitude.'

By the 21st they were steaming along in the turgid waters of the Igaraparana. From the banks villainous-looking poor-whites, revolvers on hip, strolled from their wretched huts where they lived sleazily with fat concubines and starveling plantation hands, to watch them pass. They reached La Chorrera where young Boras Indians displayed for the Commission devastating weals across their buttocks, the result of savage beatings at the hands of the overseers. A group of the latter also greeted them, and the Commission, swallowing its revulsion, dined with them. One of them, Tizon by name, did his best to flatter and cajole. But next day Tizon changed his tune and virtually admitted that things

85

were bad. And another man, with off-handed callousness, agreed that he had personally murdered five natives.

They pushed on, cramped and uncomfortable in a launch, and pausing constantly to take depositions. Tizon accompanied them and was allowed to join their evening bridge games. On the 29th they got to Occidente. One Velarde, the local plantation boss, organised a huge dance, for which over 1,000 Indians flocked in. Most of them were naked, or almost so, and the scars of their beatings were all too visible, the sight depriving the visitors of much of their enjoyment of the occasion. Casement had to speak sharply to Gielgud who had taken to addressing him informally as 'Casement', a circumstance which Casement himself looked upon as 'infernal cheek'.

The Commission continued to amass testimony, many of those interviewed being coloured Barbadians. One of these, a man named Stanley Sealy, told of 'awful and hellish acts' committed by two half-castes named Jimenez and Caucta in May 1908, of which he said that he had been an eye-witness. This witness produced an especially profound effect on the Commission, as they were convinced of his good faith. But by now Casement was taking a poor view of Gielgud, and their relations were definitely strained. Not only that, but Jimenez, one of the suspected arch-rogues, was present, and was taking his meals with Casement and the others.

On October 11th Jiminez saw them off again, bowing and waving his cap with mocking exaggeration. 'Pity we cannot wave his head—the scoundrelly murderer!' reflected Casement. On the 18th they encountered the notorious Normand[1] for the

[1] Normand was regarded as the biggest scoundrel of them all, capable of the most nameless depravities in any field. So that after diaries of a perverted nature were found in Casement's London lodgings in 1916, it was suggested by Casement's well-wishers that these were actually Normand's diaries, which Casement had copied out in his own hand for the benefit of the Foreign Office. This view is still held to-day by such staunch pro-Casement men as Mr. Bulmer Hobson and Mr. P. S. O'Hegerty.

first time. He turned up surrounded by a large harem of native women and cheerfully joined them in the plantation house where they had been put up, leaving the women to camp outside.

October dragged by and it was a strain on them all, especially perhaps Casement, since he had seen it all before in the Congo. The travel was uncomfortable, the weather and the food bad. They were forced to see a good deal of Normand, and association with so evident a thug can have been none too pleasant. But above all, the constant tales of cruelty and horror and sadism, and the constant parade of its visible results, in the persons of wretched, emaciated Indians, their cadaverous bodies covered in scars and weals, was almost more than could be stomached.

Later on there were not to be lacking cynics who pointed out that the Peruvian approach to such matters was by no means as squeamish as that of Europe; and that what was going on in the Putumayo might well be found to have been enthusiastically duplicated in other parts of South America; to point out, moreover, that the Indians, given the chance, were just as cruel to each other as was a mob of international whites and near-whites to the Indians; and that to make a fuss about a state of affairs which was far from exceptional was to reveal naïveté. In the England of 1910, however, such sophisticated reflections would have been considered not only in shockingly bad taste but in any case untrue.

In mid-November the Commission started the homeward journey, and on the 19th they were out of Peru and had reached the first Brazilian frontier post. By January 1911, Casement was in London, to tell Sir Edward Grey all about it.

When the Commission of Inquiry, of which Casement was the moving spirit, visited the Putumayo, the Indian population, which had been estimated as recently as 1908 to number between 40,000 and 50,000, was down to 12,000. Casement thought that in another six to ten years the entire population would be wiped out, if things were allowed to continue in the way they were going. He considered that the cruelty shown by the Arana firm was 'the certain cause of this depopulation; however high the

87

deaths from smallpox, etc., may have been, the deaths from violence and hardship consequent upon the enforced tribute of rubber have been much higher.'

The Commission operated under the severe but perhaps not too significant handicap that none of its members could speak or understand the local languages. In Iquitos Casement recruited a Barbadian, Frederick Bishop, a former employee of the Arana company, to act as interpreter, and he accompanied the commission on the whole journey. He was twenty-nine, and had been in the Putumayo for five years. Like most of the other twenty-nine men whom Casement interrogated, he readily confessed to having himself flogged and maltreated the Indians, but—as did all the others—maintained that it was invariably under direct orders from the 'blancos' of the company (the various station managers).

The fact that virtually the whole body of the evidence for the Putumayo Report was extracted from men who had themselves, as they freely admitted, been guilty of very bad behaviour (in some cases even of murder) may well have been the reason why this second great report of Casement's was treated at first with some reserve, and why the Foreign Office insisted that he should make the long journey back again to Iquitos to check on his facts.

Casement's report alleged that 'The firm of Arana Bros. do not appear to have scrupled to lay the burden of feeding . . . the employees very largely upon the surrounding population, who were compelled by illegal force to labour in a variety of forms for the maintenance and profit of the company. . . .' Murder, flogging and torture were used in the exercise of this illegal compulsion.

He describes the system prevalent in most of the Amazon region—'peonage, which is not tolerated in civilised communities. It consists in getting the person working for you into your debt and keeping him there; and in lieu of other means of discharging this obligation, he is forced to work for his creditor upon the latter's terms, and under various forms of bodily constraint.' The Indians were first tempted by the white men's trade goods and when they had accepted a few, found themselves slaves for the

88

rest of their lives. Similarly, the Barbadians whose duties were to coerce the Indians into working the rubber, were encouraged to buy from the Company stores and have the payments deducted from their wages. When their debts were large they found that a man in debt was never allowed to leave the Amazon rubber districts; 'the creditor makes out the accounts, the debtor frequently does not know how much he owes . . . accounts are falsified and men are kept in a perpetual state of bondage, partly by their own thriftlessness, which is encouraged, and partly by deliberate dishonesty.'

Casement quoted four specific cases of 'criminal ill-treatment of the [British] Barbadian employees; two were cases of flogging —fifty lashes with tapir-hide thongs, at the orders of Armando Normand, the arch-villain; two others had been put in the "cepo", or local version of the stocks. These stocks had very small holes for the legs, small even by Indian standards, and to get the Barbadians into them at all involved cutting into their flesh with the heavy cross-bar which formed the top half of the stocks. One Barbadian, Joshua Dyall, still had the marks on his ankles, although they were three years old when Casement took his statement; the other stocks' victim had suffered this punishment on three separate occasions. A fifth Barbadian, Frederick Bishop, the interpreter, had been "put in guns", by order of the Chief Agent of the company. "Putting in guns" is a form of punitive detention in general use in the Peruvian Army. It consists in trussing a man with his legs and arms closely bound to a triangle formed by several crossed rifles, and leaving him in this posture for many hours.'

All the Barbadians told Casement that they had been bribed by the Peruvian-Amazon Company managers in an attempt to persuade them not to tell him of their ill-treatment. They also said that since the officials had got wind of the early arrival of the inspecting commission, much improvement had taken place at the various stations, with the stocks being hastily dismantled, and so on.

Fourteen Barbadians with four Indian wives and four children accompanied Casement to the coast when he left the Putumayo; they left the employ of the company for good.

When Casement reached the end of his report, dealing with the matters concerning which he had originally been instructed, he went beyond his terms of reference and immediately followed it with a supplementary report 'dealing with the methods of rubber collection and the treatment of the Indians in the region dominated by the Peruvian-Amazon Co.'

The first declaration which Casement made in this was that in the Putumayo 'an evil usage, of which the maxim is "The Indian has no rights" prevails'. As an instance, he said that Indian women were provided as 'wives' to the Barbadians, or 'white men taking up service with the company. One negro had nine, each new wife being the direct gift or loan of the local authority.'

The Indians were described by Casement as having been originally docile people, and when the prospecting whites had first arrived, they had merely annexed the tracts of the forest where rubber grew, including the Indian dwellings which it contained. The Indians were then forced to cut the rubber trees and bring in the rubber. They were very roughly handled, and if they did not come of their own free will to the trading posts they were flogged or brought in in chains. Soon they grew to hate and fear the whites, and eventually would ambush and kill them with machetes.

Casement was informed of one particular occasion, when, in 1903, a party of about sixty Colombian 'slave-getters' had been massacred in their sleep by the Indians. 'Terrible reprisals subsequently fell upon those Indians and all in the neighbourhood for many years afterwards.'

Once killing had been alleged against the Indians, fresh barbarities were perpetrated by the would-be slavers, particularly if rifles were thought to have been stolen. 'The only Indians who were allowed rifles were young men or boys—"cholitos"—who were being trained to oppress their own countrymen. . . . These "muchachos" were generally young Indians taken from one tribe and used in acts of terrorisation against another district.' If 'a muchacho did not maltreat his brother Indian at the bidding of the white man he might himself be murdered.'

'The remuneration of the chief of section was not paid by salary but by a percentage on the quantity of rubber he could obtain from his section. These men were all armed with Winchester rifles and never moved a step from their stations without their rifles.' 'These men were murderers and torturers by profession—and as their crimes swelled, so did their fortunes.' Casement's reply to the argument sometimes put forward in defence of the company, that they would never kill the Indians since they constituted 'the goose that laid the golden eggs', was that it would have force if 'applied to an estate it was designed to profitably develop. None of the freebooters on the Putumayo had any such limitations in his view or care for the hereafter to restrain him. His first object was to get rubber, and the Indians would always last his time.'

Casement calculated that there were about 100 armed whites in the Putumayo, plus about 200 armed 'muchachos'. Flogging was a useful and plentifully used method of coercion with the Indians, because it was thought that they particularly disliked it. 'This had been prohibited for some time, and representatives of the company sought to convince me that it actually ceased,' but Casement could use his own eyes.

He saw about 1,600 'native Indians', men, women and children, not counting the Indian staffs at the different stations visited. As these Indians all went naked, it was easy to see if they were scarred by the lash, and Casement noted that 'all classes of the native population—young and old—women and children, youths and girls—were marked on the buttocks and thighs, some lightly, some with broad and often terrible scars. In more than one case young men were brought to me with raw scars upon their hinder parts, with requests that I might give some healing lotion.'

'From direct testimony laid before me I learned that six weeks before my visit a native chief had been flogged to death and had died in actual confinement in the station stocks between his wife and one of his children. . . . Flogging was one of the least of the tortures inflicted on the failing rubber-gatherer, but it was the most universal.' One of the Barbadians was quoted as saying, 'The Indian is so humble that as soon as he sees that the needle of the scale does not mark ten kilograms he throws himself on to the ground to receive punishment. Then the chief or his subordinate advances, bends down, takes the Indian by the hair, raises his head, drops it face downward on the ground, and after the face is beaten and kicked and covered with blood, the Indian is scourged.'

Later in the report, Casement says, 'Senor Normand, it was clear from the evidence of the Barbadians, had for years been engaged in hunting Indians who had fled across the Caqueta to escape from the inhuman cruelties he inflicted on them in his efforts to make them work rubber for his profit. . . . The crimes alleged against this man dating from 1904 up to the month of October 1910 when I found him in charge of the station of Matanzas seem well-nigh incredible. They included innumerable murders and tortures of defenceless Indians—pouring kerosene oil on men and women and setting fire to them; burning men at the stake; dashing the brains out of children, and again and again cutting off the arms and legs of Indians and leaving them to speedy death in their agony. These charges were not made to me alone by the Barbados men who had worked under Normand, but by some of his fellow "Racionales", and Senor Tizon himself, the company's chief representative, told me he believed N. had committed "innumerable murders".

'Senor Tizon also told me that "hundreds" of Indians perished in the compulsory carriage of rubber down to La Chorrera on the river. No food is given by the company to these unfortunate people while on these forced marches, which take place roughly three times a year. I witnessed one such march on a small scale, when I accompanied a caravan of some 200 Indians (men, women and children) that left Matanzas station on October 19th. . . . The total journey forced upon each carrier was not less than sixty miles. The path to be followed was one of the worst imaginable, a fatiguing route for a good walker quite unburdened.

'For two days I marched with this caravan . . . men with huge loads of rubber weighing, I believe, sometimes up to seventy kilos; their wives also loaded, their sons and daughters, down to quite tiny things, who could do no more than carry a little cassava bread, as food for the march. Armed "muchachos" with Winchesters were scattered through the long column and at the rear one of the "racionales", Negrete, beat up the stragglers. Behind all, a day later, came Senor Normand with more armed "racionales" to see that none fell out or slipped off home.'

After twelve hours' march on the second day they arrived at Entre Rios where 'there was a large rest-house and even food was available, but Negrete drove the Indians on into the forest beyond "to spend the night". This was done in order that a member of the company's commission (Mr. Walter Fox) who was also at Entre Rios should not have a chance to look too closely at the condition of these people—particularly that we should not be able to weigh their loads.'

They did however manage to weigh the load of one straggler and it was fifty kilos. Some days later Casement 'saw many of these people on the way back to their homes, returning footsore and utterly worn out. They had no food with them, and none was given to them at Entre Rios. All they brought had now been eaten and for the last two days they had been subsisting on roots and berries and the leaves of wild trees they had pulled down on their way. In some places the path was blocked with branches and creepers they had torn down in their search for food and it was only when Senor Tizon assured me that this was done " by Senor Normand's Indians" in their hungry desperation that I could believe that it was not the work of wild animals.'

Flogging was prohibited indeed when Casement visited the Putumayo, though it did not cease, but Casement found that in deference to this new regulation the Indians were sometimes 'chastised with strokes of the machete', or pinioned and taken to the river and 'held under water until they became insensible and half-drowned', since these alternative tortures left no marks.

93

Stringing up to trees or beams by the neck for many hours, and deliberate starvation were among other tortures. Indians 'were kept prisoners in the station stocks until they died of hunger'; some were said to have been seen in 'their extremity of hunger in the stocks, eating the maggots from their wounds'.

Another class of crime 'was of a purely private or personal malice, not directly connected with the larger crime of lawless rubber-getting. These crimes mainly arose from the prevailing immorality that led every agent to help himself to Indian women.' Casement cites a case told him by Frederick Bishop on September 6th, 1910. This concerned an Indian girl kept by a section chief named Martineugui; the girl was found to have venereal disease. Martineugui had her tied up and flogged in the station yard and then made one of the Indian boys 'insert burning firebrands into her body. Bishop did not like to say where, but indicated with his hand.' Casement asked him if he had actually seen that, and he replied, 'Yes, sir; I saw that done with my own eyes. The boy ran away, sir, we never saw him again.'

Of Martineugui it was also alleged to Casement 'that during his term of service at Atenas, he had wasted that region, and so oppressed the Indians that they were reduced to a condition of wholesale starvation from which they had by no means recovered. When we visited the region in October, those Indians who were ordered to act as carriers for the English commissioners were many of them living skeletons, and filled us with pity at their miserable condition.'

A Colombian employee, Torres, 'constantly committed murders. . . . Among other practices he cut the ears off living Indians, a pastime that to my knowledge was indulged in by another man still employed by the company at the date of my visit, Alfred Zegarra.'

Casement also took a statement from a Barbadian, James Chase, who had been present on a retaliatory march about May 1910, when seven Indians were decapitated, one little girl, a boy, a woman, and four men.

Some of the Barbadians whom Casement questioned 'declared

that they had known Indian women to be publicly violated' while held in the stocks.

Three months elapsed while the Foreign Office digested Casement's Putumayo revelations. Then they started to get them printed, and on March 17th Casement received a letter from the Foreign Office which said, in part, 'As regards the question of toning down some of the expressions, I naturally feel the greatest diffidence in offering any remark at all; the report is yours, and you are the best judge of what you want to say. If the report was going to remain for ever within the four walls of this office I should feel no hesitation in saying Let It Alone; but when one comes to consider that it will probably find its way to others outside this office, e.g. the U.S.A. and *perhaps* the Peruvian Government and P.A.Co., I venture to suggest that the report would in no wise lose in dignity or strength if the expressions used were a little softened. Mind, I don't want to offer this as advice, I only want to say that I think that it would be quite as, if not more, effective if some of the expressions—though abundantly justified —were slightly modified; but if you think differently, please pay no attention to what I say. The tale is ghastly and horrible enough, whatever the language used.'

Apart from this, Casement still had the Congo on his mind, and, to his surprise, found that the Morel Testimonial Appeal, which had been launched just before he left for the Putumayo, was hanging fire rather badly. He wrote from Liverpool, on his way to spend Easter with Mrs. Green in Ireland, that the best efforts of the C.R.A. secretary in Manchester had yielded in donations from the public a laughable £7 10s. od.—and he noted frowningly that he himself had had to pay for the hire of the room in the Manchester Town Hall at which Bishop Weldon was to make an address in support of the Testimonial.

In June, writing to Cadbury, Casement spoke with—for him —surprising enthusiasm about the efforts the Foreign Office were making in regard to his Putumayo report. But he was gloomy about the prospects of United States support. 'The U.S. have already been appealed to in the Putumayo. Long before I went out, Sir E. Grey turned to them—but they were no good then. Since my return, the report and all the documents have gone to Mr. Bryce' [British Ambassador in Washington, later Lord Bryce] 'for communication to the State Department. They will do nothing. Some of their people care—but far more don't care—especially where it is a question of "injuns"! And anyhow Peru would not care very much for representations from the U.S.A. on humanitarian grounds! She would retort. She would refer to burnings alive of Negroes, and lynchings, and would talk of 9,000 murders in one year—such was last year's statement (quite incredible, it seems!). Peru considers herself quite as highly civilised as the U.S.A. So far my chief hope is the fear of publicity. If Sir E. Grey publishes my report and the revolting evidence on which it is based, there will be a slump in Peruvian credit she will not readily recover from. Her credit, her vanity, her good name in the world are at stake—she thinks so at any rate—and so her government is trying hard to convince ours of its zeal. So far with little success. Not one of the criminals has been caught—although one of them actually came into Iquitos.

'I think the Monroe Doctrine is at the root of these horrors on the Amazon—it excludes Europe (the Mother of Western Civilisation), with 500,000,000 white people, as against U.S.A. (with less than 80,000,000 whites) from her proper correcting and educating place in the whole of South America. That vast continent of nearly 7 million square miles, has only 40 million inhabitants—and this after close on 400 years of Iberian civilisation. . . . I have talked it over with U.S.A. diplomats and Ambassadors and I find the underlying belief always the same, viz: that Uncle Sam is to inherit the New World. Well, I don't agree, and I don't think that belief or its fruition good for mankind . . . Germany in South America . . . the Teuton on the Amazon—would work more amazing things than the British in India. . . .'

On June 15th Casement got a pleasant letter from Grey, telling him that he had been given a knighthood. And then it was that Casement responded in a manner which could scarcely have been more fulsome. To Mrs. Green he wrote of the matter thus:

'My dear Woman of the Good Woods—Your congrats have been the best, for you *alone* have seen that there was an Irish side to it all. What you say is true—although few will believe it, can possibly believe that I have not worked for this—for a "distinction", and "honour"—or whatever they call it, instead of in reality deeply desiring *not* to get it. In this case it was like the C.M.G.—I couldn't help it at all—and could not possibly fling back something offered like that. Yes, it was Sir E. Grey—I had a charming letter from him telling me that it was he who did it. But there are many in Ireland will think of me as a traitor—and when I think of that country and of them—I feel I am. . . . How should I have rejoiced if I could have said to the King what is really in my heart instead of the perfunctory words of thanks (cold and formal enough) I have said. I want you, please, to keep always writing to me just as "Roger Casement"—will you?. . . . If Irish hearts that know my real feeling will keep on addressing my letters in the old way, it will be a little consolation—for, oh! you don't know how I hate the thing. . . .'

What Casement describes as perfunctory, cold and formal read as follows:

The Savoy, Denham, Bucks.
19th June, 1911.

Dear Sir Edward Grey,

I find it very hard to choose the words in which to make acknowledgment of the honour done me by the King.

I am much moved at the proof of confidence and appreciation of my services on the Putumayo, conveyed to me by your letter, wherein you tell me that the King had been graciously pleased upon your recommendation to confer upon me the honour of Knighthood.

I am indeed grateful to you for this signal assurance of your personal esteem and support, and very deeply sensible of the honour done to me by His Majesty.

I would beg that my humble duty might be presented to His Majesty, when you may do me the honour to convey to him my

deep appreciation of the honour he has been so graciously pleased
to confer upon me.

I am, dear Sir Edward,
Yours sincerely,

I do not think that there can be many who would agree with
the adjectives used by Casement to describe this letter.

Tyrrell wrote saying he was thinking of getting the Catholic
Archbishop of Westminster to set the Putumayo revelations going
in Europe, since that might prove to be the most effective method.
Casement had asked whether he might show his report to a select
few, and Tyrrell said yes, but warned him against the possibility
of leaks or premature publication, since 'we should not be acting
fairly with Peru, and should lose our leverage with them'.

On July 1st two small Indian boys, whom Casement had chosen
while he was in South America, arrived in London to stay with
him at 110 Philbeach Gardens. Casement for some time contemplated educating the boys in England at his own expense, and
arranging for them to make their lives in England. It was a kindly
thought and he seems to have wanted to do something to improve
the lot of at least two of the persecuted race. But in the end he
came to the conclusion that they would, after all, be happier in their
own country in the long run, and he paid their fares home again.

But upon their arrival, Casement proudly showed the two boys
off to his friends, and to the members of the board of the Peruvian
Amazon Company (the new name for the Arana Company);
and Mr. (later Sir) William Rothenstein agreed to paint their
portraits in his Frognal studio. Rothenstein reported to Casement
that when they came for their first sitting, the boys 'put on their
ornaments with care, almost with pedantry, with the help of
combs and water and looking-glass, and then stood like rocks. . . .
I will hand over fair wages to you, to invest for them as you think
fit, so following your advice with regard to giving them no
money personally. You will not forget your own promise to give
me a sitting, will you?'

Casement was still apt to be seized by moods of great despondency. At these times he felt that only a miracle could save Ireland—and that only another miracle could persuade the Foreign Office to do the right thing by his report. He was trying to see the Archbishop of Canterbury about the Putumayo; and he also sent a message to Sir Edward Grey, urging him to send a copy of the Putumayo report to Carnegie, in the hope that the Scottish-American multi-millionaire might be moved to provide funds to put a reorganised and rehumanised company back on its feet and make all well again.

In addition to sending his sycophantic letter to Grey, Casement had been casting about for someone else to thank for his knighthood. A letter, signed merely 'A.M.C.', postmarked The Warren, Abingdon, Berks, but written on Foreign Office notepaper, says (July 20th, 1911):

'It is very good of you to think that I deserve any thanks in connexion with your "honour". I fear I can lay but little claim to anything of the kind, though naturally I did what I could. But indeed there was small need for me or anyone else to "push" the matter, since it was the general feeling that you deserved some small recognition at least of what you had done and what you had gone through. . . .'

Now Casement was faced with a startling paradox. His efforts in the Putumayo had already served to force into liquidation the London office of the Arana company—but far from helping the Indians, it looked as though the consequence might be to worsen their plight. He wrote in perplexity to Cadbury: '. . . the Chairman of the London Board called on me on Friday morning and stayed two hours. He seems to think the Coy's financial position quite hopeless and that practically nothing can save them. To-day I got a letter from Don Julio Arana (the Peruvian vendor of the Putumayo and founder of the Coy) stating that he had 608,493 Ordinary (£1) shares, and 50,000 Preference Shares he is willing to make over—for a consideration! The more I inquire into the possibilities of getting control of the Putumayo, the clearer it is to me that the task is one far beyond the powers of anyone, save a Carnegie perhaps.

'I was staying with the Duke and Duchess of Hamilton and they are trying to help in the Mission matter. To-morrow I shall see the Archbishop of Canterbury, and later the Archbishop of Westminster as to the hope of getting a Mission founded. The Mission seems far the easiest thing to work for, and if once established, it could prove of enormous benefit to the Indians.

'Unless a Millionaire (the Duke of Hamilton is trying Carnegie) appears from on high, there is no use wasting more time with the Company. They will probably liquidate this month.

'The fear is that Arana & Co. will sail for the Putumayo and re-establish their pirate camps in the forest, and complete the destruction of the Indians within the next six years. I know the Iquitos head of the firm—Pablo Zumasta—contemplated this; and is even suggesting it to Julio Arana here in London. How to save the remnant of the Indians, only Providence can show.

'The Foreign Office are doing and have done everything a Government Department could possibly attempt—they have been splendid in the matter. I certainly see no way out at all and yet I cannot despair. It seems incredible that in this period of human development we should be faced with such a state of things in a nominally Christian state, and be quite powerless to save these gentle human beings from so ghastly a fate. . . .'

Cadbury sturdily encouraged him. 'I am much interested to hear of your further experience in the Putumayo affair. . . . If the Company "goes to pot", I suppose there will be a chance of reconstruction on new lines, as against any offer they obtain from Arana, and it is there that Carnegie's means would come in. I feel most strongly with you that the matter must not rest, and that we must at all costs help you to find some means of following up the interests of the Indians on the spot. . . . I am glad to think you are going to stick up for these people, until you see some more decent administration—I am sure you will win. Do not fail to let me know if you need further funds for your campaign. . . .'

At this point the Foreign Office sent Casement all the way back again to Iquitos! I suspect that the more they studied his first report, the more they felt that the extremely serious, not to say bloodcurdling, charges it contained, required more precise and substantial evidence, and perhaps rather more reliable and solid witnesses than the sometimes irresponsible Barbadians (some of whom often irritated Casement himself by having second thoughts and varying their evidence disconcertingly). The ostensible reason for undertaking the arduous voyage for a second time was that Casement was to install a new vice-consul in Iquitos.

Casement explained to his friends that since he was still the Consul-General at Rio, he was in duty-bound to return to Iquitos to try by his presence to obtain redress for the innocent, the punishment of the wrongdoers and to instil some sense of urgency—until now woefully lacking—in the Peruvian authorities. (The Foreign Office were to find the Peruvians much harder nuts to crack than the Belgians.) An official named G. M. Mitchell was to succeed as vice-consul. Casement took to him and considered that he should do well in the post. However, Mitchell was not due in Iquitos for some months and meanwhile Casement would be on the spot 'while the trials (of the guilty) are going on' as he hopefully put it.

He wrote an au revoir note to Cadbury as the R.M.S.P. *Magdalina* took him across Channel to Cherbourg. The two Indian boys were with him. 'My landlady at Earl's Court,' he wrote, 'was *very* sorry to lose them. She says they behaved "so gently and nicely and never a thought of bad".' The Rothensteins had been at Waterloo to see the three of them off, but unfortunately, due to the untimely return of the boys, their portrait was never quite finished. Casement added in his letter to Cadbury that the Foreign Office had sanctioned that his route back to South America should be by way of Barbados, to enable him 'to get hold of one of the black interpreters again'.

Once again he met disappointment, for 'my old Putumayo Barbados men', from whom he had hoped to obtain an interpreter, 'are all scattered and gone'. But worse—in Hastings, a suburb of Bridgetown, the capital, Casement discovered to his indignant fury 'one of the Putumayo Peruvians—settling down and buying a house here! He means to start a hotel—he does not know that there is a warrant out against him in Iquitos!!!' Nor, one supposes, did the former rubber trader greatly care. This confrontation on neutral territory of Casement and his elusive prey must have been worth seeing, and one cannot help wondering if it could have been Jimenez, of the mocking Putumayo send-off, who had thus emigrated to start a new life in the Caribbean.

But the main point of this particular letter to Cadbury was to ask for money. 'If you feel disposed to help further in the matter of the boys, I will accept your help—for they have cost me much. I have not done what I wanted with them, but still they have been of service in the cause of their kinsmen—and one cannot tell whether good fruit may not come out of it yet. If you think the cause one to justify further expenditure on your part, another £50 would ease me a good deal. I have kept accounts of all my expenditure on their behalf and I will, in any case, send you a statement so that you can see how your contribution was spent. . . . If, then, you think the money is not wasted and you care to add another £50, you could pay it into my bankers—Williams Deacons Bank, Ltd., 20 Birchin Lane, E.C. I know your good heart.[1]'

Casement sailed from Barbados on September 5th and by October 30th was once again installed in Iquitos. Nothing of great moment took place while Casement paid his return visit, and indeed, nothing much ever happened further, about the Putumayo scandal, other than great excitement when Casement's report eventually received publication. Unlike Casement's Congo efforts, which led to large and positive results, he was in the end almost totally frustrated over the Putumayo.

[1] Casement was very conscious of expenditure and kept the most laborious personal accounts, noting down such trivial items as pennies for bus tickets, how much he gave to street beggars, expenditure on public conveniences, etc. He gambled with enjoyment and occasionally lost sums which, while not in themselves of great moment, might, had they been known to his benefactors, have somewhat weakened the impact of his appeals for funds for his crusades. In the month of June 1911, for example, his personal expenses totalled nearly £200, at that time a great deal of money.

The Peruvians played an effective waiting game with the Foreign Office. Any measures which they took to bring the evil-doers to book were almost contemptuously perfunctory and ineffective; and their dilatory tactics met their reward when the 1914–18 war broke out and the last vestige of interest about what was happening on the Putumayo was engulfed in far larger pre-occupations in London.

Casement left the Putumayo again in the late autumn of 1911 and, on official instructions, went to Washington to try to help to stir up American interest. Bryce, the British Ambassador, intro-duced him to President Taft at the White House, and he had some talks at the State Department. He was pressing for the establish-ment of a U.S. consul in Iquitos. Bryce telegraphed Whitehall that Casement had been able to create 'a personal interest in the matter among the higher authorities, which gives strong ground for believing that the publication of the report will be welcomed by the United States Government'. Later, Washington, having first counselled delay, indicated that it would agree to publication, provided that their own delaying advice were published at the same time, and this was done.

On January 29th, 1912, Casement was back with the kindly Miss Cox at Philbeach Gardens, and writing to Cadbury that there was still a good deal of work which the Foreign Office wanted him to do in connection with the Putumayo. But now that he was close to Ireland once again, his thoughts hovered in-creasingly over the steadily fermenting situation there. In February a speech by Grey at Manchester pleased him—'I liked Sir E. Grey's reference to Ireland and Home Rule yesterday. The cause is advancing—surely—and I look for sanity of mind yet, even in Belfast on this great subject.' A lecture by Mrs. Green on Ireland was well attended—'among others, the Librarian of the H. of Commons came to sit at her feet!'

In May 1912, after he had returned from a motoring tour of the Continent in the company of a friend, Casement was asked by the Foreign Office to put in some more work on the Putumayo Report, and he accordingly retreated to the Green Bank Hotel,

Falmouth, to tackle this. He told Cadbury that he had got up a committee to see about the money for the Putumayo Mission—£15,000 was needed to match a pledge from the Vatican—but he was worried at the prospect that 'Protestant firebrands' of his acquaintance might 'set up an opposition cult' when they heard that the Catholics had their eye on the Putumayo.

On July 17th, the Putumayo Report was at last out (*The Blue Book on Infamies in the Putumayo*, price 1s. 5d., at the Stationery Office). Once again, as in post-Congo days, the ensuing international fandango was of gargantuan proportions. The sober-sided *Times* remarked in an editorial that 'Sir Roger Casement has deserved well of his countrymen and mankind by the ability and zeal with which he has investigated, under very difficult conditions, an appalling iniquity. His selection for the work, and the able treatment of the whole question . . . are greatly to the credit of Sir Edward Grey, whose patient and conscientious diplomacy is responsible for all the progress towards reform yet made. . . .' The accompanying news story said that 'The Report reveals a systematised barbarity not equalled by King Leopold's infamous régime in the Congo.' The Dictionary of National Biography says that the publication of the report 'created an immense sensation, enhanced by the authority which the writer had already acquired'.

Casement had done it again. Only one or two of the German newspapers attempted to find fault, contending that although the cruelty had been laid bare by a British investigator, the British themselves, in the persons of English traders, had been largely responsible for them in the first place. But the chorus was overwhelmingly complimentary. Again Casement was the hero of the hour.

The Rev. H. Hensley Henson, rector of St. Margaret's, Westminster (and subsequently Dean of Durham) devoted a great sermon in the Abbey to a consideration of Casement's report. In this the Rector stressed the point that Britain was perfectly entitled to take an active hand in what might appear at first blush to be the internal affairs of a sovereign and independent nation, because British subjects in the persons of black Barbadians were involved. The sermon was a spirited affair. Henson named names from the pulpit, including those of the Arana Company directors. Of Casement, he told his congregation, 'Sir Roger, who has fully earned the right to direct us, holds that the establishment of a Christian Mission in the Putumayo will be good.'[1]

In spite of all the uproar over the Putumayo, public response, when it came to cash, was again disappointing, and Count Blücher, honorary co-treasurer of the Putumayo Mission Fund, was able to report the intake of only a modest £1,557 8s. 6d. by the end of July.

But by mid-August the press correspondence over the Putumayo had resolved itself into a gentle bickering about the denomination of the proposed mission, and the Catholics appeared, as Casement had hoped, to be in the lead. However, a strong bid was put in by the Evangelist Union of South Africa, and one Perry H. Brown wrote to *The Times* to make the not impractical point that 'in all this controversy on religious matters, people are losing sight of the urgent needs of the Indians'.

Apart from all the other calls upon his attention and energies, Casement had some family worries on top of the rest. His brother Tom, out in South Africa, wrote reporting a most precarious fiscal situation. 'I trust he will be able to pull through, with the help I am able to give him,' Casement wrote to Cadbury. Casement was also trying to find a job for Elizabeth Bannister, a sister of his cousin Gertrude. She was after a job at the Birmingham High School, and since Cadbury was living just outside the city, it was to his long-suffering friend and patron that Casement once again turned. In return for Cadbury's many kindnesses, Casement had brought back from his tropical journeys a selection of exotic gifts, among them a blue macaw, which was referred to in the correspondence as 'good old Polly Blue Bird'. Casement described to

[1] The report of the sermon appeared on the main page of *The Times*, flanked by a description of the arrival of King George V and Queen Mary at Cowes, and that of the marriage of Lord Anglesey and Lady Marjorie Manners.

Cadbury the scene at the London station when he was bringing the bird north to Birmingham. Polly Blue Bird whipped out of the open carriage window and perched on the roof of the carriage, in front of a gathering crowd of travellers and porters, which was presently joined by Sir John Simon. 'You never saw a funnier scene,' reported Casement. 'The platform was quite in an uproar. She *eloped* through the window, chortling and chuckling, and on getting back from the ticket-office I found my carriage besieged. Sir John Simon had with him two beautiful—quite lovely—ladies, and Polly held an audience.'

By July 29th, 1912, Casement's optimism concerning his brother Tom had slumped. From The Savoy, Denham[1] he despatched an enormous letter to his benefactor Cadbury, pouring out the tale of Tom's tribulations ('I have helped this brother many times. He is *not* a waster, but an extraordinarily unbusiness-like human being—*much* worse than I am'). Tom, whom Casement described as 'everybody's friend—extraordinarily reckless, amusing and unconventional', had, it seemed, become owner of a hotel at a mountain resort called 'Mont aux Sources'. He had also married a lady artist. If Tom could get a little capital he could turn it into a paying proposition. What Tom needed was £1,200, and Casement was suggesting that this sum might be contributed in three equal amounts of £400; one each from Cadbury, Herbert Ward, and Tom's newly acquired father-in-law, a Mr. Ackermann. Casement described the matter as 'a hideous family disaster' and he asked Cadbury's forgiveness for 'falling on you with this horrible request . . .'

Ackermann had already committed himself to the dismal venture; and I have an idea that Cadbury too showed his usual generosity. What Herbert Ward's reactions were we can but guess.

About this time Casement had a brush with Lord Northcliffe. He seems to have irritated the famous newspaper proprietor by one of those changes of mind to which he was subject. Northcliffe

---

[1] At a much later era to house none other than Sir Oswald and Lady Cynthia Mosley.

coldly took him to task (October 11th, 1912) '. . . for first accepting the invitation to write in my newspaper, *The Daily Mail*, then declining, and finally inserting an article in a review.' Northcliffe added that since this placed him in a considerable difficulty, *The Daily Mail* was entitled to some explanation. Casement's explanation was that he had contracted to do the review piece long before there was talk of the *Mail* article.

Casement spent the late summer and most of the autumn of 1912 in Ireland, but in November he had to go back to London to attend hearings—'I shall be the *pièce-de-résistance* next Wednesday'—of the Parliamentary Select Committee on the Putumayo atrocities.

VI

CASEMENT'S health was giving him and his friends cause for renewed anxiety, and although there was occasional talk at the Foreign Office of his return to the Consulate-General at Rio de Janeiro, Casement himself had finally dismissed any such prospect from his mind. His thoughts turned increasingly to retirement, and he appealed for help to J. H. Morgan, later to become one of the world's foremost authorities on constitutional law (and who helped in the defence of Casement at his trial).

Morgan readily agreed to lunch with Casement in his flat in Ebury Street. '. . . You may feel assured that I will do anything I can with the utmost pleasure. I had a long talk with the Prime Minister at lunch in Downing Street to-day, and had I known what your difficulty was I might have said something. Grey I know but slightly, but Haldane I know very well (and he is a great friend of Grey's) and if it is a question of moving those in high places I may be able to be of use.

'I shall be delighted to meet Morel. But I'm disturbed about your health—what you tell me sounds rather serious—I hope you will be guided by your doctor and will rest.'

Casement then wrote to Mrs. Green, asking her to arrange an appointment for him with Sir Lauder Brinton, an eminent physician, in the hope that the subsequent medical report would convince the Foreign Office that, far from taking up the thread at Rio once again, he ought to be allowed retirement from the service on pension.

Sir Lauder Brinton's report was as follows:

MEDICAL REPORT OF JAN. 1913 ON SIR ROGER CASEMENT
  Age: 48
  Heart: Normal

Liver: Full and very tender
Spleen: Full
Lung: Curious creaks on respiration, as if from an old
    adhesion
Appendix: Tender. Ovoid swelling, like $\frac{3}{4}$ inch rope near ileum
Bowels: Constipated
Tongue: Furred, and turns slightly to left
Appetite: Very bad
Flatulence: A little
Nausea: None
Piles: Operated on for obstruction
Nervous system: Sleeps well
Headaches: Slight

All this—annoyingly, in a sense—seemed to show that there was nothing very seriously the matter, but Casement decided to take no notice of Sir Lauder's unwelcome findings, and again wrote to Mrs. Green to say that he was sure that he had appendicitis and was off forthwith to the Canaries for a rest-cure. For his part, Sir Lauder, marvelling no doubt, as others have done, at the waywardness of his bearded patient, said stiffly that all he could further do was to provide him with some notes for use by some other doctor should occasion arise.

Casement asked Sir Edward Grey for sick leave, and it was instantly granted by telegram. He informed Grey that his pains had recently been getting worse and that he feared a total breakdown. He said that he had been X-rayed for possible kidney stone but that the results had proved negative.

And with that Casement was off by German boat to seek the sun. H. W. Nevinson wrote in his wake from his Hampstead studio to say how grieved he was to hear of the illness, especially as Casement had seemed to stand up to his last journeys so well that he (Nevinson) had 'hoped that you were quite case-hardened to tropics and London equally. But I suppose it is indignation kills you, as it kills us all. . . . If we could cease from cruel rage we should all be well. . . . '

At the end of January Casement, now in Teneriffe, wrote to Mrs. Green saying that a doctor in the islands had been found who agreed about the seriousness of his condition, and that he could not go back to Rio without the grave risk of 'this disease becoming permanent'. (I am not clear to which disease he was referring, but I think, by now, arthritis.) There was more talk of his being pensioned off, and Casement compared the conquest of the Canaries by Spain with that of Ireland by the British. Spain, it is perhaps unnecessary to add, came out of it, in his view, much the better. There was the utmost indignation at the discovery that he had been placed on half-pay. There was evidently a strong protest, for in Las Palmas he received a letter, signed by Gerald Spicer of the Foreign Office, saying that he would look into the 'cut' of which Casement had informed him, and the Treasury would be asked to let him go back to full salary.

Casement now began to feel better, and he booked onward passage for Capetown, there to see for himself how his brother was managing to resolve his various difficulties. Just before he left he got a letter from none other than Gielgud, now living in Oxford-and-Cambridge Mansions, Marylebone. '. . . The committee' [presumably the Parliamentary Select Committee] 'has been having another go at me this week, and in view of the favourable evidence you were so good as to give as to your opinion of me, I think it only right to let you know that the suggestion in the minds of some of them seemed to be that I had been bribed by Arana to conceal the real state of things in the Putumayo. I need hardly assure you that this is not the case, and the Chairman very fairly allowed Astbury to give me an opportunity of giving a categorical denial to any such suggestion. You may be amused to learn that I have been informed privately that Arana has asserted that I attempted to blackmail him! . . .'

Aboard the *Grantully Castle* to Capetown, Casement railed at the Foreign Office anew. They were 'Anglo-Britannic swine' now, because they seemed to insist on his return to Rio ('the doctors all say it would be madness'), and because they had 'cheated' him of half his pay. 'They never said a word to me, either! I only found out from my bank! Aren't they beauties? I pray God—and Erin—that the Turks may yet drive them out of Egypt. Their perfidy to Turkey to-day is really a fine object-lesson to "La Perfide Albion's" ways. . . .'

But though he castigated the Foreign Office so violently, Casement decided to ask for longer leave, and he also explained to Mrs. Green ('Dear Woman of the Three Books') from St. Helena that an anti-British piece which he had written and submitted to the *Fortnightly Review* had after all better not appear over his own name, as he might 'get into very hot water at the Foreign Office. I thought at first of letting it go, but I fear it would lead to an explosion, and as I am applying for longer leave of absence, I had better not provoke them! . . . I shall soon be going up-country to my brother's place at Witzie's Hoek, in the Orange Free State, where it is warm and dry and peaceful.'

In South Africa Casement heard from Lord Dufferin of the Foreign Office, who dealt with his query as to how much pension would be due to him if he were to retire forthwith. Lord Dufferin informed him that £440 a year was the figure, and added that they would all be sorry to lose him, if he so decided, but that he realised that consular service had many drawbacks. He also reminded Casement that since he was still far short of sixty, his application for permission to retire must be accompanied by a suitable medical certificate 'strong enough to satisfy the Treasury'.

Casement duly made his way up to Witzie's Hoek and 'Mont aux Sources', but our curiosity remains unsatisfied as to the out-come of his efforts to settle his brother's affairs and those of the erstwhile Miss Ackermann. However a letter which Tom sent to Roger, after the latter had left 'Mont aux Sources' and was on his way home again, suggests that Tom shared some of Roger's flair for bungling matters; for Tom described how his favourite pony had fallen over a cliff, while a picnic was in progress, and hurt itself so badly that Tom, having climbed down to investigate, decided that there was nothing for it but to despatch the hapless beast on the spot. It required no fewer than four shots at point-blank range to do so, 'and after the second shot,' related Tom, 'the poor fellow got up and looked at me with a strange expression. The look haunts me still.'

The African climate worked wonders for Casement's health and spirits. 'I can laugh arthritis to scorn, lock, stock and barrel', and he meant to go back to London 'and square things with the Foreign Office'. 'Mont aux Sources', perched high in the mountains, had greatly pleased him—'I shall part with it with a pang—London, with its noise and worry and strains will be absolutely hateful; while Rio—ugh! I shudder at the thought.'

But there was to be no more Rio. Casement got back to London in mid-May and then went over to Dublin, where he sat for a portrait, commissioned by the Cadburys and painted by Miss Sara Purser. But hardly were the sittings under way than there came another heart cry from Tom, so serious that Roger actually considered undertaking the long journey to South Africa all over again. As he explained it to Mrs. Green: 'I should never forgive myself if I did not try to save that sinking home.' In the end he did not go, and was soon writing to Mrs. Green, untroubled seemingly by any thoughts of the despatch he had sent to the Foreign Office thirteen years earlier, 'I lunched yesterday with Major MacBride, who led the Irish Brigade in the Boer War. He did splendid work there, and I begged him to *write* that story....'

At the end of June 1913, after some interchanges with the Foreign Office, a satisfactory medical report was arranged, stating that Casement's health would be permanently impaired by arthritis were he to continue in the Foreign Service (but it is strange that Brinton had made no mention of this threat barely six months earlier), and Casement wrote to Sir William Tyrrell: 'I have put off taking a step that necessarily fills me with much regret and much pain until the last moment. I was hoping perhaps that I might see a way out that would still allow me to stay in the Service, while getting away from Brazil.

'As, however, my leave of absence expires to-morrow and I do not feel justified in returning to Rio de Janeiro, it would seem to be my duty to not longer defer sending my resignation of that post and making application for permission to retire on the grounds of ill-health.

'I feel it would be quite useless for me to return to Rio, both for myself and for the Service, my health is now so permanently impaired I could not hope to efficiently discharge the duties of Consul-General there. Under these circumstances I shall make official application for leave to retire from Rio, and as you say the Secretary of State will support that application I trust it may be possible for my retirement on the grounds of ill-health to be sanctioned by the Treasury. Whether I am doing the best thing for my own interests is hard to say, but I feel convinced that as I should only completely break down at Rio I am acting rightly to the interests of the public Service, and that the Rio Consulate can only gain from my retirement.

'I have to indeed express a very keen regret at severing my connexion with a Service I have for so long been associated with and still more at severing ties with persons from whom I have so often and continuously received marks of much friendship and esteem that I shall not forget.

'Believe me, Yours always,'

These warm sentiments scarcely found an echo in a letter to Cadbury, written just two days later. '. . . I have resigned from Rio. There was no use trying to go back there—both my own feelings and the doctor's advice coincided, and so I resigned on June 30th, with the sanction of the powers that be, who prefer to accept my resignation from Rio to offering me a post elsewhere in a healthier climate.' (Even if Casement had forgotten, the 'powers-that-be' probably recalled all too vividly what happened to their last attempt to get him to go to a healthy post at Lisbon.)

From Morel there came the expectable eulogy. '. . . I can't but feel you have done right in resigning from the Foreign Office. But I do most sincerely trust that you will get such a pension as may express, however inadequately, the magnificent work you have done for that Department. Your two exploits are the bright spot in a record of foreign policy marked by some disgraceful episodes . . . I know of no living man who deserves so much at the nation's hands as you do.'

Parminter had turned up in England, and Casement wrote to Cadbury forcefully, generously and well, on behalf of his old friend who was heartily tired of life with the coffee people in Santos and sought home employment instead. Casement maintained that Parminter was 'horribly treated by the Foreign Office', especially by Sir Eric Barrington, who was the man he characterised as 'a fierce cad'. Evidently Barrington's sword-crossing with Casement over the Lisbon business was never forgotten nor forgiven.

Casement was full of various projects. Writing now from Denham, now from Dublin and now from Ebury Street, he talked of living permanently in the Union of South Africa in order to be near his brother, perhaps taking up a travelling post for the Anti-Slavery Society, perhaps even wandering through Angola and other parts of West Africa in order to gain the material for a travel book.

But all this was as nothing compared with his growing absorption and participation in the cause of Irish Nationalism. His long letters to Mrs. Green at this period are almost always of political meetings held, or about to be held; of plans and plots and a determination to see Ireland liberated. This had been the case right through 1912, and now through 1913—there were dozens of letters to Mrs. Green and Miss Bannister, not to mention many other recipients, and they all repeat the refrain.

In September 1912, while he was still employed by the Foreign Office, Casement had contributed an article entitled 'Ireland and the German Menace' under a *nom-de-guerre*, to the *Irish Review*, newly started by two Dublin poets, Joseph Plunkett and Thomas MacDonagh; and in July 1913, barely had he resigned from the Foreign Service and started to draw his pension from the Crown, than he followed this up with 'Germany, Ireland and the Next War', an essay which put so extreme and violent a view that it was later reprinted in pamphlet form as valuable propaganda for the cause of Sinn Fein. He had also been writing anonymously in

Irish Freedom, the paper edited by Bulmer Hobson, and in other publications. His reiterated theme was that an Anglo-German war was absolutely inevitable and, when it came, it would be Ireland's grand opportunity to free herself once and for all from the Saxon thrall.

The fact that while he lived Casement was almost completely unknown among the Irish as their protagonist in Ireland is an ironic fact—but it was a fact which in no wise deterred Casement from regarding himself as a figure of great importance in the movement. Throughout his career he showed no inclination to underrate himself, and this period was no exception.

At this point in the narrative I am confronted by two difficult alternatives. One is to embark on a massive attempt to explain the immensely complex and controversial Irish historical-political situation as it obtained while 1913 ended; the other is to over-simplify.

I choose the second. Let it be said that the long, nearly always tempestuous, often disastrous and unfortunately sombre history of Ireland was now, after several centuries of blood and tears, moving quickly to a climax which seemed bound somehow or other to produce 'Home Rule' (Independence) very soon.

It had to come. On that everyone was agreed. But how? By constitutional and peaceful means, was the prayer of men of good-will on both shores of the Irish Sea.

The murmur of such prayers was, unfortunately, being drowned out by the combative sounds of the extremists on both sides—by the thump of inexpert feet bearing their owners in clumsy, clandestine drill; by the clatter of nocturnally landed arms; by the hoarse shouts of 'action now' men at public meetings. Nor was it a straightforward matter of England and Ireland, dangerous and difficult as that would have been. Probably no other country could have produced the fantastic complication of a situation where the six northern counties, known as Ulster, were not only determined to retain the English connexion, but quite genuinely prepared to fight anybody and everybody in order to do so.

Parliament was juggling with the hot potato Home Rule Bill. When it reached the Lords it was thrown out. It would inevitably get up to the Lords again in two years at the most—and at the second time of asking the Lords would be bound to pass it; for although the upper house of Parliament still retained some veto power, it had recently been modified.

Ulster was full of noise and defiance and open preparation for war. Gun-running was in full swing and a part-time citizen army in civilian clothes, Australian-type slouch hats, and bandoliers, carrying any sort of rifle, drilled with great gusto. Ulster's god was Sir Edward Carson, M.P., a brilliant, fifty-nine-year-old Dublin-born lawyer, whose fixed purpose in life it was to keep anything to do with Home Rule out of Ulster. He was a former Solicitor-General of Ireland, and his brooding, lined and rather melancholy cast of countenance was known to everyone from Antrim to Londonderry, and Donegal to Down. In London, he was the toast of the Tories.

At his side was Frederick Edwin Smith, M.P., then just over forty. His fantastic brilliance was soon to procure for him the position of Attorney-General of England. He was elegant and unhurried. He seemed to take everything in stride with indolence and nonchalance. But when he felt the moment had come, 'Galloper' Smith was as quick as a rattle-snake and just as lethal.

Together these two master cross-examiners strode the northern scene, exhorting, defying, mobilising. The smell of civil war hung acrid in the air of Ireland.

Insofar as they had a champion, the remaining Catholic, twenty-six, non-Ulster counties of central and southern Ireland possessed one in the person of John Redmond, M.P., the leader of the Irish Nationalist Party. On him had fallen the mantle of the great and already legendary Parnell. But although a man of energy and a convincing speaker (and for that matter, a much better fund-getter than Casement, since he once, on sheer eloquence, raised £10,000 for his party's war-chest during a short speaking trip in Australia), the former Clerk in the House of

Commons, now sixty-two, was no giant. On the contrary, he was the sort of moderate, reasonable, compromising man, who in the long run may be seen as playing a part more helpful to humanity than the firebrands may have done—but who is not at all likely to appeal to his own extremists, least of all Irish extremists. Redmond, although sincere, and longing for the day of Ireland's freedom, nonetheless pursued, from the British point of view, an honourable course. When the war with Germany came, he was strictly loyal to the British cause, whatever anguish may have been the result for him; and far from helping the attempts to interfere with recruiting for the Irish regiments of the British Army, he did his best to raise new divisions. To the Sinn Feiners, descendants of the old-time Fenians who had raided Chester Castle and tried to blow up Clerkenwell Jail in the 1860's, and to the men of the Irish Republican Brotherhood; to all the ardent young revolutionaries spoiling for a fight—to them Redmond was anathema, or at best a well-meaning middle-of-the-path man, who was old and soft and had lost his nerve.

To a man like Bulmer Hobson, Redmond must have seemed as painfully unattractive politically as it was possible to be. For example, Redmond always frowned on the Irish Volunteers. This was a body formed in the South as an answer to Carson's Ulster Volunteers who were so loudly rattling the sabre in Belfast and its environs. To Redmond, the existence of a few sketchily armed and ill-trained bands on his own side of the border could do no good, and could easily do harm far out of proportion to their numbers. To the Sinn Fein it was not only the manly and patriotic thing, but the logical thing to offset the cursed Ulster Volunteers with a counterpart unit of their own. Were they not red-blooded Irishmen too? What was wrong with the man Redmond? Could it be that he had stayed too long at Westminster and acquired some devious English ways? Ah, to hell with it, boys—let's go on up there and shoot some of those damned Orange Protestants.[1]

[1] At Casement's trial, his chief counsel, Serjeant Sullivan, made the point that the Irish of the South had been forced by naked fear into forming their own version of the Volunteers. In the spring of 1914,

A further reason for Redmond wishing to eschew any form of ill-considered and futile violence was that he was sure that Home Rule would come eventually by constitutional means, in spite of the House of Lords having dashed his hopes the first time. Since Ireland had already waited half a thousand years for her liberty, was it really asking too much of his followers to wait just a couple of years more? That's all very well, they replied in effect, but do not you realise that you are being tricked by these English yet again? They have done it before, and of course they are willing to repeat it. Lies, deceit, craft, treachery are the recognised and traditional British techniques. Next time it won't be the Lords, but some other excuse—you'll see, Redmond.

Alarmed by the general prospect, the Sinn Feiners went ahead and organised a Provisional Committee, a sort of political action organisation, designed to protect themselves in what they thought was to be some very dismal in-fighting—against Ulster-backed-by-Britain primarily, but also to see that Redmond did not step too far out of line. Professor Eoin (John) McNeill was a founder-member of this committee.

General Sir Arthur Paget, G.O.C., from 1911 to 1917, British troops in Ireland, defied a War Office order to move some of his men from the Curragh, in County Kildare just south-west of Dublin, northwards to Ulster, where they were supposed to guard munitions' depôts against the anticipated raids of rifle-hungry Ulster Volunteers. Paget regarded as 'unthinkable' any suggestion that his forces should find themselves in armed collision with anyone in Ulster, a sentiment which was echoed by his officers and by whoopers-up over in London. Paget's non-co-operation with his superiors in the War Office was followed by a gesture so close to mutiny as made no odds. Nearly sixty officers of the Lancers, including a Brigadier, announced publicly that they would resign their commissions rather than risk possible action in Ulster. They were recalled to London for a lecturing, and then sent back, otherwise unscathed, to the Curragh, where they were received with an ostentatious display of military honours. Uproar ensued in the House of Commons and there was a number of hasty resignations in the War Office.

In those days the Irish in Ireland found themselves in something of the same position as that occupied by the Jews of Israel thirty years after. They might have their troubles, and bad ones too, but whenever things threatened to get too tough, they were able to console themselves with the reflection that over there, in big rich America, there lived millions of their co-racialists and co-religionists. There were, for example, far more Irish in New York City than there were in Dublin, and most of the exiles were sentimentally and financially on their side; moreover they were in a position to exert, through such organisations as Tammany Hall and its counterparts in all the great cities of America, a very important political pull, if need be right up into the White House itself.

While some emigrant blocs entertained only hostility, or perhaps a mild indifference, towards the country of their origin, the Irish turned nothing but eyes of love and warm, cherishing hearts towards their native land. What is more the Irish in America quickly found that their original anti-British bias, not that it needed much stimulus, was backed up and fed and encouraged, actively or passively, by the rebel climate of the U.S.A. itself. Here was a race which had been brought up in the tradition of rebellion against England; and when the Irish went across the Atlantic it was to find themselves in a great country which had been born in revolution against the self-same England. It was hard to know which retained the more bitter or more carefully fostered memories about the Redcoats, the Irish or their American hosts.

America just before the 1914–18 war, and indeed for many years afterwards, was full of anti-British feeling. There was mistrust and hatred of 'the Imperialists'; and the American shared with the Irishman his dislike of the British 'stuffed shirts' and 'snooty monocle-wearers' who turned up in the New World; so that any inclination which Irish-American emigrés might feel to try to forget Cromwell and the Famine and absentee landlords was quickly halted as it encountered larger memories of Bunker Hill and the burning of the White House. The Irish of Boston and

Philadelphia and New York's East Side would undoubtedly plump for Bulmer Hobson and Professor McNeill, if given the choice, rather than Honest John Redmond.

Across this darkling and bewildering scene Sir Roger Casement came straying in 1913 and 1914. The old-time supporter of the Gaelic League and gay Feis in the glens; of cottage industries and the writing of cheques in Irish, now wished to try his hand in one of the toughest fields of activity which the modern world has to offer, that of politics. If any man was apolitical it was surely Casement. In the rough jungle of politics he was the innocent abroad. Casement was the born amateur. It happened that while he worked for the Foreign Office this fact could remain concealed, for the most part at any rate; but once he tried to get into politics the awe-inspiring limitations of his contribution were all too cruelly revealed. In Ireland, in the U.S.A., and finally in Germany the rest of the story was to be a series of woeful miscalculations and bunglings—a case history of amateurishness.

But no such daunting considerations disturbed Casement as he swung avidly into action in the autumn of 1913. From Ardigh, the Belfast home of his lawyer friend Mr. Biggar, he wrote that September to Cadbury: 'The Carson campaign is in full swing here now—and a Commander-in-Chief has been appointed for the Ulster Volunteer Army. It is spoken of openly as an Army, and the bands are termed "regiments", etc, etc. Carson openly proclaims its illegality and glories in it, and defies the Government to touch a hair of their heads.

'And so the fight proceeds—and most people wonder what will be the next step. If the Liberal Government quails before this open defiance of law and Parliament, the King, the Whole Realm, then there will be an end of Liberalism for one thing—and of orderly government for another. Carson will find many imitators—and the National party here will become a definite anti-English party —what it by no means is to-day. . . .'

The restraint of Casement's communications to Mr. Cadbury, who although, like his fellow-Quakers, a man of peace and conciliation, was nonetheless a patriotic Englishman, is in vivid contrast to this outburst to Miss Bannister, written from Belfast at about the same time:

'I *love* the Antrim Presbyterians—Antrim and Down—they are good, kind, warm-hearted souls; and to see them now, *exploited* by that damned Church of Ireland—that Orange Ascendancy Gang who hate Presbyterians only less than Papists, and to see them delirious before a *Smith*, a *Carson* (a cross between a badly reared bloodhound and an underfed hyaena, sniffing for Irish blood in the track) and whooping Rule Britannia thro' the streets is a wound to my soul. . . . Sometimes the only thing to bring a boy to his senses is to hide him—and I think "Ulster" wants a sound hiding at the hands of her that owns her—Ireland's hands. Failing that—I pray for the Germans and their coming. A Protestant Power to teach these Protestants their place in Irish life is what is needed—and as England is too paltry, too political, too timorous to play the great rôle needed, then pray God the heads of Europe step in and end this affront to the civilisation of the world. . . .'

In November the Sinn Fein Political Committee held their first public meeting in the Dublin Rotunda. It was a matter of standing-room only, in order to hear Patrick Pearse, and of overflow meetings in the streets nearby. Afterwards, thousands hastened to sign on for the Irish Volunteers, and every available hall in Dublin was hired for drilling. Colonel Maurice Moore, who had fought in the British Army in the Boer War, was appointed Inspector-General of the Volunteers.

Casement who was at the Rotunda meeting, wrote to Mrs. Green about it: '. . . Do contrast this fine spirit of the *Irish* Volunteers and what Eoin McNeill writes of the cheers for the Unionist Irishmen at the meeting, with the mean, atrocious appeals to hate and contempt of the English "Aristocracy". What a sordid, cowardly gang of curs they are at heart—and, oh! how I sometimes in my heart long for the thud of German boots keeping guard outside the Mother of Parliaments! And *The Times* office as the head of the German Intelligence Division . . .!'

The Secretary for Ireland in the British Liberal Government of the day, was Augustine Birrell, a former Liverpool barrister and past-president of the National Liberal Federation; an essayist of repute, and the author of a life of Charlotte Brontë. He was a well-meaning man, then aged sixty-three, with the virtues and defects of liberalism, whose main political interest lay in the field of education. It was a pity that it should have been Birrell who attempted to rule the tornado, for there can be little doubt that a far stronger hand was required on the tiller. But Birrell it was, and he continued in office until the Dublin Rising of 1916 obliterated him politically.

In that December of 1913 Birrell acted, however, as best he could. He proclaimed that all arms imports, into both northern and southern Ireland, were banned. This move signally failed to appeal to the south. They had scarcely begun to gather weapons about them, whereas Ulster had had a start so long that it might well prove decisive. Ulster was openly cockahoop. The Sinn Feiners were frustrated and alarmed. Redmond did his best to counsel moderation and patience. But almost immediately both sides started to redouble their efforts to run in guns clandestinely from the Continent. Civil war seemed to hover even more closely.

At this point there followed two episodes in Casement's bungling later career which are so characteristic of the man, so much in keeping with the pattern in which his highest enthusiasms seemed fated to crash in dismal anti-climax, that one does not know whether to laugh or weep.

Both took place in Cork. On December 15th, Casement and Professor Eoin McNeill turned up there to address a mass meeting in the City Hall. Things went fairly well, although as a public speaker Casement was not nearly as convincing as in conversation among a few people in a drawing-room; and McNeill, although a man of high scholarly attainments, was no spell-binder. It is likely that the fervent, volatile, enthusiastic Cork crowd would in any case have gone home a little disappointed, but Casement and McNeill put the lid squarely on matters with a *gaffe* which only two political babes in the wood could have achieved.

At the meeting's end, Casement and McNeill stood up on the platform and smilingly called for three cheers for—of all people—Sir Edward Carson. Later they explained to astounded friends that their reasoning had been that Carson, for all that he was on the other side of the fence, had shown great courage in rebelling against the rule of order and in striking a firm blow for his political beliefs. He was, in fact, an admirable and independent Irishman. While this sort of sophistry might have appealed to a group of dons sitting round their port, the proposition was far too subtle for the audience of good Cork men who were ready to cheer, if anything, eternal hell-fire for Carson; and in putting it forward, Casement and his companion were but revealing their lack of knowledge of even the most elementary rules of the game. It was a little like calling on a gathering of fanatical Pakistanis for three hearty cheers for Mr. Nehru.

All those present jumped to their feet in rage and the next moment the air was full of flying chairs. There was an ugly rush at the platform. Casement and McNeill were lucky to find a handy door through which to make a smart, if undignified, getaway.

Casement's next bout of windmill-tilting, which followed immediately, was to plunge into the situation which had developed over the withdrawal by the Cunard and White Star companies of calls by their ships at Cork harbour. The shipping companies maintained that the harbour had become unsafe for such giants as the *Lusitania* and *Mauretania*; and until matters were remedied they feared that Cork must be abandoned. This was a serious matter not only for Cork itself but to some extent for the commercial interests of the whole of southern Ireland.

While the Cork Harbour Board and other interested bodies were pursuing an orthodox policy of trying to induce the British shipping people to relent, Casement suddenly thought he saw a wonderful chance not only to do Cork a power of good, but also at a stroke to cement the Irish-German relations on which he was by now so set, and cause Whitehall grave concern and embarrassment into the bargain.

He determined to get Herr Ballin, the famous Hamburg shipmaster, to direct his ships of the Hamburg-Amerika Line to call regularly at Cork and Queenstown in future, thus scoring heavily off 'The Fat Man of Europe', as Casement had now taken to calling England in his letters to intimates. And if Ireland could thus possess herself of an entirely non-English transport link with the New World, and a German one at that, the implications both in peace and war were enough to make Casement's easily stirred heart thud with excitement.

This plan was no sooner thought of than tried. At once the familiar rhodomontade started whirring into the letter-boxes of his friends, here, there and everywhere. The dossier built up fast— telegrams, postcards, as well as the multiple-page letters that were standard form. 'I am fighting Hell and all its Angels over the Cork and Queenstown route to the U.S.A., and may go to Hamburg next week. The Anglo-Saxons are in a blue funk—a regular panic, and are trying every dodge they know to keep the German line off—but the O'Scrodgie has got them hip and thigh—and if the Germans *do* funk it (and I don't think they will) then he has another card up his sleeve!' (To 'Gee', December 19th, 1913, on notepaper headed 8 Onslow Gardens). Also from Onslow Gardens on December 22nd, Casement wrote to Mr. John J. Horgan in Cork[1] saying that the Germans definitely meant to start calling at Cork and 'are keen on it' but did not think it wise to make too big a splash about it at first 'and they hope it won't be treated in an anti-English light'.

Inconsistently on the 31st he wrote again to Mr. Horgan, this time from Belfast where he was staying with his friend Biggar, 'I see that the first call of the Hamburg-Amerika Line is fixed for January 20th, with s.s. *Rhaetia* (a small ship I knew in Brazil). I trust the Harbour Board will send at once their invitation to the Captain, etc., to lunch, so that there may be no possible hitch . . . I will come too, if you ask me . . . I suggest that you should also get the Board to invite the Baron von Horst "and party". He is the London representative of the German line, has big business concerns in England, and hopes to extend some of them to Ireland. . . .

[1] See Appendix I.

124

Do all in your power,' adds Casement, vicariously warming to the work, 'to make the occasion a success, and to show this friendly German ship that the Continental tradition of "Irish hospitality" rests on something more than a memory of the Middle Ages. By the way, why not ask Mrs. Green to this historic luncheon . . . ?'

On January 7th Casement, intoxicated with delight, announced to Horgan that Baron von Horst had telegraphed saying that the Hamburg-Amerika Line had agreed to a civic reception when the *Rhaetia* made her first call at Cork. Casement charged off into a mass of detailed suggestions—his 'not too big a splash' completely forgotten—for the great day. German flags were to be flown by all the ships in harbour ('*at the fore!*'), a brass band would be handy to play 'The Watch on the Rhine' (in preference, apparently, to the German National Anthem). Biggar promised to bring a bagpipe band down from Belfast. The prospect, as Casement saw it, was of 'a regular feast of commercial reason and flow of Irish soul' commemorating 'the advent of the first Great Continental Steamship Service to Irish waters'. And 'by the way, don't omit a *real* Irish flag—none of your spalpeen things, with a Union Jack in the corner, but the real old true-blue green'. Finally there was to be a message of cordial sympathy and congratulations from the Italians of New York City, 'So now we have a new Triple Alliance, of Ireland, Germany and Italy . . .!'

By January 12th there was an ominous turn of events. The Germans were now saying that they would prefer there to be no reception and, above all, no demonstration. Casement was piqued, and talked of cancelling the charter of a large tug on which he had planned to entertain his friends in the harbour. Quickly the Germans backed up their request with a much more peremptory message—the shipping company would be forced to abandon the Cork call altogether unless they received categorical assurances that there would be 'no fuss'. Casement hinted darkly at 'political pressures'. Finally came total disappointment when the Germans backed out altogether.

Casement's mortification was deep. '. . . I shall certainly go to the U.S.A. *now*, to burn all boats and raise this issue through all the land. We'll wreck the Anglo-Saxon Alliance anyhow . . . I know the agency that moved in the matter—I know its power—it has again locked the door and shut us off from the friendly people coming to our shores. . . . The pretext for the public is "no passengers booked"; the real reason is undoubtedly what you suspect' (to Mrs. Green, January 20th, 1914).

Probably Casement was wrong in his estimate of the reasons for his latest frustration. At the start of 1914 war between England and Germany was obviously very near. But until the guns actually started to go off, neither side wished to do anything but seem ultra-correct and non-provocative. Thus it was probably unnecessary for anyone in London to concern themselves overmuch with the proposed visit of the *Rhaetia* to Cork, or to try to bring pressure on Ballin and the Baron. The German company either decided to call the project off on its own account—especially in view of Casement's plans for making a carnival out of it—or else it received a quiet word from the Wilhelmstrasse.

The Irish free-for-all continued with undiminished strenuousness and by April 1914 it was doubtful which war would break out first, that in Ireland or that on the Continent. Most of the general public would probably have given you long odds on Ireland. On the 24th the Ulstermen triumphantly landed 40,000 German Mauser rifles at Larne, Donaghadee and Bangor. 'An unprecedented outrage!' cried Mr. Asquith, the Prime Minister, but this observation did nothing to quell the lively fears in the Sinn Fein breasts, and feverish preparations went forward to cap the Ulster gun-running with one in the south. Bulmer Hobson changed his name and took command of the operation. Someone rushed over to Germany to see if there were any spare Mausers left. The novelist, Erskine Childers, who had written a best-seller called *The Riddle of the Sands*, all about mysterious goings-on in a yacht off the German North Sea coasts, now cruised off the German coast in his own yacht, all agog for real-life drama.[1]

[1] Childers was executed during 'the troubles'. It was alleged that he had been found carrying a concealed weapon.

The place designated for the landing of the Sinn Fein arms was Howth, a pretty little summer resort with a ruined abbey, eight miles north-east of Dublin. But despite the extreme urgency of the hour, and the dread that haunted Hobson and his men lest they be attacked while they still remained virtually naked in a military sense, the earliest date on which the arms could be expected was in mid-summer.

Casement skirmished about on the periphery of all this, desperately seeking to get into the heart of the matter. Germany was still the trump card for Ireland, he felt. But meantime perhaps there was something he could usefully achieve for the cause over in America? Perhaps he could raise some money among all those rich people with which to buy the arms his comrades so sorely needed. Casement was undeterred by the somewhat indifferent success which had hitherto attended his money-raising efforts.

He continued to rail against England, wrote some more articles for *The Irish Review* under the pseudonym of Shan Van Vocht (the 'poor old woman'—Ireland—a piece of whimsy which was to cause intense exasperation later to John Devoy, the hard-headed Irish-American leader) and continued to draw his pension from the Crown. He applied for and drew it for the last time on June 30th, 1914; although he made formal application for another quarter's pension, on September 30th, from New York, he did not in fact draw any more money from the British Treasury after the June instalment.

He also continued to interest himself in a charming project, that of bettering the facilities of the poverty-stricken little school in the hamlet of Carraroe, in County Galway. Casement had visited the place on one of his Irish holidays many years before, and did what he could to help the school. In return he stipulated that the children must be taught Irish. I believe that his name is still remembered there with gratitude.

Casement probably paid his last visit to London—before that on which he arrived in handcuffs—in May 1914. The occasion was richly ironic. On April 24th, while he was staying at Malahide, he received a letter from his acquaintance Lord MacDonnell explaining that he was the chairman of a Royal Commission inquiring into the organisation of the Foreign Office and the Diplomatic and Consular Services which was then holding hearings in London. MacDonnell asked if Casement would be prepared to give evidence about the conditions in the Consular Service, with suggestions on the improvement of its recruitment, promotion and general organisation. If Casement agreed, he could charge travel expenses, plus £1 a day for out-of-pocket expenditure. Casement accepted, and on May 8th he was writing back to Miss Bannister from Ebury Street to say that he had arrived safely and would start to give his evidence the next morning.

I like to think of that final formal scene, the last contact between Sir Roger Casement, still the highly respected ex-consular official, full of prestige and authority, the great emancipator; and the worthy civil servants and functionaries who sat there questioning him politely, even deferentially. Here was London in May—the start of the Season; the last few moments of that world which would not be seen again; the few moments which were still to run before even they started to disintegrate. No doubt most of those present at the dignified meeting sported frock coats and would reach for top hats as they went off to lunch at the club. But the handsome giant who sat there that May morning, helping these painstaking gentlemen with their inquiries, was already in his heart and mind a traitor.

VII

CASEMENT returned to Ireland, went to Glasgow and thence, on July 4th, 1914, sailed aboard the s.s. *Cassandra* for Montreal and New York. He listed himself as 'R. D. Casement' and none of his fellow-passengers suspected his identity, although one of them asked idly whether he were any relation of 'the well-known Irish baronet'. Although he did not like the accents of his Scotch fellow-travellers, he quite enjoyed the twelve-day voyage, which was, for him, unusual. (He wrote later that the only people who knew that he was going were 'Mrs. G.—vaguely and not precisely—Bulmer Hobson (precisely), F. J. Biggar (precisely) and possibly Erskine Childers'.)

As the *Cassandra* made her way up the St. Lawrence, whose vistas reminded Casement in some respects of the Amazon, his thoughts, so he recalled some months later, went something like this:

'Some day I may try to write the story of the Congo, and how I found Leopold; of the Putumayo, and that abominable London Company, and of the "inordinate wild Irishman" ' [the quotation is not attributed] 'who went out on both quests in the garb of a British official, with the soul of an Irish felon. If the English had only known the thoughts in my heart and the impulses I obeyed, when I did the things they took pride in, I wonder would their press have praised my "heroism" and "chivalry" as they did; or would that expatriated patriot T. P. O'Connor have referred to me at the Reading election last November as "one of the finest figures in our Imperial history"?'

In Montreal Casement boarded a train for New York, which he reached on the 18th. 'The journey was long and hot and quite stifling. The windows of the carriages or "cars" open only a little way up from below, and some of them will not remain open, but slide down again slowly and have to be constantly re-hoisted. Mine was one of these, so to breathe at all, I had to put a hat-box in below the lifted sash—to the scandal of the guards and of some very uninteresting passengers. The dullest looking lot imaginable. But the scenery compensated for the want of the picturesque in the human environment.'

A long look at Lake Champlain as the train followed its banks recalled to Casement memories of the days when 'Mohicans and the Six Nations had here a hunters' paradise'. That did it—'Poor Indians! You had *life*—your white destroyers only possess *things*. That is the vital distinction, I take it, between the "savage" and the civilised man. The savage is, the white man has. The one lives and moves to be; the other toils and dies to have. From the purely human point of view, the savage has the happier and purer life— doubtless the civilised toiler makes the greater world. It is "civilisation" versus the personal joy of life.'

In New York Casement registered at the Belmont Hotel, and on a stroll down Broadway that evening, he picked up a young Norwegian sailor, named Adler Christensen. This unlikely character attached himself to Casement, and was to play a prominent, though largely farcical, rôle in Casement's German sojourn for the next year or more.

Next day Casement met John Devoy.[1] The ancient Fenian cast a somewhat fishy eye over the newcomer, for he was as tough as a precinct station-sergeant and about as romantic as a Jersey City petty politician. Casement's appearance and windy rhetoric can have evoked small response. However, Devoy took him along to lunch at Moquin's Restaurant, and afterwards he met the Irish-American leaders John Quinn and Bourke Cockran. Cockran asked him to stay with him out at Port Washington, a Long Island suburb of New York; and Casement also went down to Philadelphia to meet a local stalwart named Joe McGarrity. There was a trip to Norfolk, Virginia, where Casement addressed a shirt-sleeves-and-fan audience provided by the Ancient Order of Hibernians. Casement, taking his courage in both hands, eulogised

[1] See Appendix I.

the Ulster men, but this time 'to the evident contentment of many' (who presumably themselves hailed from Ulster), and there was no repetition of the Cork fiasco.

The United States in which Casement found himself that July of 1914 was a country so vastly different from that of to-day that it is very difficult for those who know only the modern American colossus, with its decisive participation in the affairs of the world, its assumption of the Royal Navy's former dominant rôle in trying to maintain world peace, its genuine and sympathetic concern with the affairs of foreign nations, and its inescapable influence on the lives of millions of persons on our planet, to appreciate how poky and parochial, how ignoring and ignored in the realm of international affairs was the America of just over forty years ago.

At that time 'isolationism' was not merely a political instrument wielded occasionally by a rapidly dwindling group of mid-Western congressmen; it was a deep-rooted instinct of the entire people, who then numbered ninety-two millions, or little more than half the American population of to-day. The aeroplane was a toy. Guided missiles and H-bombs were the exclusive property of Jules Verne. If one thing was quite certain in an uncertain world, it was that the U.S.A. was utterly and forever immune to physical attack from without. At the back of every American's consciousness, colouring all his thoughts, was the comfortable knowledge of a twin fact; the existence of the Atlantic and Pacific Oceans. Whatever might happen in the world outside, however grossly Europe and Asia might contrive to mismanage their affairs, it was certain that nothing but a distant echo or a very faint rumble, harmless as the reverberations of a summer storm far away, need disturb Americans.

In the material things, the gadgets and labour-savers, in the matter of motor-cars, and astonishing luxuries, in industrial production, the making of films, the entire concept of 'Hollywood' (then a virtually unknown and ugly hamlet on the edge of an uncomfortable desert), in the vast and complicated and sometimes exaggerated sweep and rush and volume of the standard of living which has now become America's—in all this, America was only just starting to draw away from and ahead of Europe. Like Ford, the magician of Detroit, America was on its way; but only just.

In the world of Roger Casement there were no air-conditioners, no hydramatic cars, nor TV, nor holidays with pay. The New Deal, should some bold seer have attempted to interest anyone in so revolutionary a notion and explain what it was, might well have sounded as implausible as interplanetary travel. New York in July 1914 was to Casement an uncool, uncomfortable, unlovely, unsympathetic and uninteresting spot.

In these surroundings, Casement concentrated as best he might on the Howth gun-running attempt, which he had been told before he sailed was due for Sunday, July 26th. That day he was in Philadelphia, killing time through the long, hot Sabbath hours with McGarrity, and waiting tensely for the arrival of news of the venture. At last it turned out that the guns had indeed been landed, but at the cost of casualties among the Volunteers when the British troops opened fire.

On the 29th Casement wrote to Mrs. Green: 'Dear Woman of the Ships! How can I tell you all I have felt since Sunday! I can never tell you. I was in anguish first—then filled with joy—and now with a resolute pride in you all. We have done what we set out to do! And done it well. The Irish here are mad with anger but filled with pride, joy and hope. All else is swept aside in these feelings—old J. D. says with a glow of joy, 'the greatest deed done in Ireland for 100 years'—and keeps repeating it. Well, Woman of Three Cows, Afra, you see our plot did not fail—and all has turned out well—and "Napoleon" too planned well—we have struck a blow for Ireland will echo round the world. Were it not for the Stupendous War Cloud, the press here would be filled—as it is they give much—although they are a *bad press*.

'A real bad press, uninstructed, fumbling, stupid and unenlightened on everything but baseball, American finance and politics. Their "interviews" are ineptitude condensed. The Irish here would make me into a Demi-God if I let them. In Philadelphia they have christened me, a deputation told me, "Robert Emmett"! They are mad for a Protestant leader. At the

Hibernian Convention, when I opened the ball, and said I was a Protestant, they cheered and cheered and cheered, until I had to beg them to hear me. And after I had done, a man sprang into the stage box and called for cheers again and again—and then "priests and people" came round to "shake" and pledge their support. Redmondism has no real support here at all. It is all bunkum. The "promises" of money to him are fakes—and the only subscribers who materialise are Shoneen Irish who have made a million or two and want to get into English Society, and so find Redmond respectable and "loyal".

'Oh, Woman of the Stern and Unbending Purpose, Autocrat of all Armadas, may your knee never be bowed—may it be strengthened and may the God of Erin put rifles into the arms of Irishmen and teach them to shoot straight. My grief is that I was here and not on Howth Road last Sunday—and my blood is hot with wrath when I think of that bayoneting and bulleting—but God bless you and *Mary of the Yacht* and all who helped the noble gift of arms—and those two Irish lads, who shipped as hands aboard. May this bring a new day to Ireland—I see it coming— New Hope, new courage on the old, old manhood.

'Yours devoted and always,

'The Fugitive Knight.'

Until then Casement had not quite burned his boats. Even at that point, with England on the very eve of war with Germany, there would still have been time to turn back, and probably no questions asked. In the U.S.A. he had thus far committed no overt act against Britain, any more than he had in Ireland, since his retirement. That he should have wished to travel across the Atlantic without revealing his identity was his own affair.

But now things began to move too fast. Publicity caught up with him, something which, while more than welcome in 1904 and 1912, was to be shunned just now. Joe McGarrity all too enthusiastically organised a monster meeting in Philadelphia to protest against the Howth shootings and—without telling Casement about it or giving him the chance to avoid the event—tipped the newspapers off that Casement was to be the star speaker. Casement pondered this and noted, 'So, whether I liked it or not, I was now in it up to the neck. I would have wished to keep quiet, but from every national point of view it was necessary that this meeting be held, and if held, that it lack no support that I could give it. So I reluctantly agreed to a step already taken in my name.'

This was a feeble piece of vacillation if ever there was one. Casement had gone to the U.S.A. ostensibly for the purpose of raising money to buy arms for Ireland. He had gone secretly. Yet, before he had done practically anything to further his self-appointed task, he threw everything aside in order to take part in a meeting, which could have no real effect on the long-range fortunes of Ireland—a meeting which had been fixed up for him by some blundering fool, and which could scarcely fail to bring him abruptly to the notice of the British authorities.

Casement continued: 'The next day, Monday the 27th, I was interviewed by some of the Philadelphia papers—and photographed, and the interview appeared in full in the evening papers, particularly the *Bulletin*. In this conversation I spoke very strongly of the lawless action of the British authorities in Ireland, culminating in the murder of women and children . . . and I put the blame fair and square on the shoulders of Mr. Asquith.

'The interview gave general satisfaction to the Irish of the city, while I learned that it greatly incensed the loyalists, some of whom wrote stupidly irate letters to my host.'

On August 4th Britain declared war on Germany, and on the 11th Casement wrote to Miss Bannister: '. . . Here I am, marooned on a desert island, Manhattan! Surrounded by 5,000,000 strangers. God save Germany! I got here in peace and began a nice campaign for the Irish Volunteers and would have got probably £40,000 or £50,000 for rifles—when this War of Devils broke loose. I have sincere, good friends here and am staying with one, John Quinn, 58 Central Park West, a great friend of Gaelic Ireland. . . .'

On September 14th, Casement wrote again to both his faithful women friends, Mrs. Green and Miss Bannister. He had meanwhile visited the former President, Theodore Roosevelt, and to Mrs. Green he fulminated, '. . . The average American has no ideals, no national mind or spirit, and is a gas-bag to a great extent. I saw Roosevelt, and warned him that "England will be supreme". He grinned and said, "*She* won't—*because she's finished*." I laughed and said, "You are wrong—she will swell to bigger things yet, and in the end inoculate *you* with the virus of her own disease. You will become Imperialists, and join her in the plunder of the earth. . . ." '

At about this time Casement was in Washington when, by arrangement with Devoy, he saw Von Bernstorff, German Ambassador to the United States, and decided on his forthcoming visit to Germany.

To Miss Bannister he wrote, again: '. . . Well, I can't tell you anything about myself because I expect this letter will be opened. I have not been idle, and in many ways things are better than could be expected. The Redmond conspiracy has failed here. The Irish say eight out of 10 in the U.S.A. are all for Germany and against the Coward and the Assassin, and the Union of friendship and goodwill between Irishmen and Germans in this country has become fast and sure and will bear future fruit. Any attempt by G.B. to get the U.S.A. in on her side—she is trying it secretly— would provoke a civil war here—and President Wilson knows it. He would get shot right away! John Bull is trying all he can to corral the States and if he has one naval defeat (as may well occur) he is going to put up a howl for Anglo-Saxon solidarity.

'I saw Roosevelt and others. I don't admire them. It is all self, self, self—all the time—and intrigue in place of principle. The poor Germans! God help them—"God Save Germany!" I pray night and day. . . . Oh! how I long for a chance to strike a blow as the Irish did at Fontenoy and there are thousands here the same! Had we a War Chest we could give the Hyena some new spots. But God in *some* day of payment will do that—and probably Russia will be the paymaster. When the Anglo-Saxon Corpse comes it will not be so brave a sight or so fine a corpse as the Teuton one of to-day.

'God save Germany!'

On September 17th, 1914, in New York City, Casement took the irrevocable step, and one which could not possibly be ignored by the Foreign Office, whatever its doubts may then have been as to the mental stability of the man who had for so long played the *enfant terrible* with the Barringtons and Tyrrells and Dufferins.

He issued a statement, which he dubbed an Open Letter to Irishmen. It made his position perfectly clear, underlined it and repeated it. He announced that he had been a founder of the Irish Volunteers, told the Irish that they ought not to join the British forces in a war against Germany, complained that Ireland had suffered at the hands of 'British administrators' a more prolonged series of deliberately inflicted evils than any other civilised country, and jeered at the British contention that the U.K. had entered the war because of the violation of Belgian neutrality. It was published in the American press, and, after an interval, in the *Irish Independent*, in Dublin on October 5th.

The stately riposte was not long in coming. A letter signed by Arthur Nicolson, then permanent Under-Secretary of State for Foreign Affairs, took him to task as follows:

'Sir—The attention of the Secretary of State has been called to a letter, dated New York, September 17th, which appeared in the *Irish Independent* of 5th October over your signature. The letter urges that Irish sympathies should be with Germany rather than with Great Britain and that Irishmen should not join the British Army. As you are still liable, in certain circumstances, to be called upon to serve under the Crown, I am to request you to state whether you are the author of the letter in question.

'I am, Sir,
'Your most obedient, humble servant,'

The day on which he wrote, or at least issued, his Open Letter, Casement wrote to Mrs. Green, enclosing a copy of it, with the following covering letter:

'My dearest Woman—Could you get this evidence in favour of Germany by any chance published in Ireland? I know the stream of atrocious lies that is flooding Ireland—to get Irish boys entrapped into the Army in defence of the Religion—the nuns, priests, etc., outraged by the German savages. The time has come when, if we can do nothing else, we should go to jail! I *request* and *order* you to start an anti-enlisting campaign. I will come and join and go to jail gladly. I began to-day with a public protest here to John Bull against Redmond's shameful appeal on behalf of the other Bull. It cannot be out till to-morrow or next day. I will send you copies. Meantime I send this. We *must* mark this awful debauch. *What* element of national life can survive if Ireland responds to this atrocious call? I see the *doom* of Irish nationality in this War and the destruction of the spirit of Irish nationality on the fields of plunder abroad. We were slaves in the Napoleonic War—we are free now, and not forced to fight.

'If Asquith and his ally come to Dublin, they should be shot— were I at home, I'd do it. I trust someone will. It is said by hundreds of Irishmen here. My blessing on you.'

His last letter from America to Mrs. Green was dated October 11th. '. . . Sir E. Grey should be hanged far higher than Haman. Of all the villainous fools British greed of Empire has yet produced, that wicked, stupid, obstinate fool is the worst. The tool of a gang of unscrupulous anti-Germans (Tyrrell, Cartwright, King Edward, Bertie, Delcasse, etc., etc.) he has as fully committed his country to this war as the Czar, Kaiser or any other autocrat—and yet the horrid thing's given to the world as a "democracy"! . . . Money will go. Some has gone. Do not hesitate to help Bulmer; he is a good, honest, hard worker—about the only one! . . . The Irish here, fully eighty-five per cent of them, now sound and are dead against Redmond. They and the Germans are joined hand in hand in active citizenship to keep this country out of the sea-serpent's coils—and to keep it American. I shall probably end my days here—as an Editor! I have been already offered the direction of a paper to be founded and shall probably accept—but on conditions I can't tell you anything about. . . . The immediate, the vital issue for Ireland is to keep her hands clean, to keep her conscience clean. This war is no concern of hers. It is *England's* war—for sea supremacy and world trade against a people who have no thought of hurting us in their hearts, heads or plans—unless, like the Belgians, we willingly play the game of their enemies.

'A large "Irish Army" in the field against Germany will be the climax to our own woes—a gratuitous gift of our last blood to a bad cause. . . . Should England be beaten—as she richly deserves to be, for her criminal conspiracy against Germany—let *her* pay the cost! We should be safe. I know whereof I talk. I have, perhaps, done more for Irish safety (and Irish virtue too, for that matter) than you will ever know. At any rate, here in America the Germans now love, honour and respect the Irish. They say so openly everywhere—in the streets, at meetings, in the press—"One people has been brave enough and chivalrous enough to not fear the odium of supporting the under-dog—all hail the brave Irish!". . . Let Ireland avoid all. Let her stay in her cabbage garden and try to keep the children safe. That is about all we can do. My policy is not mean or paltry—it is wise. It is the *only* way we have to-day of assuring our nationality, and the *only* way of perhaps safeguarding it. . . . It is really pathetic and makes one smile to hear now on *every German lip*, "By God, if Germany wins this war, we are going to free Ireland!" '

The supposed editorship cannot have materialised, for three days later Casement was off to Germany. He sailed from New York on October 15th under the name of James Landy armed with the passport of the real Landy, with credentials provided for him by Von Bernstorff, and accompanied by Adler Christensen, whom, according to his own account, he had 'befriended' after their chance encounter. Christensen was a plump twenty-four year-old, who had expensive tastes and used make-up. For a couple of days before they sailed on the Norwegian ship *Oskar II*, Casement, calling himself 'R. Smythe, of London', and Christensen went elaborately to ground in a New York hotel, taking various measures to throw any possible antagonists off the trail. What the luckless Casement did not know, either then or later, was that nearly all the messages passing between Von Bernstorff and the

138

Wilhelmstrasse in Berlin, were being intercepted and read by the British, a fact which lent an added touch of futility to his efforts over the next eighteen months.

Aboard the *Oskar II* Casement was regarded with lively suspicion by his fellow-passengers, most of them Germans, Austrians and Hungarians. This Mr. Landy, who claimed that he came from upstate New York, was like no New Yorker that anyone had met before. His accent was English and his manner and dress were those of a dude. Soon a rumour swept the ship that Casement was in reality a British spy, and he was given a wide berth.

To try to make up for his lack of American accent, Casement wrote from the ship a long descriptive letter to his sister Nina, who had by then gone to the United States, in what he apparently conceived to be American vernacular, and pretending that he and Christensen were both women. This, he felt, would serve to throw the British off the scent, should it fall into their hands. The *Oskar II* was in fact intercepted by the Royal Navy and taken into Stornoway. Here is Casement's account of matters, as relayed to his sister:

'We steered further north, and the dear, kind captain, such a nice Dane, with a beard just like cousin Roger's, told me he hoped to go up by the Faroe Islands, and get past those cruisers. . . .' [When the *Oskar II* was duly intercepted by H.M.S. *Hibernia*, Casement dumped some of his diaries and other papers through a porthole—'that dear Norwegian girl helped me stow away all the old hairpins'—and the prize crew came aboard.] 'Now, when I saw *Hibernia* on the caps of the men I nearly kissed them—it took my breath clear away. What followed did too. First they cut the Marconi connexion slick—right away, the moment they got to the Captain's bridge, and then they brought the Marines on board. . . . We steamed away south-south-east and that Saturday night's dinner was the sorriest, saddest dinner for some of those folk you ever saw. They looked fair scared to death, and when they looked at me—Gee, they did look queer. You see, they all thought I had done it!

'They had it going I compiled reports from the other two

spies as to all the people who were fakes on board and that I sent a wireless to have the *Oskar II* cut off. And no one knew who was who, or who would be taken and who left. I laughed, and one poor old German nearly had a fit and came to tell me how he loved the British.'

At Stornoway, 'The day passed very drearily. We knew it was Sunday—a Scotch Sunday. You could hear the Sabbatarian sanctity of those islands all round us, and I guessed they were eating heavy Sunday dinners in London and would be slow in answering' [the messages sent by the captain of the *Hibernia*].

That night was an uneasy one aboard the *Oskar II*. Casement reported in his letter that he was still the subject of suspicion on the part of his fellow-passengers, despite his protestations. Next morning six of the men were taken off the ship as prisoners, among them the ship's bandmaster. 'I was *furious* about the bandmaster . . . I ran to the side and waved adieu to them all, and then I got up a subscription for them among the passengers and we raised 247 kronen, or about 65 dollars, and sent it ashore to be distributed among them. . . .'

Nobody from the Royal Navy bothered Casement, and soon the *Oskar II* was on her way again. 'They were all pleased that I started the subscription—and that act of mine as well as the clear proof that all those in fear for themselves were safe on board, proved to everyone that I was not the British spy they had thought me. And so they came round me that night and the Tuesday and you never saw such changed faces. And some of them looked at me with such a knowing smile I felt there was something else too. . . . Owing to fog we did not reach Christiania until just midnight. And the first news we heard was that De Wet and Beyers had joined Maritz in South Africa—and do you know, dear sister, some of those wicked men [Austrians of the Embassy party] and some of the others who had been frightened of poor me, got champagne and drank to the "South African Republic"!

'And then the notice was posted up that the steamer would leave at 6 a.m. and it was then 1 a.m., so I had to hurry up and get ashore. The Norwegian girl was very useful and got me a cab and got my things through the Customs, and I bid everyone good-bye at 1.30 a.m. and drove up to the Grand Hotel at nearly 2 a.m. with the Norwegian girl. I made her sleep next door to me and we both went to bed very tired—it was then Thursday morning.'

But although Casement had eluded the Navy at Stornoway, any sense of elation or relaxation he may have felt on landing in neutral Norway was quickly dispelled. He was up early, went to the German Legation and presented his letters of credence to the Minister, Von Oberndorff, and was told to come back again the next day, because Von Bernstorff's letter of introduction from Washington was said, rather unconvincingly, to be in a cypher which the Legation did not quite understand.[1] He returned to his hotel and got busy with his interminable writing, whereupon there occurred the start of an episode which eventually assumed in Casement's estimate such undue significance that it can be said to have preyed on his mind.

What happened was that the British Minister in Norway, the late M. de C. Findlay, made a fairly spirited attempt to have Casement kidnapped. British agents got hold of Christensen and took him to see Findlay, who tried to bribe him to deliver Casement into British hands, finally offering him £5,000—very big money at that time—personal immunity, and a free passage back to the U.S.A. if he would take it on. Christensen seems to have been loyal to Casement in everything having to do with this affair, at least to begin with. He promptly reported back to Casement, who was flung into a fever of nervous excitement and apprehension. There followed a sort of cloak-and-dagger travesty, with much taking of trams going in the wrong direction, jumping out of moving taxicabs, hunted glances over the shoulder, and finger-on-lips instructions to Christensen. Casement's peace

[1] When he went back to the German Legation next day, Casement was told that it was quite all right and the cypher had been found the night before. To which he pleasantly rejoined, 'Why didn't you tell me yesterday that you wished to confer with Berlin about me before acting? I should have understood it and not been offended.'

of mind was not helped by the fact that strange men kept accosting Christensen in the hotel lobby or out in the street—one of them offered him some beer—and the luckless Casement must have been hard put to it to determine whether these were more British agents or merely casual admirers.

At one of Christensen's interviews with the British Minister, Findlay, according to Casement, 'instantly plunged *in medias res*, and unfolded his intentions towards myself with a boldness that, as Adler says, quite won his admiration—though not his sympathy'. Findlay appears to have remarked to Christensen at one stage: 'If someone knocked him (Casement) on the head, they would not have to work again for the rest of their days'—which was, to be sure, a forthright approach.

VIII

FINALLY Casement got away from Christiania with the maximum expenditure of nervous energy, and after displaying agility
in switching from one railway carriage to another in an attempt
further to bamboozle the British, he crossed by ferry into Sweden
and reached the sanctuary of Germany at Sassnitz, where he was
made welcome by Richard Meyer, special representative of the
Wilhelmstrasse and brother of Prof. Kuno Meyer, sometime
professor of Celtic studies at Liverpool University and a notorious
Anglophobe. Once again any temptation to relax which Casement may have felt was short-lived; for he was first of all the
object of unsympathetic treatment at the hands of the German
border guards ('stupid peasant reservists') and then fell foul of two
Junkers in the train to Berlin ('One with an excessive Prussian
beard, divided into two extraordinary waves that stuck out at
right angles from one another. Both were ugly.') because he was
speaking English. Poor Casement—that was to be only the first
of a long series of slights and exhibitions of hostility that he was to
endure during his German stay.

Instead of dismissing the Findlay kidnapping attempt from his
mind in favour of more pressing and far more important matters,
Casement was only starting to get worked up about it. It became
an obsession. A vast rigmarole grew up—affidavits by Christensen—challenges to Findlay to have it out in the Norwegian courts
—an enormous letter of protest, copies of which were sent to all
the foreign diplomatic missions in Berlin—the despatch of Christensen back to Norway to see what else he could find out—protests—even, if it can be believed, a letter of protest to Sir Edward
Grey himself, resoundingly denouncing the lack of ethics involved. The Germans were at first politely uninterested, then
puzzled, then infuriated by all this; and it must have seemed to his

exasperated hosts that Casement was devoting far more of his time to the wildly irrelevant Findlay affair than to the formation of an Irish Brigade, the task which had brought him to Germany.

Even before Casement was being glared at by the Junkers in the train, two of his fellow-passengers from the *Oskar II* were tipping off the German authorities that they considered Casement a suspicious character, or at least someone who merited investigation. One was a Major Lothes, the other a young man who was returning from South America to fight for the Fatherland, named Walter Muller. Muller's information was immediately passed to the chief of the Hamburg police. The report from the police chief's underling stated that 'On board the steamer which brought Muller from New York there travelled also under the assumed name of J. Landy the leader of the Irish living in America, Sir Roger Casement. He succeeded under his assumed name in evading the pursuit of the English, and landed in Norway.' So much for Casement's alias. It must have been a near thing at Stornoway if others on board knew who he was. One wonders if it got about through Christensen elevating his master to a position he never held, or through the vainglorious and talkative Casement himself.[1]

Later on, during that first German train ride into Berlin, there was another episode during which the charming side of Casement's nature emerged. 'A lady who had got into our carriage saw my *Times* and *Daily News* which I had bought in Christiania, and asked to look at them. She explained to me in excellent English (this only after my "American" status had been pro-

---

[1] The British authorities seem to have been determined to do things the hard way. The Navy had Casement right under its nose for 48 hours at Stornoway, when his identity was known to some of his fellow-passengers. Six men were taken away for internment—but not Casement. No sooner did he reach Christiania than the British Legation embarked on the rather delicate operation of trying to kidnap a man in a neutral country in wartime. Anybody else but Casement would have laughed heartily at the fact that he had twice succeeded in slipping through the British fingers, and blessed his lucky stars. But not Casement. Self-pity gushed at the thought of Findlay's wickedness.

claimed) that she had an aunt, an Englishwoman, now practically a prisoner in Germany, and she would like to show the papers to her. So I gave them to her, although I had not read them, and was keeping them for the dreary nights in Berlin which I knew must be before me. . . . She was all smiles and good humour and niceness and had a very friendly little dachshund who nestled against me and ate the remains of my bread and sausage from the wayside station.'

Berlin and journey's end at last. Casement, Christensen and Meyer trudged down the platform, noting as they went a trainload of German wounded from the eastern front, and took a taxi to the Continental Hotel. 'Meyer got rooms for me under the name of "Mr. Hammond". I had decided to bury "Mr. James Landy" on the shores of the Baltic. The management were impressed by Meyer and all were smiles and bows—and so I was duly registered as "Mr. Hammond of New York", and they were told they would be responsible to the German Foreign Office if anything unpleasant occurred to me. . . .

'Meyer soon left me for the Foreign Office to report our arrival and to arrange for me to see some of them to-morrow. He begged me not to go out, or let Adler out, until the police had been advised—as English-speaking men, without papers, etc., and unknown to the police, would surely get into trouble. . . .

'At last in Berlin! The journey done—the effort perhaps only begun! Shall I succeed? Will they see the great cause aright and understand all it may mean to them, no less than to Ireland? To-morrow will show the beginning.'

But the next day was a Sunday and Casement's spirits sank as he whiled away a dreary day in the hotel, writing letters. The first two people he selected to write to were Major Lothes and young Muller—who had both informed on him to the police. Casement notes: 'I was sorry afterwards that I had written these letters so soon—but the inertia of a whole Sunday in this dreary hotel was too much for me.'

On Monday Meyer walked Casement down the Wilhelm-strasse to the Foreign Office, at No. 76. 'You have to ring at a wooden gateway and the door opens. We went upstairs and a manservant took our coats and hats and sticks. So different from the London Foreign Office where I have been so often *chez moi*! The waiting-room into which we were shown was a fine salon, well-furnished and large, with fine oil paintings of King Frederick William III and the old Emperor William. Meyer told me I was to be received first by Herr Zimmermann, Under Secretary of State, and then by Count Georg von Wedel, head of the Foreign Office English Department. Meyer left me alone for a few minutes. Some officers came and went, cavalrymen in grey. Strange thoughts were mine as I sat on a big sofa in this centre of policy of the German Empire. No regrets, no fears—well, yes, some regrets, but no fears. . . . If I fail, if Germany be defeated— still the blow struck to-day for Ireland must change the course of British policy towards that country. Things will never be quite the same again. The "Irish Question" will have to be lifted from the mire and the mud and the petty, false strife of British domestic politics into an international atmosphere. That, at least, I shall have achieved. . . .'

Much more in the same vein ran through Casement's mind as he sat on the sofa, but finally Meyer returned and introduced him to Zimmermann and then Von Wedel. Casement took to them both—Zimmermann had 'a very good-natured face, with a warm, close handshake,' and he struck the right note by ejaculating 'Dastardly!' as Casement promptly poured out his account of the Christiania kidnapping effort, and added sagely, 'They stick at nothing!'

Von Wedel too had 'a charming personality—a man of upright build; frank, straight brown eyes and a perfect English accent'. They got right down to Casement's plans for suborning the Irish prisoners-of-war. 'I made it plain beyond all misconception to Wedel that my efforts with the soldiers must be strictly defined as an effort to strike a blow for Ireland—not an attempt merely to hit England. I described the character of the Irishman and of the Irish soldier, and pointed out that any Irishman might commit treason against England for the sake of Ireland, but that he would not do anything mean or treacherous. He would put his neck in the noose, as I have done, for love of Ireland; he would not "desert to an enemy" or forsake his own colours merely to assail England. In fact, he must have an active cause, not a negative. If thus Germany made the declaration I sought as to the fortunes and future of Ireland in the event of German victory, I had little or no doubt that scores, perhaps hundreds, of Irish prisoners would follow us.'

This was not a bad start. Von Wedel himself went off to see the head of the Berlin Secret Police, who immediately gave Casement a *laissez-passer*, which said that he was a 'Mr. Hammond of New York' and 'not to be molested'. Christensen, it turned out, needed no such card after all, since he was a Norwegian, and thus 'not an offensive personage'. Taking no chances, Casement despatched Christensen to buy two tiny American flags, which they both thereafter sported in their lapels.

Casement ended his day's entries in his diaries on a note of triumph: 'Now I am fairly launched on Berlin—and to-day sees me take up a definite position. "Mr. Hammond of New York—not to be molested"!'

Over in the Wilhelmstrasse, Von Wedel sat down and wrote the following report to the Reichs Chancellor, Von Bethmann-Hollweg:

'The Irish Nationalist leader Sir Roger Casement who is known to Your Excellency from earlier reports has arrived in this country from America, with a letter of introduction from Ambassador Count Bernstorff, and has paid a visit here. He makes a reasonable and trustworthy impression.

'His proposals are set forth in the enclosed paper on "German Relations towards Ireland and Irish Prisoners of War in Germany". They can be summed up in the following two points:

'(1)—Formation of an Irish Legion from British P.o.Ws. in Germany of Irish nationality and Catholic religion.

'(2)—Public "Proclamation" by the German Government to the effect that Germany has no intention whatsoever of bringing Ireland under German domination and that it will, moreover, in case of conclusive victory over England, stand for its liberation from the English yoke and for its independence. An idea of what such a Proclamation should amount to, in Sir Roger Casement's opinion, appears in the document.

'Sir Roger Casement expects these two measures to cause, first of all, a considerable set-back to English recruitment in Ireland, which, if not made immediately impossible, would be considerably restrained and rendered much more difficult. A further consequence would be immediate and open support from all Irish-Americans for the German cause. In view of the political influence of the Irish in the United States, "which should not be underestimated," he thinks he can count on a certain reorientation of American public opinion in our favour.

'Ambassador Count Bernstorff has repeatedly recommended in his reports that consideration be given to the proposals of the Irish as soon as the stage is reached when it no longer matters whether the differences with England are exacerbated and when it is clear that England intends to pursue the struggle until complete mutual exhaustion supervenes.

'My personal impression of Sir Roger Casement inclines me to give serious consideration to his proposals. If Your Excellency takes a favourable view, may I suggest that the responsible military authorities be directed from Supreme G.H.Q. to the effect that the Irish P.o.Ws. of Catholic faith from the various camps be assembled in one camp in order to make it possible for the Irish Catholic priests and for Sir R. Casement to exert their influence upon them.'

For his part, just before turning in, Casement sat down to write to someone in the U.S.A., possibly Devoy, but I cannot be sure as only a fragment of this letter is extant:

'. . . Saw two important friends to-day. All goes splendidly. No need to give you particulars here as to shipment. They will themselves make the arrangement. All we have to do is to prepare the reception at the other side. There you and the friends at home come in. I shall stay on here for the present, but hope to get off from the Schleswig coast or one of the small islands there by a boat my Norwegian can arrange for me. I am glad I brought him indeed—he has been a treasure. And now I can arrange through him a means of getting across that cannot excite suspicion. The only danger will be from the mines. That bumptious ass Winston began the war you remember by an appeal to Christendom against Germany mining the North Sea Coast. Now these seadog swankers are mining not the coastlines only but the whole sea right up to the Faroe Islands nearly! Of course they mined the Irish seas long since—a convincing proof of Irish "loyalty".

'However, I have no fear I shall get across—the thing can be done and I'll do it and be there at the time agreed. No more now—R.'

He also sent a cable to Judge Cohalan, one of the top Irish-American leaders in New York—a cable which seems to have interested German as well as British censorship. In this Casement wrote that 'Landy's' identity [i.e. his own] had been 'discovered by the enemy, who are greatly alarmed and taking steps to defend Ireland and possibly arrest friends. They are ignorant of the true purpose of my coming to Germany but seek evidence at all costs. . . . Send messenger immediately to Ireland fully instructed verbally. No letters on him. He should be native American citizen, otherwise arrest likely. Let him despatch priest here via Christiania quickly. . . . Also let him tell Biggar, solicitor Belfast, conceal everything belonging to me.'

Having broached the plan for the Irish Brigade and obtained at least the appearance of German interest in it, Casement, accompanied by Meyer, paid a quick visit to German G.H.Q. at Charleville, to try to gain the attention of Von Bethmann-Hollweg, the Chancellor, and Von Jagow, Secretary of State. The Kaiser was also at G.H.Q. at the time, and it may well have irked Casement that no audience of the All-Highest was forthcoming.

At this point Franz Von Papen, then a rising young attaché under Von Bernstorff in Washington, enters our narrative with the following memorandum on 'The Irish' to the Wilhelmstrasse:

'Referring to the Under Secretary of State's misgivings, and in accordance with the opinion of the Imperial Ambassador already communicated by cable, it should be pointed out that no untoward pro-English effect on American public opinion need be feared.

'That [American] public opinion is mainly governed by widespread misconceptions about the true causes of the war. The fact that Germany sponsors the achievement of independence by small nations could, indeed, only influence it favourably. In order, however, to avoid any odium, I propose announcing the formation of the Irish Brigade (or if this proves impossible, a smaller, independent unit) formed by its own initiative, in order to bring this fact to the notice of the public. In this connexion the Press might discuss the Irish Question in the desired sense. The moral effect, that the Irish are volunteering to fight England, will be great.

'One or more prominent Irish-Americans would leave here for Germany to help in the formation of such a volunteer corps. It would also be advisable to separate the Irish P.o.Ws. from the English and to provide Catholic priests for the former.

'According to Intelligence from Ireland, 200,000 men for the new British Armies are to be drafted in Ireland. But despite strenuous efforts, no enrolments are taking place in the South and South-East.

'The way in which such recruiting as there is has so far been successful is as follows: (1)—People were told that Protestant Germany had invaded Catholic Belgium, that priests, nuns, etc., were murdered, etc. (2)—By bringing to a standstill all branches of industry and by laying mines on all coasts, thus preventing their inhabitants from earning their livings.'

On December 2nd, Casement wrote to Miss Bannister: 'The Germans deserve to win. They are making heroic sacrifices—without a word. . . . No one complains, all go out to die for Germany. The lies of the English Press are colossal. The "atrocities" in Belgium, etc., are a horrid lie.[1] I've been there and seen with my own eyes, and in France too. Everyone is sorry for France and

[1] After Casement's prolonged personal war with Belgium, the King of the Belgians and the Belgian-dominated Congo Free State authorities, he was the last man to be moved by anything to do with the troubles of 'gallant little Belgium'.

Belgium; it is only England, the originator and plotter of the war, they loathe, and rightly.'

A week later Casement was noting in his diary: 'When I look at this people, at their manliness of brow and bearing, their calm front and resolute strong chests turned to a world of enemies, and then read the English columns of trash about Prussian barbarism and English heroism, I regret I am not a German.'

Casement had been fretting because the official German announcement about him and his plans seemed to be held up. But at last it came, and Casement was able to revel in the front pages of the evening papers. 'The article contained,' he notes with satisfaction, 'not only a sort of biography of me but a eulogy as well.' The Germans stated that they would never invade Ireland, but if their troops ever found themselves on Irish soil, due to the fortunes of war, it would be in a spirit of goodwill only.

From the German Ambassador to the Vatican came a message that two pro-Nationalist Irish priests had been procured to work among the Irish P.o.W.s and were on their way. They were Father O'Gorman and Father Crotty. From America, too, 'dependable' priests were coming. Bernstorff cabled that the Rev. John T. Nicholson of Philadelphia was leaving for Germany via Naples. 'He is in every way qualified. Speaks Irish well. Has visited Germany and is in full sympathy with the work we want done. Born in Ireland but is an American citizen.'

Meanwhile the Germans were quietly checking up on Christensen, who had made an odious impression in many quarters. Von Oberndorff, the German Ambassador in Norway, was asked to make inquiries in Christensen's home town, and he wrote back to Von Wedel saying that Christensen had caused his parents a good deal of trouble as a boy, but was said to be 'talented'. He claimed to have a wife living in America and to have once been a secretary to a millionaire. He had gone to Germany 'for business reasons'.

Casement was seeing quite a lot of Count Blücher, the former honorary co-treasurer of the Putumayo Mission Fund. At the outbreak of the war the Count had returned to his native land, together with his English-born wife.

There is some disagreement about the terms on which Casement and the Blüchers found themselves after their Berlin re-encounter. Before the war Casement had been a frequent guest at their London home, and, the Princess recalls, he once entertained the company to a post-prandial rendering of 'The Wearing of the Green', sung with great feeling.

Princess Blücher (the Count inherited the Princedom half-way through the war) says that her husband almost at once had a heart-to-heart talk with Casement, trying to make him see that he was, to put it mildly, in a dreadfully false position, and that the only possible thing for him to do was to get out of Germany without delay. But Casement would not listen. Later, states the Princess, the Blüchers refused to have anything to do with him, partly because of his conduct politically, but especially because of the highly unsavoury rumours of which he and Christensen became the centre.

The Princess tells me (London, March 10th, 1954) that Casement's perverted tastes quickly became evident in Berlin and caused scandal. Christensen's appearance and mannerisms were very feminine, and he habitually made up. The last point we have confirmation of from Casement himself. A year later he wrote a letter to 'dear, good, faithful old Adler', chiding him on his extravagance. 'Don't go and be foolish with money or you will not have a cent. You are fearfully wasteful of money, much more so than I am, even, because you buy things you don't need at all, like that raincoat and gloves, etc. I have *no* gloves, and you have about six pairs! And face and complexion blooms!'

December drew on. Berlin was as yet scarcely affected by the war, and a traditional German Christmas was in the making. The lights glittered brightly on the shopping streets and there was quite enough to eat, for the British blockade was not yet making itself felt to any great extent. There was nothing to fear from the skies. The heavy defeat on the Marne and the disappointment at not getting Paris was largely offset by Hindenburg's vast defeat of the Russians at Tannenberg. The defeat of the English at sea by Von Spee in the Coronel engagement was almost immediately cancelled out by the annihilation of Von Spee's South Atlantic squadron by Sturdee off the Falklands. It was stalemate.

Christensen was sent back to Christiania to see what he could discover of Findlay's intentions. He extracted 500 kroner from the British Minister as a down payment and arranged to see him again. Casement girded himself for his first confrontation of the prisoners of war. The priests had arrived. All was set. Casement was pleased with the prospect. 'Everyone in the hotel now knows who I am and they are fearfully civil. They do everything for me—and the old manager himself now comes up to my rooms with papers and things. It is amusing, because I am still officially "Mr. H.".'

Blücher had not yet broken with Casement. On the contrary he was being helpful about sending Casement's mail. 'To Blücher at Hotel Esplanade at 6, and left a letter for John McNeill, enclosed in one to Mrs. G., and this in one to Wambersin & Son, Rotterdam—this finally to go to Herr Ballin in Hamburg, who can get it through to England unopened. So Blücher says—this is the route the Princess of Pless takes, and it is on her advice.'

On Thursday, December 3rd, Casement was in Frankfurt-on-Main, on his way to the first of the prison camp trysts. He wrote: 'There has been little to record in the past few days. Tuesday I was unwell and stayed in my room all day. Professor Schieman called late at night with disquieting statements about Adler that were unwarranted and malicious. Poor Adler! God knows, he is bad enough without these professional inquests on him. I was annoyed beyond words—and disgusted.'

Assuming that his attachment to Christensen was morally innocent, what was Casement, a diplomat of two decades' experience in various parts of the world, doing in Berlin at that supremely difficult moment in his career, accompanied by a youth whom he had casually picked up in New York, and who, rightly or wrongly, was regarded as highly disreputable by nearly all who encountered him?

The morning after Schieman's startling call, Casement took the opportunity of telling Blücher 'of Schieman's remarks about

Adler—and then of the truth—of Adler's confession to me the night before he left for Christiania. Blücher agrees with me about him, that there is an innate sense of honour and courage that make amends. I went to Von Wedel at seven to tell him too—I felt it necessary to be frank. . . .'

We are not told what this confession of Christensen's was all about. And although Count Blücher is represented as agreeing that Christensen's innate sense of honour and courage make amends—we do not know for what it is thought to make amends.

It is perhaps easy to guess why Casement at that point thought frankness essential. Professor Schieman was a political agent of the Wilhelmstrasse, and his visiting Casement and warning him was no idle gesture. Casement was being served notice that he had better be careful. If his follower was so quickly gaining a scandalous reputation in Berlin, it was obvious that he himself might be implicated. Casement got the point, and rushed off to Count von Wedel to tell him all about it, including the 'confession' of Christensen.

That night in Frankfurt Casement was already beginning to feel so restive—and after only a few weeks in Germany—that he was willing to compare Britain and Germany to the disadvantage of the latter. 'It is strange no word comes from Von Bernstorff,' he notes. 'Indeed, so far as I can observe it, "German Diplomacy" deserves many of the hard things Billy Tyrrell said of it in the Foreign Office in 1912 at our historic meeting. But the real German diplomats are not in the Foreign Office but in the German armies and navy. The brains of the country and its best character are of necessity there, and the civil power is left to fish for inferior intelligence with less attractive bait.'

The assembling of the Irish prisoners of war from other camps into one large group at Limburg was still in progress at the beginning of December. At that point the men had no inkling of what was afoot. They were of course delighted to find other Irishmen to talk to. At the Sennelager Camp, from which many of them had been brought, German generals had recently been giving them pep talks, some of them wrapped in hazy historical references which puzzled the men. There was talk of better food, a relaxation of regulations, opportunities for sport, and Mass every morning, to be conducted by O'Gorman or Crotty. The Bishop of Paderborn delivered a sermon all in English. But the Irish at Sennelager had struck entirely the wrong note by sending to the Camp Commandant a memorandum, signed by their N.C.O.s, saying that while they appreciated the spirit in which these concessions were proffered, they felt they had to ask that they be withdrawn unless they could be extended to all the other prisoners, 'as, in addition to being Irish Catholics, we have the honour to be British soldiers'. For good measure they asked that the message be relayed to the Kaiser. This was indeed a dubious climate for Casement's approaching attempts at suborning.

Casement's first try probably took place about December 4th or 5th, 1914. It was a sampling rather than a full-dress affair. The N.C.O.s at Limburg were gathered into a hut, and after a long pause Casement arrived with two senior German officers. He was noticeably on edge, spoke briefly, made a passing allusion to the formation of an Irish Brigade and then handed round copies of the *Gaelic-American*. The N.C.O.s were non-plussed. They were uncertain as to Casement's identity and the object of his mission. But as he drove back to Frankfurt, copies of a document which was to be produced at his trial were being posted all over the prison camp. This asked the Irish if they were willing to fight for their own country instead of England, and to fight for the National Freedom of Ireland under the Irish flag. It added that recruits to the Brigade would be treated as 'guests of the German Government', and that at the war's end any member of the Brigade so wishing would receive an assisted passage to America. Those not willing to join the Brigade would be removed from Limburg.

By December 6th Casement was in an almost rebellious mood. The Germans, he felt, were treating him far too casually, and he was not to be trifled with—especially as regards the Findlay affair.
'De Graeff' [G.O.C., Frankfurt area] 'advised me to see either

Von Bethmann-Hollweg or Von Jagow quickly and not be content with Von Wedel, who he said was merely "a letter-carrier"; and I should insist on the heads of the Government seeing me. I wrote to Von Wedel a letter saying something of this, and sent it off by special post. . . .

'I have decided, perhaps finally, on one thing. It is that I shall insist on seeing either Von Jagow or the Chancellor. Both are in Berlin. If I cannot get an interview with them, I shall take it as proof that the German Government is not sufficiently in earnest for me to go on further.

'I will not accept the responsibility for putting a couple of thousand Irish soldiers into the High Treason pot, unless I get very precise and sure promises both in their regard and for the political future of Ireland.

'If I learn that neither Von Bethmann-Hollweg nor Von Jagow can see me, and I care not what the reason assigned may be, I shall decline to continue our "conversations" and shall ask for my passport, to enable me to go to Norway or Sweden.'

Casement then makes the assertion: 'From the point of view of the Irish Cause, I am not sure that the case against Findlay is not more telling than would be even the formation of an Irish Brigade. Of course, for the Germans, the Irish Brigade is the most important. It shames John Bull's Army and it knocks recruiting on the head in Ireland.

'The Findlay business has no interest for them and they do not appreciate its significance rightly—or the vast effect it would have on public opinion in Ireland and the U.S.A. But even if they did, it would be for me only and not for them; and they are keen only on the things I can do that will help them. Quite naturally. But equally quite naturally, I mean to convict John Bull's government of being what I have always termed it—criminal conspiracy. . . .'

Casement was ill during his Limburg visit and was in bed for a day or more. That was a foretaste of the patchy health which was to dog him through much of his German stay.

A couple of days later relations with Count Blücher were

showing signs of strain. 'Blücher is quite impossible. He has arranged for me to meet the "Minister of Colonies" (I put it in quotes because the German colonies to-day are mainly possessions of Britain, Japan or France) to-night at six. I was to have met Erzberger, an influential Reichstag deputy, to-morrow, but as I refused to discuss the Irish Brigade with him—having no liberty to do so—he got very huffy and talked angry nonsense and altogether behaved as I expected. Blücher's interest is solely in himself, and his chances of besting his unscrupulous old father, the Prince, and getting control of the palace and estates while his father is interned at Herm.'

To add to his depression a copy of *The Times* reached him containing a New York despatch about German peace feelers in the U.S.A. which, while listing a number of small nations which must be given the right to frame their own post-war destinies, omitted Ireland from the roll. Casement indignantly took up this omission with Von Wedel. Von Wedel said he thought the *Times* report must be inaccurate. *The Times* inaccurate? At this suggestion the Irish rebel was temporarily submerged by his years of training as a British official. 'Impossible!' thundered Casement. 'I have no doubt that the statement was made—and that the omission of Ireland from the list of friendly states was intentional, and a part of the German *mot d'ordre* to commit themselves as little as possible to the Irish cause in public—so that retreat and "accommodation with England" may always be possible.'

'In my heart I am sorry I came,' Casement confides to his diary. 'I do not think the German Government has any soul for any great enterprises—it lacks the divine spark of imagination that has ennobled British piracy. The seas may be freed by these people, but I doubt it. They may do it in their sleep—and without intending to achieve anything so great. . . . England supplies all the necessaries—ships and brains—Germany thinks to do it by ships alone, and without brains, and resolute far-seeing purpose. A fixed, unchanging Irish policy is essential to freedom at sea of every power competing with England. That is the first rule to master.

'These things I should like to say to the Colonial Minister this evening—but I shall be wholly debarred from saying them by the presence and constant interruption of Blücher, who has become a very tyrant of speech too. He talks without pause—and mostly irrelevancies.'

On Sunday, December 13th, Casement was first flabbergasted by the announcement that Britain had appointed a Minister to the Holy See ('She reverses the Reformation!'), then made a quick recovery as he reminded himself that 'this is really the most convincing proof of the far-reaching character of my coup. We have actually forced them to a step hateful to "every good Englishman" ... It is an unprecedented step—and if the German Government had brains they would see how deep they have already struck.'

The new Minister was taking with him as his personal assistant J. D. Gregory. 'Ghosts of the Putumayo Indians!' muses Casement. 'How strange it all is! Gregory, who collaborated with me in the Foreign Office to get the Franciscan Mission sent out by the Vatican, and who was the first in belauding me at Rome and in London, now goes to Rome to aid in belabouring me and in enslaving Ireland! English rule is assuredly the master-piece of dissimulation in the world. I await with amusement the forthcoming comments of the English world on my "treason"—but, oh! God Save Ireland!'

Adler Christensen now got back from Christiania again and proceeded to delight Casement with his account of new conversations with Findlay. Findlay, it seemed, had by now increased his offer for Casement dead or alive to £10,000, and had gone to the length of giving Christensen a private key to the back door of the Legation. 'Oh, it is quite delicious!' cries Casement, enchanted. 'And I am to hear more to-day. Adler says that if I go to Norway, Findlay will "go bug house", an American euphemism, I believe, for "going off his chump" ...'

Casement's mercurial temperament encouraged him to make another change in his estimate of the Germans. 'At six I went with Blücher to call on Dr. Solf, the Minister of the Colonies. Found him (after long wait) a fine type. Once Governor of Samoa. Knew Nigeria too. Very charming. Great big, strong man. I told him they would have to knock England out—there was nothing for it but that—they must use all their brains and intelligence for that. He agreed—and confessed their brains diplomatically were inferior to the English, and that they were not trained to cope with English statesmen, "pirates in evening dress". (I had called them "very charming men, hereditary pirates of long descent", and he had laughed approval and said, "Yes, I see—pirates in evening dress!")

'I got a better impression of the German official world from Solf than from any of them. He confessed too that they had all been deceived by English "nice manners" and "hearty hospitality", and cited his own reception in Nigeria many years ago—and the speeches of "goodwill and cousinship" exchanged—or professed, rather, by British officials. I assured him that was all part of the game—and said it would have paid Germany well to have engaged a few Irishmen as guides to the British character in international affairs. An Irish Imperial Chancellor would not let John Bull wall up the German Michael[1] as we see him now.'

Whatever the truth of Casement's suggestions, they were somewhat patronising, and Solf must have possessed considerable tact. Casement purringly continues: 'He was greatly interested in my explanation of the international value of Ireland to Europe and the freedom of the seas. He said he would speak to Von Jagow and arrange a meeting. . . . He also said that the Declaration on Ireland was "an entirely new departure in German foreign policy" —that until that statement was issued, Germany had never said or done anything that implied a desire to meddle in "the internal affairs of another country". It is a new departure indeed. . . .'

Casement wasted most of the next three days in huge discussions with Christensen about Findlay. The two of them sat down

[1] 'German Michael' was the cartoon equivalent of John Bull or Uncle Sam. He was the symbol of the Germany of those days—a farmer's boy wearing a peaked cap, honest, sturdy, hardworking, the embodiment of all the peasant virtues.

to prepare a wordy report on Christensen's Norwegian experiences. But Casement was not sure whether to be gratified or annoyed when Christensen quoted Findlay as having said of Casement: 'He is a very clever and very dangerous son-of-a-bitch. But he *is* a gentleman.' Casement paused to remark in his diary: 'It is a pity I have no copy of my "friend" Conan Doyle's letter,[1] referred to in the Daily Chronicle, wherein my mental malady is diagnosed! What strange people the English are! When I served them, I was a "hero"—"the most chivalrous public servant in the service of the Empire, etc". Now that I dare cut myself off from them and do a far braver thing and surely a more chivalrous one, I am at "the most charitable view" a lunatic—and in my case "a rampant traitor". I like that; as if I owe any loyalty to that cowardly, cringing Bully, the British Empire!'

Meanwhile the 'secure route' for mail, as recommended by the Princess of Pless, proved less reliable than hoped. For the letter to John McNeill, one of the revolutionary movement leaders in Dublin, the letter which had been secreted inside so many others, like the endless toy boxes, was being pensively pondered by British Admiralty Intelligence, before they sent it on its way.

So the British authorities learned that Casement (1) wanted McNeill to get maximum publicity in Ireland for the German declaration about their intentions towards Ireland, (2)—wanted him to tell the world of German good will towards Ireland, (3)—wanted more Irish priests to join him in Germany as undercover

---

[1] To allude sneeringly to Sir Arthur Conan Doyle as a so-called friend was completely unjust. Sir Arthur's petition in support of the movement for Casement's reprieve, after his conviction, was one of the most telling of all; and it must have been about this time (the letter bears no date) that Conan Doyle wrote to Morel from his Sussex home near Crowborough: 'What is this about Casement? His friends must inquire and put it right. It is quite incredible and impossible that so noble a man could have proved a traitor to the Government whose salt he had eaten. I don't and won't believe it. But I wish you could get something solid to connect it with. I confess that C's last letters to me from Belfast made me acutely uneasy as to his health. They seemed wild.'

men, carriers and agents, (4)—promised German arms and ammunition for Ireland in due course, 'and good officers, too,' although it is difficult to think of any source which may have given him that idea. The Germans never for a moment intended to send any of their officers.

Whitehall now saw a fascinating two-way stream of enemy communications. About this time, interested British officials were also having a look at the latest batch of cables from Von Bernstorff to the Wilhelmstrasse. Bernstorff reported that an agent had, as previously requested, safely arrived in Ireland; that the German Declaration of intent had gone down well in the U.S.A.; that the complaisant priest, Father Nicholson, was starting soon; that Judge Cohalan was reluctant about the advisability of publishing any statements on the Findlay affair until there were 'actual proofs'; that Casement's money remittances from the U.S.A. were being arranged; and that arms had been bought for delivery to India and Turkey. (The Irish in America did not think it feasible to dodge the British blockade in the Atlantic, and so some of their funds were spent at points from which they might be brought in with less trouble if events proved favourable.)

As far as I can determine, Casement's protestations that he 'never took a penny of German gold' were probably true. He regularly received quite large remittances, of $1,000 or $2,000 at a time, from the Irish in America, forwarded by John Devoy. However his own improvidence and the often wayward extravagance of 'poor Adler' got through it fairly fast, and while in Berlin Casement was often hard up. It seems unlikely that, had the Germans themselves been financing him, he would have been short of money.[1]

On December 18th Casement's vanity at last obtained some balm when Chancellor Von Bethmann-Hollweg received him at what was apparently a genial and expansive interview. (Another great virtue of the occasion, where Casement was concerned, was that the Chancellor let him do most of the talking.) They

[1] The last remittance from Devoy for Casement arrived in Berlin after Casement had already left Germany by U-boat for Ireland.

touched on the Brigade; the irritating way in which the Royal Navy barred access to Ireland; and, inevitably, the Findlay affair. Afterwards Casement strolled round with Von Wedel to the latter's office, where the two had a good gloat over the bombardment of Scarborough, Whitby and the Hartlepools by German cruisers. 'Who are now the rats in their holes?' queried Casement rhetorically.

Casement passed on to Von Wedel a fantastic project, originally Christensen's idea, for trapping an entire squadron of British cruisers. These were to be summoned, by means of a false report passed to the eager Findlay, to a sea rendezvous, under the impression that they would catch Casement in the act of boarding the yacht of a rich American friend (Norman Armour, the meat-packing king). Von Wedel was sufficiently impressed to put this up to the German Admiralty, and although, as Casement notes, 'They were at first naturally surprised by this "bombshell", I got a 'phone message from Von Wedel to say that they were considering the matter.'

Suddenly Christensen himself became suspect in Casement's mind. 'Alas, I am not sure of Adler! His air and manner have greatly changed since he came back—or rather, since he went away. He confesses that he "now admires Findlay! Findlay is a man—he sticks at nothing—he would roll these god-damned Germans up!" For the Germans now, since they held him up at Sassnitz, Adler has only scorn and a sense of outraged pride. They treated him badly there, stripped him, split his gloves open, took his gold coin and gave him paper money instead, extorted seven marks per meal, while he was detained forty-eight hours their prisoner, pending the order from Berlin to release him, and read aloud to the crowd my letters to my American friends. This last extraordinary piece of stupidity it was that chiefly affects Adler. He says "They are fools"—and that they are trying to fool me and get advantage of me and Ireland and give nothing in return but empty words.

'There is also the resentment he feels, the very deep resentment, at the allegations against himself and his conduct while in Berlin, to which Schieman referred and which Blücher told me had been conveyed in a police report to the Foreign Office. I told Adler of this report last night—giving it as the reason why I found it impossible to take him with me to Limburg and the Irish Brigade.'[1] (One feels that the appearance of Adler at Limburg would have been all that was needed to touch off a full-scale riot among the P.o.W.s.) 'I think it would be far safer for all concerned to send Adler back to Norway and let him return to the U.S.A., to work there. I told him much of this last night.'

It was soon time for Casement to make another visit to the Limburg prison camp. There the Irish were being congregated in force, and in fairly attractive quarters. The mystery attending Casement's first visit was still being discussed. It had been suggested that he was a Boer. And not only was Casement about to face a hostile audience among the Irish, but many of the German guards were themselves shocked, and said so, at the idea of trying to seduce captive soldiers from their allegiance. Already one or two of the men, who had shown some signs of having been tempted by Casement at his first visit, had had a poor time of it from their comrades.

Casement passed a dreary hotel Christmas, his gloom deepened by a letter from Kuno Meyer in New York, reporting that every one of the Irish-American leaders had strongly deprecated any publicising of the Christiania business. He tried to encourage

---

[1] When Christensen mentions his resentment at Schieman's allegations, nothing is said about whether Casement reminded Christensen of his 'confession'. Nor are we told whether Casement ever informed Christensen of his visit to the Foreign Office to tell Von Wedel of the 'confession'. It must also be borne in mind that there is a considerable difference between the Berlin diaries of Casement, and those which dealt with other parts of his career. The Berlin diaries were written with a view to possible publication. Casement met a Dr. Charles E. Curry, an American who was living in Munich in May 1915, and struck up a warm friendship with him. Long after Casement's death, Curry published parts of Casement's Berlin diaries. The other diaries of Casement were not meant for publication.

himself with preposterous notions that such incidents in the war as the bombardment of the English east coast would be taken by Findlay, and hence by Whitehall, to be due to his influence; or that 'harsh repressive measures in Ireland', as reported in the Swiss press, were 'panic steps taken by the British Government to forestall any move by me there'.

His spirits revived when, on December 27th, he was sent for to attend the Wilhelmstrasse, and there was Zimmermann all ready to affix the seal, with due portentousness, to the document which Casement had drafted, setting forth the terms under which the Irish Brigade was to be raised and would operate; and which Casement himself now signed with a flourish.

He planned to pay his second visit to Limburg on New Year's Eve. He accordingly left Berlin on Wednesday, December 30th, by the 10.36 train for Frankfurt. It was an all-day journey, the train getting in at 7.30 p.m. Casement had a cold, due, he says, to the sharp thaw after Christmas, and on arriving in Limburg, he went straight to bed and stayed there for a while.

On January 2nd, 1915, Casement, still no doubt feeling groggy from his chill, but well bundled up in overcoat and scarf, drove up the steep roadway which led to the hill-top camp, ready for his second confrontation with his uniformed compatriots. Also, as though in almost compulsive fidelity to his former employers, he carried a neatly rolled-up umbrella over his arm.

The men were waiting for him; the Munsters, the Fusiliers, the Dragoons, the Rangers and the others. 'Here comes the Boer again,' murmured some of them, while others were saying out loud, 'Ah, 'tis the bloody Fenian, boys!' The great liberator did not on this occasion enjoy good public relations.

In spite of this reception, Casement, with his sick-bed pallor, gathered himself together, strode over to where about eighty (out of 2,400 Irish prisoners) stood in a sullen knot, and clambered up on to the table which formed a makeshift dais. Private John Cronin, 2nd Battalion, the Royal Munster Fusiliers, was there that day. And here, in the unadorned, laconic style of the court of justice in which he later described the proceedings, is his account.

'He said that he was going to form an Irish Brigade, and he said "Why live any longer in hunger and misery in this camp when you can better yourselves by joining the Irish Brigade which I am going to form? You will be sent to Berlin as the guests of the German Government." He said that in the event of Germany winning a sea battle, he would land the Irish Brigade in Ireland, and Ireland would equip them. They would free Ireland from England. If Germany didn't win, then they would be sent to America; they would get £10 or £20 pocket money and a free passage.

'He was asked who he was, and he said he was Sir Roger Casement, the organiser of the Irish National Volunteer Movement. He could go wherever he liked, and he went around the camp with papers, one called the *Gaelic-American* and another called the *Continental Times*. . . .'

John Robinson, of the R.A.M.C., another there that day, considered that Casement got 'a very poor reception'. He was struck and pushed. There were boos. Casement swung the umbrella at his tormenters, and someone tried to grab it from him. German guards intervened, conceivably without much enthusiasm. Casement's speech lasted between fifteen and twenty minutes.

So there, in that wintry camp in Germany, Casement tasted the bitter dregs of complete humiliation and rejection. In Berlin the Germans sneered. In Limburg the Irish jeered. What had happened to the great spell-binder, to his 'irresistible personality', his 'beguiling voice', his 'charm', his 'utter sincerity' and so on? Whatever it was that Casement had possessed in the pre-war drawing-rooms of London and Dublin signally failed to emerge when he talked to cold and hungry Irishmen in German prison camps. They saw him—and so did the Germans—as a man of straw. There are few romantics in prison camps.

He lingered on in Limburg for a fortnight or so, fretting about various matters, including the fact that neither Von Wedel nor Meyer bothered to write. He had embarked on the draft of an open letter to Sir Edward Grey about Findlay's iniquities, and this perhaps helped to take his mind off the Limburg fiasco. He went back to the camp nearly every day, only to be met with renewed insults and derision. Father Crotty, a redoubtable figure, was now hard at work in the camp, and Casement took to trailing round with the priest as he went his rounds, smiling ingratiatingly but himself saying little or nothing.

Finally Casement became so appalled at his reception by the Irish prisoners that he was ready to throw in his hand. He wrote (January 9th, 1915) to Von Wedel: 'Dear Count—As you will have gathered already from my notes to Mr. Meyer, and from the report of Bryan Kelly, *my hope to find the Irish soldiers willing to enrol in an Irish Brigade must be given up.*

'The favourable impression conveyed to me early in December by the small number of men I then met in the camp and the apparent willingness they displayed to fall in with my views have not been realised in the much larger number since brought together.

'*I daresay a sham corps of sorts could be formed by tempting the men with promises of money; but an appeal to their patriotism is an appeal to something non-existent* . . . All thought of enrolling the men, I fear, must be abandoned—*they are mercenaries pure and simple and even had I the means to bribe them I should not attempt to do so.* . . .

'Believe me,

'Yours sincerely,

'Roger Casement.'

Nevertheless five days later he wrote to Count von Wedel:

'Since writing you I have had long talks with General Exner on the subject of the Irish prisoners here and the projected Brigade. General Exner thinks it may be and should be possible to get possibly some hundreds of the men to enrol, if time is given. I think so too. Much will depend on the arrival of Father Nicholson.

'. . . Gen. Exner suggested yesterday getting 2,000 small Irish flags! My own idea at the first. He thinks they would be very helpful. . . .'

This letter goes on to suggest putting more meat in the

prisoners' soup, the provision of a harmonium and maps of Ireland in each prisoner's room as morale-boosters.

Casement now returned moodily to Berlin, where he immediately had a row with the Foreign Office because they insisted on retaining Findlay's formal and personally signed offer of £5,000 for Casement's delivery—written on British Legation notepaper —in their own files, instead of handing it over to Casement. How far anyone concerned was taking seriously the whole preposterous fantasy of Christiania it is difficult to judge.

By January 24th Casement was pettishly referring to 'this stupid, pig-headed German Government', and to their 'wretchedly run Foreign Office! Truly they merit all the opprobriums Billy Tyrrell heaped on them in the London Foreign Office that November day in 1912 when he was discharging his soul into my ears—and Lichnowsky outside the door, and announced as he spoke! It is almost impossible to have true dealings with them. You never know their minds—save that if there is a wrong way to tackle a human problem, they are likely to choose it.'

Count von Wedel wrote to Count Oberndorff, who had been anxiously cabling from Christiania to know what his own position was in this unorthodox imbroglio:

'Personal. To be decoded personally.

'Direct relations between Your Excellency and Christensen shall be limited to the indispensable.

'If possible please send urgently sample of your English colleague Findlay's handwriting, e.g., a letter or something of the sort, from which comparison regarding handwriting can be made.'

[1] The German Foreign Office filed Findlay's offer of the bribe immediately beside a letter which Findlay had written to his opposite number in Christiania, Von Oberndorff, some years before the war, offering condolences—in a perfectly proper diplomatic manner—over the loss of a German destroyer in a storm. Presumably Von Oberndorff found this letter in his own Embassy files, and sent it to Berlin in response to their requests for a sample of Findlay's handwriting. The two letters matched perfectly, and there seems to be not the slightest doubt that Findlay did in fact make the offer to Christensen.

'Few days ago Christensen brought a letter written in Findlay's hand on paper with the imprint of the British Legation at Christiania, the authenticity of which seems certain, and in which Findlay offers Christensen £5,000 in the name of the British Government if he makes it possible for the English to get hold of Sir Roger Casement.

'Mr. Findlay is therefore already so compromised by this letter which is in our hands, that the danger of Your Excellency becoming compromised is hardly to be reckoned with.'

Just before he paid his second visit to Limburg, Casement had visited Ruhleben, where the Germans ran their main prison camp for allied civilian internees. He had talked to some Irishmen interned there, and this gave him an idea. On January 27th, he wrote to Von Wedel (from the Esplanade Hotel, where he had now apparently moved in beside the flinching Blüchers):

'I take this opportunity to suggest that a very favourable impression indeed throughout the world might be produced by the notification to-day that certain Irish civil prisoners now at Ruhleben might be released forthwith as an act of imperial (and national) goodwill to the Irish people. . . .

'The effect, not only in Ireland but in America and in ecclesiastical quarters in Rome and all over the Catholic English-speaking world would be very great. . . . I need not add that not the least of the favourable results to be anticipated would be the effect produced on the minds of the Irish *prisoners-of-war*, when they learn of this generous manifestation of German goodwill to Irishmen. I am sure the very happiest results will accrue to our just cause if you will be guided by me in this. . . .'

This proved to be one of the few suggestions by Casement on which the Germans acted favourably and promptly. The three civilian internees selected, William David Coyne, of Ballharris, County Mayo, a student; Thomas Gerald Hoy, of Dungannon, County Tyrone, a teacher; and John Patrick Bradshaw, of Ballymoney, County Antrim, a business agent; were duly released and were back in the British Isles in the spring of 1915. But an unlooked-for circumstance was that Hoy, on May 12th, 1915, turned up in London, and volunteered a long statement to Admiralty Intelligence. Among the information which Hoy passed on was that Casement was closely guarded by German secret agents, because it was feared that British agents were plotting an attempt on his life. This seems highly unlikely. There is not even the most fleeting mention of this in Casement's diaries or other writings.

On January 27th Casement wrote to Von Wedel: 'I am sure that to-day in America many of my countrymen are associating themselves with yours in expressions of sincere respect and regard for the German Emperor and the German people on the occasion of His Majesty's birthday. May I, as an individual Irishman now in Germany and as one who has striven to promote both in Ireland and America sentiments of goodwill and esteem between Irishmen and Germans, be permitted to associate myself in these universal feelings, and to offer my earnest prayer for the welfare of His Imperial Majesty and His people and for the righteous triumph of the German arms in this great war of National defence forced upon a peace-loving, peace-keeping and a peace-seeking people.

'I beg that you will do me the honour to convey this poor expression of a very sincere feeling to the proper quarter, since I am confident that in so speaking I utter the sentiments of many Irishmen, not only in Ireland but throughout the world.

'I am, dear Count von Wedel,
'With much regard,
'Yours very sincerely,
'Roger Casement.'

The fulsome, not to say sycophantic terms in which this letter is couched are uncomfortably reminiscent of the letter of acceptance of his knighthood to Sir Edward Grey three years earlier.

A few days before this, on the 24th, Casement recorded: 'I told Von Wedel last night that were I sure of getting over, I should return to the U.S.A., but the risks are too great. And yet I know not what to do. To stay in Berlin or Germany, idle, inactive, and with the huge disappointment of the Irish Brigade failure staring me in the face and with no hope of further action by the German Government anent Ireland—is a policy of despair. Besides I have not the means to live here. Life is very expensive and I must stay at expensive hotels and incur constant outlays. It would be better to return to Norway—convict Findlay up to the hilt, get H.M. Government exposed, and if necessary return to Germany, should Father Nicholson succeed with the soldiers. I shall talk things over with him to-day—and decide quickly.'

On January 29th the open letter to Grey about the Christiania affair was finished and was being typed, and Casement thought that he was on his way to Norway. 'All hurry and haste now to get ready for the flight to Norway. Decided to go myself on Sunday with Adler. Meyer said he would get three good private detectives to go with me—and so protect me and do all they could to help. Von Roeder and Blücher very much against my going to Norway. Meyer has a silly scheme for me to go there and try to get Findlay to kidnap me, and then, through my private detectives, to catch him and his, and hand them over to the police. I rejected this, on Roeder's and Blücher's advice—and decided to go to Norway openly, as myself, to challenge Findlay and invite the Norwegian Government to investigate the whole affair.'

In all this windy nonsense the Irish Brigade, the one thing that had any relevance in Casement's German visit, was pushed into the background, while Casement pursued his obsession. By now Von Wedel and his colleagues may well have been cursing the day when Casement took it into his head to go to Berlin. If Meyer was serious in suggesting to Casement that he should try to embroil Findlay by encouraging him to make an actual attempt at kidnapping with violence, one cannot help wondering if it was in the hope that whatever happened up in Christiania, the Wilhelmstrasse would see the last of the ineffective Irishman.

Casement was now once again involved in a muddle, this time over a small matter, for when Meyer brought along twenty copies of the Grey letter to his hotel, they were so full of mistakes that

Casement angrily returned them for re-typing. Then there was a mistake about the time their train was to leave for Sassnitz. When Casement and Christensen met at the station (for by now the two were staying at different hotels, although no explanation of the separation is offered in Casement's writings) early on a wretchedly cold day, with snow on the ground, it was to find that they should have gone the night before and would therefore have to wait until the evening. The time-table had been changed, and the reason for the change was disquieting—British submarines had become active in the Baltic, and in consequence the mail boat for Sweden was now crossing from Germany by daylight only. Meyer was none too pleased to learn of the hitch when he in his turn arrived at the station with the promised escort of three burly detectives. But that evening back they all came again, and this time Meyer gave Casement a special message from the Admiralty hardly calculated to enhance his morale: it was thought possible that a British submarine might try to stop the mailboat at sea and demand the surrender of Casement. 'If a spy is at Sassnitz,' broods Casement, 'they will surely do it. But I said I should go on, and if this happened, I'd resist and not be taken alive.' Meyer assured him that the detectives were tough and would fight too—'to the death. Adler also agreed, and so we left Berlin on the 7.18 . . .'

Close on midnight they reached Stralsund and Casement went to bed in his clothes, 'greatly upset and wondering how best to proceed'. He was not, he writes, afraid of any submarines, but of the possible actions of the British Government in Norway, their influence there, their power and gold in contrast to his own penniless and defenceless position. 'To go out single-handed, to thus challenge the mightiest government in the world and charge them publicly with infamous criminal conspiracy through their accredited Representative, is a desperate act. . . .' He got no sleep.

They went on by train early and put up at the Monopol Hotel in Sassnitz, to sit out the morning until the mailboat should leave at 2 p.m. But in those few intervening hours Casement's nerve cracked. He decided to throw in his hand and go ignominiously back to Berlin.

This decision was reached after a long and rambling discussion with Christensen, who had been against Casement's going to Norway all along. The fact that Casement sought, and probably took, the advice of his servant on so important a decision is a measure of the influence which Christensen had by now established over Casement. In any event Casement panicked and burned some of his papers then and there in the grate of his hotel bedroom. He then broke the news to the three detectives that the trip was off but does not say how they took it, contenting himself with noting that they were 'armed to the teeth'. It is not difficult to believe him when he adds that he 'spent miserable day'.

The real reason for this abrupt change of plan certainly seems to have been sheer cold feet. Even if we give Casement the benefit of the doubt and accept that the reasons for the cancellation of the project are those which he advances, then there is yet another example of disorderly planning and woeful misjudgment that must have served to remind the Germans once more of what a broken reed Casement was proving to be.

A year or so later Casement advanced an entirely different reason for not having continued his journey. He gave his American friend, Dr. Charles Curry, a memorandum in which he claimed that he had had on him during his journey to Sassnitz an extremely important document (unspecified) which the Germans were wild to get their hands on. They had already 'stolen' from him, in Casement's view, Findlay's letter about the bribe, and now they badly wanted this other document; and far from being there for his protection, the main duty of the three detectives was to ensure that all Casement's papers, but especially the important one, were 'safely taken back to Berlin' if anything befell him in Norway.

In Casement's tortured and fearful mind anything, or so one supposes, was possible. As he wallowed in his almost perpetual bath of self-pity and persecution mania, fear of the German detectives may perhaps have outweighed his fear of British submarines.

The day after his decision to remain in Germany Casement trailed back to Berlin, re-registered at his hotel and went round to the Wilhelmstrasse for what must have been an embarrassing chat with Von Wedel. Later when Casement saw Meyer, the Foreign Office man impishly revealed that a German cruiser had been standing by specially to escort the mailboat from Sassnitz to Traelleborg—although why Meyer could not have told Casement about this in the first instance instead of merely scaring him with talk about submarines is not clear.

Meyer also informed Casement that that very day a German-Irish Society had been formed in Berlin and had put up a handsome 50,000 marks as a starting fund, the money to be entirely at Casement's discretion for disposal. This at a stroke removed Casement's worries that he was in no position to challenge the rich British Government in the courts of Norway, as he could now doubtless hire the best legal advice available in Christiania. Meyer, however, seems to have been too tactful to touch on this point, while Casement merely remarked that he felt himself unable to draw any of this money unless his friends in America gave their permission.

At last the Grey letter was not only written but typed to Casement's satisfaction. But it proved to be scarcely worth all the fuss. It said that while Casement was prepared to face charges in a Court of Law, he was not prepared to meet waylaying, kidnapping, suborning of his dependants or knocking on the head, all of these being expedients which had been invoked by Britain's representatives in a neutral country. It accused Findlay of criminal conspiracy and went into a history of the Findlay-Christensen conversations. It was full of such phrases as 'My faithful follower concealed the anger which he felt at this suggestion' and 'That this man was faithful to me and the law of his country was a triumph of Norwegian integrity over the ignoble inducement proffered by the richest and most powerful Government in the world to be false to both.'

It seems inconceivable to-day that Casement should have given the matter a second thought—still less that he should have tried to make an international issue of it. He ignored the plain indications that the Irish-Americans considered the matter too trivial to pursue. He was convinced that the Germans were wrong in not showing enthusiasm. Once again he was displaying the staggering lack of judgment which attended the later years of his career. Just as, having gone to the U.S.A. to raise money for his hard-pressed compatriots at home, he allowed his design to be deflected by a chance public meeting arranged by a third party, so in Germany, neglecting the main reason which had brought him there, he persisted in trying to make a mountain of a purely personal molehill.

However, special messengers rushed copies of his letter to twelve diplomatic missions in Berlin, and by safe hand, another copy went to the Holy See, with injunctions that His Holiness should at all costs be shown it.

By February 5th, Casement was sitting about, tensely waiting for reactions. 'Stayed in hotel all day—busy and very anxious. Meyer told me they would not publish here first. Only after Rome or some other country had got it out first. I agreed as wise.'

On Sunday, February 7th, Casement tried over the luncheon table to cajole Count von Larisch, of the Austro-Hungarian Embassy, into promising that the Grey letter should get good play in the Viennese press. ('Larisch very friendly, but not very intelligent, I fear'.)

Monday was another bad day. Still no news of the letter receiving publication anywhere. Casement thought that when it appeared he would be besieged by reporters, so he decided to take evasive action. Accompanied by Christensen, he went off to the Palace Hotel at Potsdam, which had been warmly recommended by Herr Klicks, the manager of the Continental in Berlin. 'But it was wretched; I got such a rude reception when they found I spoke only English that I returned to Berlin in despair.'

Acknowledgments of the Grey letter now started to trickle in from various quarters. The Swedish Minister sent a courteous reply saying that his copy of the letter had gone on to Stockholm. But the Portuguese Minister stated tartly that to forward the letter to Lisbon would be to exceed the legal rights of his Legation

—and with that, returned it. ('Ah, le cochon!' cried the sympathetic Meyer, on hearing this news.) But as all too often, Meyer proved to be the bearer of evil tidings, for he pointed out that publication of the letter in Rome would be impossible ('The Foreign Office has doubtless heard,' speculates Casement darkly). Meyer followed this up by affirming that all the papers in Italy were pro-Ally and would say nothing against England. (Italy was soon to declare war on the Central Powers.) Meyer set the following Friday as the earliest date for publication, and then only in Vienna—which was really not much better than Berlin itself.

Moved to waspish resentment by all this, Casement confided that night to his diary: 'Meyer is so secretive and lacking in frankness that he tells me nothing. I am treated by him as a sort of tool or agent—to be directed and used—but never to be kept informed or referred to or consulted. Only directed. He now wants me to arrange to have Aubrey Stanhope, Karl von Wiegand and Conger' (newspaper correspondents in Berlin) 'out to interview me on Friday (but not before!) and tell them all. I said much better do it before, so that they might be ready by Friday, not merely told on Friday . . . The wretched suspicion and mistrust of everyone that characterises all their conduct of public affairs again revealed here.'

Casement, by now thoroughly cast down, decided to enter a sanatorium, once again under the alias of 'Mr. Hammond of New York'. No sooner had he arrived at the sanatorium in the Grünewald than Meyer was on the telephone, repeating that no interviews were to be given before Friday. Casement told him wearily to bring the newspapermen out to the Grünewald for the interview. Then followed a great explosion of rage—'To-day's news is that England has prohibited all cables from the Continent! This is a fine measure of freedom of communication! My God! How much more will the world have to stand from the Bitch and Harlot of the North Sea! This measure is asserted to be in connexion with the transport of Kitchener's Army to the Continent. That may be—but if so, it would be the other way about, and no cable communications to the Continent from England—whereas it is from the Continent to the outside world which they have interdicted.'

But again, as with the shelling of Scarborough, the moves in Ireland and the sending of a Minister to the Vatican, Casement decides on second thoughts that he himself is really at the bottom of the whole thing. 'It is,' he muses, 'much more likely that the measure is part of their damned conspiracy against me. They fear mightily my charge coming out in the U.S.A. first, and before they have arranged their version and publicly branded me as a "traitor" . . . This will surely be their game.'

The next day: 'I am still in my room at the sanatorium, writing my diary and eating my heart out. An agent of the secret police has just called (11.20 a.m.) to ask for my "military pass"—I have none. I gave him the old police card of Mr. Hammond, which I happily still have and referred him to the Foreign Office for further information. It is highly possible that they will bungle things there, and I may be haled off to jail.'

It is only fair to Casement to say that he wrote in a letter to his friend Mr. Curry the following year, just before he left for Ireland, 'I often say things in my diaries that I should not like to stand for ever. It is hard to see straight even when one is well and not troubled—and I am not well in body and have not been so for long, and thus greatly troubled in mind too—so that my remarks are often unjust, and hasty and ill-considered.'

With his entry of February 15th, 1915, Casement abruptly cut off his German diaries. He later wrote: 'I stopped it when it became clear that I was being played with, fooled and used as by a most selfish and unscrupulous government for its own petty interests. I did not wish to record the misery I felt, or say the things my heart prompted. But to-day it is my head which compels me to the unwelcome task.'

Although Casement was so bitter against the German Government he ought perhaps to have borne in mind that it was at least long-suffering. When he accuses it of being concerned only with its own selfish interests, he might well have recalled that the main object of all governments is to concern themselves with what they conceive to be their primary self-interest; and to have reminded himself that virtually his own sole concern in the more than three months since he arrived in Germany had been with the completely personal matter of the ludicrous Findlay episode. Was that to be termed a selfless concern with the interests of Ireland?

The Edward Grey letter duly received some publicity, although some newspapers scoffed at the Findlay saga. I have not been able to find anything to show whether Casement was satisfied or not at the extent of the resulting publicity. I suppose that he was not. If the splash had been of truly gratifying proportions, it might well have lifted Casement from his despond and got him going again on his diary. But evidently the news continued to be drab.

By February 21st, Casement had left the sanatorium and was staying at No. 14 Harvesteruder Weg, Hamburg, then a stately mansion overlooking Lake Alster. The third count against him at his subsequent trial stated that on or about February 15th, 1915, he was again at Limburg, soliciting and inciting Irish soldiers there. But—at least as far as I can determine—the dates in this instance do not tally.

From Hamburg on the 25th, Casement turned once again to Von Wedel, but this time with something new:

'The enclosed' (which was a newspaper cutting referring to shipping under the Irish flag) 'will create a great sensation in the U.S.A. It is the weirdest act which the British Government has yet committed. I am to be hanged, and captured at all costs, because I asked *you* to recognise the Irish flag—and when you did I was denounced as a "traitor". Now, the very Government denouncing me is making use of that flag (which has no existence in International Law!) to cover their ships. It is the very best justification I could seek for my coming to Germany. Of course the British intention is an evil one. They want your submarines to blow up a ship *"flying the Irish flag"* and then say to Ireland and the Irish in the U.S.A., "You see how fraudulent was the German Declaration of Goodwill to Ireland." By a public fraud they want to get the Irish at home and abroad enraged against Germany. They will fail. But you could take the wind out of their sails splendidly if your Admiralty would say (in effect) "We welcome the recognition by Great Britain of the Irish flag on the high seas. Germany will respect that flag when England notifies the world that she will respect it." '

This seems to have evoked small enthusiasm at the Wilhelmstrasse. There was now most vexing news of a post-card sent by John Smythe, a prisoner of war at the Limburg Camp, to his mother, Mrs. M. Smythe, of Mullingar, and intercepted by the German military censors. 'Dear Mother, I was very pleased to receive your letter yesterday. Do not send anything else out, Mother. I am getting along very nicely and hope soon to be able to handle the pike again. They are hoping to form an Irish Brigade here, but we will die first—Johnnie.'

While in Hamburg, Casement was in touch with his old acquaintance Herr Ballin, the head of the Hamburg-Amerika Line, about a passage back to the U.S.A. for Christensen. 'Faithful Adler,' now in rather piano mood, paid him a visit there, but he was still proving a considerable embarrassment to various authorities, for there is no reason to suppose that he had changed his habits in any notable respect.

On March 12th, a letter was sent to Count von Wedel by the Berlin Kulturbund stating that Christensen was proposing to go to the U.S.A. as 'a German propaganda agent commissioned by the German Foreign Office', and would it not be preferable to find him a job in Berlin instead?

To this Von Wedel replied tersely: 'Adler Christensen, Sir Roger Casement's attendant, has received no orders from the Foreign Office to make propaganda for German interests in America. This office has no adverse comment to make regarding the intention of the Kulturbund to find Christensen a post in Germany.'

This must, however, have sounded too much like hard work for Christensen, and soon afterwards he took leave of Casement and sailed for New York. There John Devoy and the other Irish-Americans were not impressed by him.

In mid-March the German Admiralty sent a Top Secret message to the Foreign Office, coldly turning down a suggestion that two of the Imperial Navy's specially trained agents should be detached for special duties in Ireland. In effect the message told the Foreign Office, that (1)—It takes time and trouble to train a spy to the required standards of efficiency, that they are valuable men, and that Ireland was not worthwhile from a Naval Intelligence point of view ; (2)—the Imperial Navy's agents had better things to do than encourage the Irish Nationalist Movement. Whether or not this had something to do with a suggestion of Casement's does not emerge; but it seems likely that this snub from the Admiralty may have caused restiveness at the German Foreign Office, which in turn found expression in increased impatience with the fumblings of the visitor.

Impatience was mounting fast, indeed. Writing to Von Wedel from Wilmersdorf on March 20th, Casement frostily remarked that he had heard from Limburg that nothing had been done to carry out the understanding at which he claimed to have arrived with General Exner, the Limburg Camp Commandant, in January to the effect that the 'English-born and pro-English men in the camp should be separated from the others'. Worse, the censorship over the letters received by the men, complained Casement, was slack, so that 'misleading statements' were being allowed to reach them from their friends and relatives in Ireland. So, he ends, 'I see no object in my returning to Limburg under these conditions. . . . '

The same question of lax censorship was causing misgivings to Father Nicholson. Unlike Father Crotty, who seems to have pursued his ministrations at the camp in a correct manner, divorced from attempts at political activity, Father Nicholson, procured and enthusiastically vouched for by Von Bernstorff in the United States, was to all intents a German agent.

Nicholson took up eagerly where Casement had left off, and of course there were endless opportunities for one in his position to set about suborning the Irishmen in his flock. It is perhaps even more to the credit of the prisoners that Father Nicholson failed as signally as did Casement, when one remembers the natural veneration in which simple Irishmen would be inclined to hold a priest of their own race, and of the favourable religious climate—from the sermon to the confessional—in which an adroit and unscrupulous cleric could ply his propaganda. However, far from being swayed by the priest, the prisoners quickly started complaining about him, and there was a move among the men to boycott Masses conducted by Father Nicholson.

Father Nicholson paid a visit to Berlin, where for the benefit of the Foreign Office he listed various matters which, in his opinion, were 'hampering' pro-German propaganda among the prisoners of war. He too pointed out that censorship was not strict enough. Several prisoners had received letters and cards from home telling of a completely pro-English disposition in Ireland and about the good progress of recruiting there for the British Army. This sort of news from their homes, Father Nicholson told Von Wedel, could not fail to have a highly unsettling effect on the men just when it was being explained to them in Limburg that every true Irish patriot should look on England as the greatest enemy of his land.

Nicholson went on to say that Irish prisoners of war had lately been kicked and struck by German guards for trivial reasons, and Father Crotty had witnessed one such episode. The prisoners were also complaining that money sent to them from home was being withheld or pilfered from them by the Germans.

The outlook concerning recruitment for the Irish Brigade seemed to be going from bad to worse, and the diligent Nicholson also visited General de Graeff, G.O.C. in the Frankfurt area, and complained to him that some of the men were asking for transfers away from Limburg, as they were 'fed up' with reading the anti-British pamphlets which were constantly circulated among them. There were, summarised Nicholson, individuals in the camp who were definitely working at cross-purposes with his own endeavours.

Major Dachsieb, an aide to General Exner at the Limburg Camp, also put in a dampening report. A questionnaire had been circulated among the men with the object of finding out whether there was anybody left who might still be persuaded to join the brigade. Dachsieb stated that there was not a single man who could be considered suitable for further attempts at indoctrination. He complained that this disappointing state of affairs might be due to (1) the 'extremely low standard of education' among the prisoners, (2) the fact that there existed a pro-English disposition among them, enhanced by gifts of money sent them 'by their rich officers and the officers' wives', (3) the men fearing that when they returned to Ireland after the war, they might get into trouble if they showed that they were anti-English now. As regards Fathers Crotty and Nicholson, Dachsieb wrote cautiously, 'Since the two priests, in accordance with existing orders, enjoy free communication, without witnesses, with the prisoners, especially in the confessional, they are informed of the prisoners' state of mind. In these circumstances, this battalion command cannot report on the nature of their activities.'

Captain Nadolny, of German G.H.Q. Political Division, wrote to the Foreign Office: 'In view of conditions described' (by Dachsieb) 'it appears doubtful whether the continuation of the propaganda among the Irish prisoners of war is worth while. A statement thereon would be much appreciated.'

Casement has been accused, and it was to be so alleged at his trial, of having spitefully taken it out on the recalcitrant prisoners of war, by having caused their rations to be reduced. As with the allegation about the acceptance of 'German gold', I feel one should give him the benefit of the doubt about this. The two main answers are that since the men were promised better conditions if they would join the Brigade, it was only logical that those who did not do so should eventually revert to the ration level which obtained for all run-of-the-mill prisoners, English, French and Russian, as well as Irish; and that as the British blockade of Germany began to be felt with increasing severity, everyone in Germany had to tighten his belt, including, of course, the prisoners of war. By mid-1915 the majority of prisoners in German camps were getting nothing much beyond bread and mangolds, with some occasional watery soup.

To the objective view it seems apparent that Casement had not a cruel or vindictive nature. He ranted and raved and breathed fire in his diaries and letters—but that was on paper. He had the most disastrous defects of character and the most glaring weaknesses, but cheap revenge on fellow-Irishmen in a prison camp was not in his nature.

By April 11th Casement (back in Berlin) wrote to Von Wedel seeking an early appointment with him and Zimmermann, and saying 'I wish to discuss the later developments of the Limburg matter. There is now more than the probability of the object in view last December being successfully effected if the desire still exists, on both sides, that it should be done. . . . To the cause I represent, however, there is much less prospect of anything useful accruing from the formation of the Irish Brigade than when the idea originated.

'It is this conviction of the perception that the sacrifice would be quite useless for any practical purposes to my country that has weighed with me and caused me to leave the matter alone. This conviction is reinforced by a letter I got last night from Prof. Kuno Meyer in Chicago.'

This was followed two days later by a long memorandum asking favours for Irishmen if the Germans failed to win the war, and seeking to find out what would happen to the Brigade after a lost war, if it did after all prove possible to form it.

May 1915 was another black period for Casement. He was ill. again—he refers in a letter to 'an old malady, internal catarrh, that I was subject to in the tropics, and so I am in bed and in the hands of the doctors'.[1]

[1] The medical expenditure to which he was put rankled. In a memorandum which he handed to Dr. Curry on March 26th, 1916, Casement wrote: 'Since I came to Germany I have spent roughly £2,000, and many Germans have done well out of me. Thus Dr. Caro, a Berlin lawyer, got 500 marks for some paltry "advice" in the Findlay affair. Doctors have had a big haul. Professor Oppenheim of Berlin 100 marks—and many more. I have not found any German, I may say, (except Mrs. Gaffney's maid!) who has done anything for me for

By the 10th a report from Limburg, made to the General Staff by one of their agents, said that out of a hundred and fifty men interviewed until then, thirty-one had volunteered for the Irish Brigade. The men had to be interviewed in small groups, about thirty at a time, as it was always necessary to use personal persuasion, refuting objections, etc. Recruitment, went on the report, encountered many difficulties. 'There seem to be many English and Scots among the men, these having pretended to be Irish in order to enjoy the various advantages, such as better food and treatment. . . .'

The G.H.Q. agent returned soon afterwards to Berlin and put in a further report, headed 'Proposals'. This suggested that some of the N.C.O.s who had already said they would volunteer, should be decked out without delay in their smart new uniforms and shown off in camp. Then, it would be advisable to have enough uniforms and full accessories 'ready at hand for the first 100 volunteers, as the sight of a formation in Irish uniform would no doubt make a deep impression.' The uniform—designed by Casement himself in a spare moment—consisted of grey-green tunics and trousers, with emerald-green collar, facings and shoulder-straps. On the collar appeared a golden Irish harp. On the shoulder-straps were shamrocks. The tunics had 'golden' buttons, and there were touches of gold on the cap.

The 'proposals' went on to say that all volunteers should be immediately segregated in separate barracks, and 'no longer treated as prisoners'. And there followed the German agent's picture of the ideal C.O. for the Brigade: 'Until Irish officers are available, the assistance of a young German infantry officer (a Catholic) for purposes of command will be necessary. He should speak English fluently and have lived some time abroad, in England or America. His choice should be made carefully, with

nothing—or for love. No one has refused my "Irish gold", and perhaps the worst case was that of Dr. Muhlig, brother of the Baroness von N——, a friend in whose house I was and where I got ill. She called in her brother in a friendly way to prescribe for me, and he sent me a bill for 80 marks. A trifle—but not very gentle or distinguished!'

the object in mind that he should be able to handle these men who are so different from ours. It is essential that he should know how to make himself popular without jeopardising his dignity. He must be just, smart, in every sense a leader; therefore physically superior to the men, and always with a friendly joke in reserve.'[1]

But the whole thing was so much shadow-play. Everyone concerned, from Casement to Von Wedel and the men at G.H.Q., realised the hopelessness of the project; yet it was never quite dropped.

At the end of April Joseph Plunkett,[2] the son of Count Plunkett, arrived in Berlin via Switzerland, and Casement got him to go to Limburg to see what he could do there. Plunkett attended the 'processing' of the prisoners of war during a long day on which they were formed into the prescribed batches of thirty at a time and harangued. Some of those who had volunteered were already wearing their brand-new uniforms, and they came in for some highly uncomplimentary remarks from their unyielding fellows.

From time to time Casement himself paid a few more duty calls at the camp, but for the most part he preferred not to reawaken the boos which must still have often rung in his ears. Altogether fifty-two men were finally scraped together to form the 'Brigade', and taking the most charitable view, they seem to have been riff-raff, the dregs of the Army. Instead of showing restraint at their new privileges and comparative freedom, they got into constant brawls with the French and Russian prisoners, abused their privileges, got drunk whenever funds allowed, showed wretched discipline and altogether must have greatly strained that small stock of jokes which the German C.O. was supposed to keep on hand. The French were particularly incensed at the infuriating spectacle of these 'salauds', lounging about in their smart new uniforms, and enjoying life, so that clashes broke out almost nightly. Finally in desperation the Germans removed the Brigade to a camp at Wunsdorf, not far from Berlin, and now it was the

[1] See Appendix II for further suggestions concerning treatment of the Irish Brigade.

[2] Later shot for his part in the Dublin rising.

turn of the Brigade to be incensed, for they found that they had as next-door neighbours a horde of coal-black Senegalese prisoners, muttering unintelligibly at them through the wire.

About the only action that any member of the Brigade was to see in his new capacity was against the Germans. During the few months that they stayed in Wunsdorf, the authorities were presently forced to cancel evening visits by members to nearby beer gardens, so lively did the brawls with German soldiers become. Apparently the German troops found the Brigade nearly as objectionable as had the French, and it was only necessary for a Brigade uniform to be glimpsed entering a beerhall for an insulting chorus of 'Here comes an Englishman!' to be raised. Finally the German authorities moved them on again, this time to Zossen; but although this was supposed to be a barracks, and they to be respected allies, the general lay-out and appearance of the place differed little from that of just another prison camp.

For much of that spring and summer of 1915, while on the western front the Germans and British fought the Battle of Ypres to a standstill, and in the east the Russians, Austro-Hungarians and Germans produced titanic offensives which swayed back and forth over hundreds of miles, Casement was ill and living in or near Munich. At the end of May he went to the Bayerischer Hof Hotel in Munich, where he was introduced by an Egyptian prince to Dr. Charles Curry, the American who was later entrusted with some of his diaries and other documents. They became firm friends and Curry did all he could to help Casement, who was still completely ignorant of German and was apt in consequence to flounder into unpleasant situations as a suspected Englishman. Curry, when the time came for him to go with his family for a summer holiday to the Ammersee, engaged rooms for Casement at the nearby village of Riederau. Casement kept on the Riederau quarters as a country retreat until the start of 1916, and whenever things became too much for him, tried to get back there.

The dismal summer went past, with growing mistrust and hostility at the Wilhelmstrasse, and farce at Limburg and Wunsdorf. By August it looked as though Casement had finally had enough of Germany and was for returning to America. St. John Gaffney, the U.S. Consul-General in Munich, was persuaded, almost certainly by Curry, to interest himself in Casement's troubles, and in the best means of getting him across the Atlantic. It was even suggested that Casement might make the journey 'aboard a warship of a neutral (friendly) power', presumably American. Gaffney wrote to the German Foreign Office about this on August 7th, saying: 'I am fully aware of the immense political value of Sir Roger's arrival in the United States in the near future. Naturally he would travel incognito, and would preserve absolute secrecy as to how he landed in the U.S. after his arrival there. . . ' (There is nothing to show that in making this suggestion Gaffney had approached his Embassy, much less the State Dept.)[1]

On the same day that Gaffney wrote thus to the Wilhelmstrasse, Casement was writing to his old friend and comrade-in-arms, Morel, who was in England, although whether by the Princess of Pless's now rather doubtful route or by another method is not stated.

The burden of his letter to 'Dear Bulldog' was that anything discreditable about him which Morel might have heard was to be treated with the contempt it deserved, for Casement was the victim of 'a campaign of infamy'. 'For you and the brave men with you, there is only honour' (Morel was being roundly denounced by a section of the British press and by some M.P.s for his pacifist activities).[2] 'You are doing your duty to your country. I have been trying to do *mine* at a terrible cost to myself. . . . Do not judge your old friend harshly. Remember—I am the same

[1] Gaffney was abruptly discharged from the U.S. Consular Service not long after this.

[2] E. D. Morel, who had glowingly termed Casement 'the Bayard of the Consular Service' in happier times, was himself under heavy attack in the British Press because of his connexion with the Union of Democratic Control, a pacifist organisation, and because of his authorship of a book entitled *Truth and War*, which was held by some sections of the press to be pro-German propaganda.

"Tiger"! If you see William and Emmeline [Cadbury], say that I grieve more than I can say when I think of the separation between us. But history will perhaps do justice. . . .'

Next day Casement wrote to Von Wedel that he still had 3,000 marks by him, and he would like to leave at once via Sweden for the U.S.A., while he was still solvent. He also requested a passport.

Von Wedel was 'absolutely in favour of helping to speed Casement on his way to America. As the matter stands with the Irish Legion, he can be of no use either to the Irish or to the German cause. In America he can be at any rate active in the anti-English sense, provided that he arrives there and is not hanged by the English beforehand.'

It is evident that even Von Wedel's patience was exhausted; after nine months of Casement, he was saying in effect: to the devil with the man. It would have been fascinating if Tyrrell and Barrington, on the one hand, and Von Wedel and Zimmermann on the other, laying aside all nationalistic considerations and speaking merely as professional Foreign Office men, could have been induced frankly to compare notes about Casement.

Von Wedel continued: 'If you share my view, please instruct Assessor Meyer to get in touch with Nadolny regarding an exit permit for Casement (he should be described therein as an "Irishman" and not as a "British Subject") and inform Casement briefly in Munich.'

Across the bottom of this communication is written: 'Sir R. Casement has been informed by letter that he can at any time obtain a passport for Switzerland or for Sweden, and that he will be given every possible assistance for his journey to America.' This note was signed by Meyer.

This was one of Casement's last chances of successful flight. Had he taken it, he might well have lived. If he had gone to the U.S.A. he would have presented a problem for Washington eighteen months later when America entered the war. An Irishman wanted by Britain on charges of alleged treason could not have been handed over by the American Government very easily, even to a new-found ally, in face of outraged protests from the

U.S. Congress and the highly vocal Irish-American press and spokesmen. If he had gone to Switzerland or Sweden and stayed there, it is quite likely that either of these neutral countries would have done what the Netherlands did in face of the 'Hang the Kaiser!' outcry at the end of the war—sat tight and hung on to the man who had sought the sanctuary of neutrality. But although the Germans were willing for him to go, Casement remained. Probably the overriding, haunting dread of being taken by the British persuaded him to call it off; and I find no further trace of any efforts by Gaffney to push his remarkable scheme for sending Casement across the Atlantic by dreadnought.

In any case, by September 5th, the Germans realised, according to their official reports, that the exchange of prisoners of war with Britain had suddenly furnished the British with vital witnesses concerning Casement's German activities, which would prove highly dangerous, if not decisive, should he fall into British hands.

About this time a man named Robert Monteith, a former soldier in the British Army (he was an ordnance store conductor and fought on the British side in the Boer War) was being given official permission, by the staff of the clandestine Irish Republican Army in Dublin, to leave Ireland and sail for the U.S.A. on a special mission. In the U.S.A. he saw John Devoy and the other Irish-American leaders, who took one look at this tough, formidable fellow, with his practical knowledge of warfare, and concluded that he was just the man to offset the half-baked plottings of Casement which were by now causing them profound disquiet. So Monteith took off for Germany in his turn, and as he set sail cautiously from Hoboken one moonlit night, who should come back briefly into our narrative but Adler Christensen. The irrepressible Adler played once more a rôle which must have seemed by this time second nature to him, for when Monteith's ship was intercepted by the British and a prize crew came aboard, just as had happened during Casement's voyage, Christensen scouted the corridors, kept the concealed Monteith supplied with sandwiches and water, and distracted the ratings when their search grew warm with disarming smiles and capers. And at Christiania, while

Monteith rested in his hotel, it was again Christensen who came rushing into the room with the warning that the police were on their way to ask for Monteith's papers.

Monteith reached Berlin and then went on to Munich to find Casement. He also went to Limburg to see what he could do among the prisoners of war, but he fared no better than the others. Monteith regarded Casement with a respect amounting almost to veneration, and did his best to encourage him, and help him to regain his health. In December 1915 Casement was well enough to go to Zossen, where the Brigade then was, and even to accompany them on their make-believe route marches and drill. The men would sing Irish songs as they marched and Casement briefly regained some of his former zest. As the men fell out, Casement would call them into a wayside inn for beer at his expense, and chat animatedly with them. That there were only fifty-two who had answered his call did not, in those moments, seem to matter so much.

In spite of Monteith's arrival, on the whole things remained gloomy. At the end of December Casement went back to Berlin. His relations with the Foreign Office were now reaching new heights of unreality, and it was in a moment of exceptional folly that he made his suggestion about the possibility of the Irish Brigade seeing service with the Turks. This was a particularly serious indiscretion, for although he had long ago committed treason in the legal sense, it could still be argued with some force that he was a sincere if misguided patriot who had done nothing but try to persuade his fellow-countrymen to enrol in an army of liberation for Ireland. But to suggest that these same Irish soldiers should go off to the Middle East, there to form some sort of Catholic contingent fighting alongside the Moslems against the English and their Russian allies, was an entirely different matter.

One can only surmise the reasons which turned Casement's thoughts towards the Middle East. He was talking about sending the Brigade to Syria at almost the same time that he was writing about himself volunteering to fight with the Turks in the Dardanelles. It may have been due to a passing flight of romantic fancy; a young German friend of his was said to be going there.

189

By now the Germans were greeting Casement's every suggestion with an automatic reaction of suspicion and hostility. He had only to suggest that the Brigade, or what there was of it, should be sent to the Middle East, for the War Ministry or the General Staff to start speculating on whether the Irishmen intended to desert to the British or mutiny against the Turks as soon as they arrived. But perhaps these fears were exaggerated, the mutiny would certainly have been a puny thing. Casement thought that thirty-eight men were willing to go to Syria; but Monteith told Nadolny of G.H.Q. that only twenty-four were prepared to go.

The suggestion got as far as Enver Pasha, the Turkish leader, who said that he was agreeable to receiving the support of Casement's tiny force. At this Casement was reluctantly informed by the Foreign Office that his men could take special training courses in the use of various weapons.

This prospect appalled the German military authorities. No less a personage than General Von Lowenfeld, A.D.C. to the Kaiser, and Acting Commanding General of the Corps of the Guard, let loose the following stormy protest (February 10th, 1916): 'In view of the behaviour of the Irish—described in the report of the Commander of the manœuvres at Zossen on the 19th of January— consisting of individuals proving themselves addicted to drink and opposing the laws of military discipline and order, I agree that the proposal of Sir Roger Casement regarding the possession of rifles by the prisoners of war, which is supported by the Political Section of the General Staff, Berlin, should be rejected. I consider it utterly inappropriate, even dangerous, that these undisciplined men, who because of far too lenient treatment are constantly proving guilty of the most grievous offences, should even be given weapons.

'I am unable to repose a great deal of confidence in a gentleman like Sir Roger Casement, who raises against the Government in whose service he has stood for so many years, such grave charges; all the less so, as I cannot push aside the thought that the aforesaid propagandist might be guided by some sordid intentions.'

That was the end of the idea.

In January 1916 the German Foreign Office and General Staff sent cables to the German Embassy in Washington concerning the possibility of sabotage in the U.S.A. and Canada. The message from the Wilhelmstrasse said that the General Staff wanted 'energetic action' in order to destroy the main line of the Canadian Pacific Railway at several points. 'Provide necessary funds', this message added.

Following up with a direct message of its own, the General Staff provided the names of three men who could in turn produce a list of henchmen 'suitable for carrying out sabotage in the United States and Canada'. The three were (1)—Joseph McGarrity of Philadelphia, (2)—John P. Keating, of Michigan Avenue, Chicago, and (3)—Jeremiah O'Leary, of No. 16 Park Row, New York City. Of these 'one and two are absolutely reliable, although not always discreet. These persons are indicated by Sir Roger Casement. In the United States sabotage can be carried out on every kind of factory for supplying munitions of war. Railway embankments and bridges must not be touched. Embassy must in no circumstances be compromised.'

This was (potentially) a further grave indictment against Casement. But, again giving him the benefit of the doubt, it is possible that he was asked by the German General Staff to supply the names of completely reliable Irish-American agents in the U.S.A., and did so, without knowing or even suspecting that it was a question of sabotage in America.

It was at this time, incidentally, that Casement suffered a severe nervous breakdown and was taken back to a Munich sanatorium. When he emerged in February his appearance was described as startling. He had been marking time wretchedly and unconvincingly for nearly eighteen months and now the shadows were starting to lengthen.

The following message was sent from New York to the German General Staff, on February 16th, 1916:

'Communication has been received from the Irish that the general uprising in Ireland has been decided for Easter Sunday. No support can be sent from here. The details of the plan have been sent by the Imperial Embassy direct to the Foreign Office. The Irish Committee asks for cabled response as whether these proposals agreed there.'

Next day Von Bernstorff himself joined in:

'Washington, 17th February, 1916. Radio Telegram. To the Foreign Office. CODE.

'The Irish leader John Devoy informs me that revolution in Ireland due to start on Easter Saturday.[1] Requests arms to be sent to Limerick, west coast of Ireland, between Good Friday and Easter Sunday. Further delay impossible. I request cable whether can promise help from Germany.'

This message, of course, like all else that passed between the German Embassy in Washington and the Foreign Office in Berlin, was intercepted, read, and acted upon by the British.

In the following weeks there was a lot more in the same tenor.

During this time Casement was hanging about in Munich, seedy and neglected. He had no inkling of the messages which were reaching the Germans about the preparations for the Irish rebellion. He was the last man to be told anything of importance. When finally, in the first weeks of March, the Germans saw fit to let their Irish agents inside Germany into the secret, they contemptuously by-passed Casement and instead told Monteith. Perhaps Devoy, Cohalan and the others in America had by this time come to the conclusion that Casement was no longer worth bothering about. Or less likely perhaps, their messages to him were killed or hung up by German censorship. Whatever the reason, he was left in the dark. Monteith, clearly a capable and effective man, must have struck the Germans as somebody much more worthy of their confidence than Casement. This soldier and man of action who, thirty years later, would probably have made an admirable commando or parachutist, provided, but too late, the contrast to Casement's futilities which the Germans sorely needed.

About March 7th, Monteith was urgently summoned by the German General Staff and told that Easter Monday, April 24th,

[1] It was to be postponed two days, until Easter Monday.

was the day for the rising. He was also told that the Irish were pressing for a shipload of arms, to be escorted by a U-boat, and German officers and men, especially artillerymen. He went off at once to Munich, where he found Casement back again in a sick-room and broke the news to him.

Casement's angry reaction was: 'They always tell lies!' But he pulled himself together and, although weak and in no condition to play much part in the swift succession of events, took the train for Berlin. Now there hung over Casement the most tormenting of all the worries which had beset him since he chose his path of treachery. He knew that the rising in Ireland was at hand. But he also knew that the Germans had decided to make only a token gesture of help to the Irish patriots. Their help was hopelessly inadequate: a load of obsolete Russian rifles. Brave men could make good use of those, but they needed far more than that: some artillery, something with which to form a stockpile of munitions; above all, a few—a handful would do—professional German soldiers.

But the Germans were adamant. The discussions dragged on about the number of obsolete rifles to be consigned. Monteith and Casement pressed for two hundred thousand. They finally got twenty thousand.

Then came the question of whether Casement was to go ahead to prepare the way, or to travel in the arms ship itself. The *Aud* was a 1,200-tonner, which was to have the Norwegian flag painted on her sides, and whose captain was ordered to pretend in case of trouble that his cargo consisted of pit-props consigned for North Africa. The suggestion that Casement should go ahead was at first resisted by the German Foreign Office and Admiralty. Knowing their man as they did, they shuddered at the thought of this talkative and impractical creature being in a position to break any secrets. So they pretended that they had not got a U-boat to spare.

On March 13th, 1916, a telegram, signed jointly by Devoy and Count Bernstorff, was sent to Berlin from Washington, apprising the General Staff and Admiralty of two important code words.

To indicate that the German arms ship was on its way and would be landing its cargo, the word would be 'FINN'. But as a warning that something had gone wrong, and that the shipment had been delayed or postponed, the word was 'BRAN'.

In the autumn of 1914 a German named Wolf von Igel had set up in Wall Street, ostensibly as an advertising agent, but in reality as a German agent to further spying and sabotage. He was an official of the German Embassy in Washington, and his office was virtually a sub-bureau of the Embassy. He specialised in German-Irish intrigue. Throughout 1916, the U.S. Government was increasingly alert to the possibility of serious sabotage inside America, and on the Wednesday before Easter Sunday the police raided Von Igel's premises. The papers there seized showed clearly the intimate relations existing between the German Government and the Irish Societies in the U.S.A., especially in regard to possible sabotage. Excerpts from them were published by the American Government.

In Berlin the atmosphere was ill-omened. There was no sense of optimism. No one appears to have given the impression that they anticipated any sort of success. The thing that struck horror into Casement's heart was the realisation that the Germans intended sending not only no artillery or machine-guns, but no sort of expeditionary force, however minute. Anything at all in the way of Germans would have calmed Casement—some 'trained observers', as we call them nowadays; a 'military mission'; some 'technical experts'; a dozen gunners; best of all, a few old sweats who knew enough to heave a hand-grenade in the general direction of the enemy. But no. Nobody at all could be spared. For the first time, perhaps, Casement saw the full measure of the contempt in which he was held by those whom he had been trying to woo. As the mists of politeness and protocol shredded he perceived that Von Wedel with his polished courtesy, Herr Meyer with his effusive helpfulness, and Herr Zimmermann with his infallible punctuality, now intended to leave him all alone. This was the end of the road. Casement, as he could see for himself, was totally discarded.

As the terrible reality sank home, Casement wrote: 'I go on now because I am fool enough or coward enough—I know not which.'

While the dismal preparations went half-heartedly forward, the wretched Casement became convinced that there was only one thing for it—to call off, by hook or by crook, the planned rebellion in Ireland. To let it take place now would be to court only useless slaughter and inevitable defeat. So word must be sent to the leaders in Dublin to cancel or at least postpone the whole operation. But how?

He had rows at the Admiralty and made scenes in the Foreign Office. There was a furious altercation with Nadolny at the offices of the General Staff. He did his best to send a message through to Joseph Plunkett in Berne, but the Germans intercepted and stopped it. In desperation he turned to Irish-Americans then in Germany who might have acted as eleventh-hour couriers to Dublin. To no avail. Beside himself, he confided in a certain Noegerrath, who was an under-cover man for the Wilhelmstrasse. He twisted and turned in a final sustained bout of frustration.

Finally he burst in to see Princess Blücher, in her Berlin hotel room. She was greatly shocked by his sudden appearance. He wept hysterically and complained, amid sobs, 'They are holding a pistol to my head here if I refuse to go. But in England they have a hangman's noose ready for me. So the only thing I can do is to go out and kill myself.' The Princess, who was at first sure that she was in the presence of a madman, did her best to calm him. She accepted a bundle of letters which he pressed into her hands for safekeeping, and gave him a miniature prayer-book as a keepsake. As he went to the door, the tear-stained Casement turned and asked if he might see the Princess once more before he sailed. But, as she put it, 'feeling that there was some political intrigue on,' she said no.

Next the Germans abruptly changed their minds and told Casement that they would agree to his going ahead after all. Monteith and one Daniel Bailey, one of the staunchest recruits to the

Brigade, were to accompany him. At this the mercurial Casement's spirits lifted once more. He felt that perhaps now he might manage to get word to John McNeill and the other Irish leaders to call off the rising.

Bailey and Monteith were given some cursory instruction in the use of small arms. Then, on the night of April 11th, Casement, Monteith and Bailey, travelling in separate railway carriages, went from Berlin to Wilhelmshaven to embark in the U-boat for Ireland. In his pocket Casement had the sleeping-berth ticket with which the always methodical Foreign Office officials had provided him beforehand.

It was the final small service performed on his behalf by Count Von Wedel and Herr Richard Meyer. And it played its part in getting him hanged.

IX

THE doomed and tormented Casement had about as wretched a prologue to his final fling as could be imagined. In the two U-boats which, one after the other, conveyed him to Banna Strand, on the Galway coast, he got, as he later confided to an Irish policeman, practically no sleep for twelve nights. Casement, Monteith, and Daniel Bailey, the former Royal Irish rifleman turned Paddington porter (he was recalled to service as a reservist in 1914) found that they had to try to make do in a tiny cabin, supposed to accommodate a maximum of four naval officers—with the occupants there also. The seven men tossed and turned in this cramped misery, breathing the foul air, disturbed by the ringing of bells and the humming of engines. Casement was sea-sick nearly the whole way and Bailey too. They led a squalid existence, and not the least of Casement's irritations was that now that he had shaved off his trademark of a beard by way of disguise, he was forced, in these dreadfully confined quarters, to do more shaving than ever before in his adult life.

The Germans did their best to cheer up their unusual passenger, but for much of the time Casement lay weakly on his bunk, occasionally trying to swallow some breadcrumbs or force down a cupful of ersatz coffee. The main fare consisted of raw ham and tinned salmon, delicacies scarcely calculated to appeal to a seasick man. He was even too weak to crawl through the hatch and take a little air on deck.

The submarine which first undertook to get them to Ireland, the U-20, broke down after a couple of days. Something went wrong with the diving controls and they had to go back to Heligoland. Leaving the U-20 to get on with the repairs, the three men were transferred to the U-19, which was even smaller and her accommodation thus more confined. ·

Even for a man in normal health and with nothing on his mind, such a journey could not have failed to be hideously uncomfortable. But what can have been Casement's thoughts as the submarine twitched and bumped her way along—for most of the time on the surface—towards Ireland? He knew that he was doomed. He was sure that the Easter Rising in Dublin was also doomed. His time in Germany had been one long frustration. Even the presence of Bailey must have been a constant reminder of the jeers and insults of the prisoner of war camps.

Rousing himself from his miasma of nausea and despondency, Casement, on April 20th, wrote this letter:

'Nearing Shannon Mouth. Dear Captain Heydell—A few lines to thank you and your chiefs for the kindly hospitality of the "U-20" and later of the "U-19". We were *very* sorry to lose the "U-20" and her charming captain and officers—but OberLeut. Walther has been very kind and helpful on board this boat. I am hopeful of landing to-night in darkness near Ardfert, and meeting friends in Tralee in the morning.

'I have written to Graf von Haugwitz of the Gr. Genl. Staff about further help if possible by submarine, later on, if we can hold out.

'I think by submarine will be the only way to send us further supplies of guns, etc., after this landing—and if you hear we are holding out, then any machine-guns and a few more men may be a help.

'The next few days will settle a good deal—and if we succeed in the S.W. of Ireland we should try to keep Tralee Bay as a "*port of call*" for submarines—to bring us guns, etc.

'It will be our only chance of communication, and if we hold that part of the country for any time, your boats could be sure of friends in all the fishing-boats they might meet in the shore waters there.

'Again thanking you for your help,
'Yours sincerely ——

'P.S.—Much better than Tralee Bay would be the Shannon if

we were fortunate enough to get Limerick and hold it. Then you could send submarines up the Shannon without risk if we were in force in the City and neighbourhood.

'But the whole thing is a problem of which I can say nothing certain until I learn more on shore.'

The same day Von Bernstorff [who seems to have signed himself 'Lucius' when he wanted either to maintain some semblance of additional secrecy or else to stress the importance of the message] sent the following:

'Telegram from Washington via Buenos Aires and Stockholm, VERY URGENT.

'The Irish want to know whether submarine coming Dublin harbour. If not, they intend to block Dublin Harbour and possibly Limerick Harbour. The landing of however small a contingent of troops urgently desired. Moreover, strong, warlike demonstrations by aircraft and on sea to be staged.

'Lucius.'

And on the heels of the above:

'Cohalan desires the following to be forwarded: "Revolution in Ireland can only succeed if supported by Germany. Otherwise England capable of crushing it, although struggle would be bitter. Help necessary. Should (group indecipherable) air attack on England and naval attack simultaneously with the insurgents, thereafter landing in Ireland of troops, ammunition and possibly a few officers from aircraft, thus making it possible for Irish ports to be closed against England, for U-boat stations to be constructed, and the import of foodstuffs to England to be cut. Success of revolution may decide war.

'Lucius.'

Apart from the fact that the British Admiralty had an excellent notion of what was passing between the German camps on both sides of the Atlantic, thanks to the efficient system of wireless intercepts and deciphering, there came at the eleventh hour an unexpected confirmation of the plans for the Dublin rising. When Von Igel's Wall Street 'advertising agency' was raided by the U.S. government, the papers which were then seized provided unmistakable proof of what was planned. The Americans were still neutral, but incensed, probably, by the fact that Von Bernstorff and his staff were taking advantage of their diplomatic status to plan sabotage in America and Canada, the office of the United States Attorney-General had no hesitation in informing London what had been discovered.

At last the nightmare voyage ended and the U-boat was nosing into Tralee Bay. But nothing was going right, and there was no sign of any friends ashore. While the Germans, anxious to be off, grew visibly more impatient, Casement and his henchmen peered through the night, seeking desperately for the glimmer which would show that they were expected and would be met. In spite of the stout-hearted letter which he had written, Casement could have been forgiven for wondering, in that moment of terrible doubt, whether the Germans had betrayed him completely, and were simply getting rid of him in the way likely to give the least trouble.

Finally the U-boat commander virtually ordered the three passengers ashore, explaining that he could not, as a naval officer, risk losing his ship by dallying longer. They went below for their kit, and Casement, like the others, clumsily strapped on a belt and holster containing a Mauser pistol. Then they went up on deck, where they shivered in the cold mist. The U-boat rolled a little as she came closer to the land. Still no light. Still no friendly hail.

A rubber dinghy was obtruded from a hatch. The three adventurers tugged lifebelts on over their pistols. Casement tried to cheer his companions with a jest—'it will be a greater adventure to go ashore in this!' There were handshakes all round—but the Germans refused to let them have the outboard motor which went with the dinghy, even though Casement gave his personal word of honour that it would not be started up until the U-boat had got well out of harm's way.

So there they were; Casement ill, still probably feeling seasick and uncertain how to work his Mauser even if he had the will to do so, which was doubtful; Monteith full of resentful rage against the Irish who had failed to meet them; Bailey, who later explained that his sole object in doing as he did was to escape from Germany —probably true. (Although he appeared in the dock alongside Casement on the treason charge, no evidence was offered against him and he was allowed to shuffle off into the shadows of history.)

They were left bobbing about in the bay, alone with their apprehensions and worries, resentments and regrets. They had been provided with what was to become known during a later war as commando equipment; pistols, zeiss binoculars, wooden stocks for transforming the pistols into short rifles, overcoats, handbags containing changes of underwear, flash-lamps, note-books, sheath-knives, and golden sovereigns, British sovereigns.

Casement, the incurably inefficient, the romantic Casement, still retained something which common sense should have enjoined him to destroy—his sleeping-berth ticket from Berlin to Wilhelmshaven.

They groped about in the bottom of the dinghy and found some oars. Since there was no rudder Casement steered with his oar; the other two pulled as best they might. An hour passed and at last Casement whispered of a landfall. Next their craft was capsized in the surf and the three invaders pitched into the sea. They managed to right the dinghy and clamber in again. After a long and exhausting struggle they beached the boat and staggered ashore. Bailey went back into the sea several times to salvage their dripping gear. Casement flopped on to the sand, wet through and panting. He was so played out that he was unable for some time even to drag himself above the high-water mark. Monteith tried to scupper the dinghy with his knife but could not manage it.

Banna Strand is a long sweep of sand and shingle. Behind it a steep little bank of dunes rears up from the beach. The rushes and coarse grass on top of the dunes bend permanently back from the

harsh winds that push against them from the Atlantic. By day as
you stand there you can see Magharee Island due west, and past
that Brandon Head. The mouth of the Shannon is just round the
corner from Tralee Bay. But although there is a sprinkling of
the homes of smallholders not far inland, even nowadays and in
the sunshine there is an impression of loneliness and forlornness
about this remote and isolated place. In the small hours of that
Good Friday morning it must have seemed to the weary, dejected
and disappointed Casement that desolation marked the end of his
road.

If only someone had been there to meet them the three could
have been spirited away to any of a hundred safe hiding-places.
As it was their situation was critical. They buried, or so they
thought, their kit and weapons, retaining only their overcoats.
They wrung out their sopping clothes as best they could and
stared heavy-eyed at the pale dawn which began to lighten the
sky.

Monteith and Bailey planned to go to Tralee town, a dozen or
so miles away, to arrange for a motor car and then to come back
for Casement. He was exhausted and it was necessary to find a
hiding place for him. It is always easy to find fault with the actions
of men in a sudden emergency, but one wonders why both Monteith and Bailey went away and left Casement alone. By this time
they must have known that he was a helpless and impractical
man. They also knew that he was a man of importance to the
Irish Nationalist cause. It would have seemed the obvious thing
for one of them to remain at his side, while the other went for
help; but they elected both to go off and leave him to his own
devices. At every turn Casement was ill-served.

The three of them trudged up the strand, headed inland, then
turned south, parallel with the coast. They were forced to wade
through stinking marshes and ford streams in their painful
progress.

The sun was coming up and although it was welcome in one way,
it meant that the early-rising farming community would also
soon be up and about. And indeed, while the three of them were

looking round, seeking possible lairs for Casement, they were spotted by a farmer's lass named Mary Gorman. She leaned over a low wall and eyed them narrowly. (Later, at the trial, she was asked whether it was normal for her to be up as early as 4.30 a.m. To which she pertly rejoined that she was by habit up at four.)

The luckless three would no doubt have been taken aback to know that almost at that same moment their abandoned dinghy was being discovered on the strand, and that an hour or so later their revolvers, which they thought they had concealed, were being delightedly brandished as playthings by a small girl.

Even the arrival of the submarine the night before had not passed unnoticed, for a labourer on his way home from a visit to a neighbour had seen the winking red light by which the U-19 was vainly trying to catch the attention of the friends ashore who had failed to keep the tryst.

The discovery of the dinghy fell to a small farmer, named John McCarthy. He said later that because it was a Good Friday, he got up at two in the morning in order to walk to a Holy well and pray. At the trial, some doubts were cast on the story of the Holy well, but no better reason for McCarthy's early rising was ever forthcoming. On his way back along the beach from wherever it was that he had been, McCarthy perceived the dinghy, dancing about forlornly in the green rollers. He tried to beach it by himself but could not manage it, so he hurried home and despatched his small son to rouse Pat Driscoll, a neighbour.

Pat and John returned to the beach and duly landed the boat. Then they examined the footprints which remained as glaring clues in the sand. The ill-organised invaders had not taken the elementary precaution of walking along in single file to blur their footprints. Obligingly, they had walked side by side.

Next McCarthy and his friend saw a tin box sticking out of the sand. The sea had already exhumed the commando properties; and when they got back to McCarthy's home, whence he sent Driscoll off to alert the police at the nearby barracks at Ardfert, it was to find the seven-year-old McCarthy daughter happily playing with the Mauser pistols of the marauders.

They, in the meantime, after dodging men driving cartloads of seaweed—used in that part of the country as in many regions of Ireland and Scotland as fertiliser—had finally found a hiding-place for Casement in a spot called McKenna's Fort. The Fort would be a pretty good place to hide in if nobody were out looking for you, and you were merely seeking to keep out of the way of chance encounters. But once a hunt was on, it was far too conspicuous and obvious. But presumably Casement and his companions were under the delusion that they had covered their tracks.

In *The Times* the 'fort' was described as 'one of those circular raths or rings, so common in all parts of Ireland, possibly Danish in origin'. From the narrow road, lined by a low stone wall, which passes about two hundred yards away, there is to-day little to be seen but a wide clump of bushes. There are some remnants of stone foundations buried in thick grass, and the place is ringed by a trench and a zareba of dense thorn bushes. It stands in rough pasturage and is perhaps thirty yards in diameter.

There the three took off their still damp things and sat down to talk. Monteith and Bailey decided to leave their heavy overcoats behind when they went into Tralee. Both of them went carefully through their pockets before abandoning the coats, but even with this example before his eyes, Casement allowed the Wilhelms-haven railway berth ticket to stay where it was in his own overcoat.

Monteith found some sausage sandwich, soaked in seawater, which he gave to Casement. More important, Monteith also gave him the detailed code which he had received from the German General Staff in Berlin, and which was meant to be furnished to Sinn Fein H.Q. in Dublin. It contained a long list of groups of numbers, bearing such meanings as 'Send rifles and ammunition to . . .' 'My address for letters is . . .' 'Last wire has not been understood. . . .' 'Railway communications have been stopped', and so on.

Monteith has since explained that in going on to Tralee, he calculated that he would be in greater risk of being taken than would Casement staying on in McKenna's Fort; it was one more wrong guess. Anyway, Monteith and Bailey shook hands with Casement for the last time and pushed off for Tralee.

Meanwhile the Royal Irish Constabulary were taking a look at the dinghy and the other finds. Sergeant John Thomas Herne and P.C. Thomas Riley, when they saw the revolvers, the 900 rounds of ammunition and the daggers, decided that they might as well be armed too, just in case; so they bicycled back to Ardfert, picked up carbines from the barracks armoury, and then started on a methodical search of the district.

By 1.20 p.m. on Good Friday, when Casement had been waiting alone, for six or seven hours, the two policemen were at McKenna's Fort. Mary Gorman had come forward with her description of the unwonted strangers of the morning, and with that guidance, the Fort must have seemed an obvious spot for inspection.

P.C. Riley was tip-toeing through the brambles when he caught sight of Casement staring—it might have been wistfully— in the direction of Tralee. Riley, taking no chances, aimed his rifle at him and called, 'If you move hand or foot, I'll shoot.' Disregarding the threat, Casement, who had been kneeling on the ground, now rose easily to his feet, smiled his charming smile, and said, 'That's a nice way to treat a harmless English visitor. I've got no arms, I assure you, and will not do you any harm.'

The sergeant came up at the double and, brushing aside Casement's attempted objections to being questioned, asked him who he was and what he was about. He was, said Casement, Richard Morton, the English author, and his address was The Savoy, Denham, Bucks. Was this invented on the spur of the moment, or was he ready for some such emergency? It would have been more in character to have been extemporaneous.[1]

'What books have you written?' pursued the sergeant. To which Casement replied that he was the author of a Life of St. Brandon. ('This,' The Times was later to observe, 'was a good local

[1] In a letter written in Brixton Jail, Casement, referring to this incident, said: 'I knew poor old Dick wouldn't mind my using his name. He was far away in England, and it couldn't do him any harm.'

touch, for St. Brandon is the patron saint of the district, and Mount Brandon lies just across from Tralee Bay.') Indeed, went on Casement, he had come only that morning from Mount Brandon. But by now the sergeant's beady eye had spotted the sand on Casement's boots and the fact that 'the lower parts of his pants was wet'. Sir Roger was arrested.

It would have been a rather tedious walk from McKenna's Fort to Ardfert Barracks, but driving past at that moment came 12-year-old Martin Collins in a pony-trap. The sergeant hailed the lad, and the three men piled in and were driven to the police-station. Martin must have been a wide-awake youth. Just before they had left the fort, he had seen Casement casually put his hands behind his back, tear a piece of paper in two and drop the fragments to the ground. Holding his tongue, Martin, after driving the men to the barracks, at once returned to the fort to have a look at what had been dropped. He found that an even smaller boy had meantime started to paddle about in a small puddle, and had fashioned the two pieces of paper into boats, Martin retrieved them and was back at the barracks post haste.

The code paper was brought in by Martin just as the other damning piece of evidence was coming to light. Riley, searching the pockets of Casement's overcoat, discovered the Berlin-Wilhelmshaven rail ticket. Asked at the subsequent trial what he had made of this, Riley caused laughter by remarking, 'I didn't know what it was, but I knew it wasn't Irish.' Casement was asked about the ticket by Riley, and made the unconvincing response, 'I don't know—I've never seen it before.'

On top of this the police found a diary—Casement, ever the compulsive diary-keeper—concerning the period just before he left Berlin. In this he had made an attempt to cover things up by substituting Irish for German proper names. But it did not take a very acute mind to fasten on to the actual meanings, including the final facetious one: 'April 12th—Left Wicklow in Willie's yacht.'

A further search of the properties accompanying Casement revealed a selection which did nothing to discourage the police in their belief that their captive was someone to be held on to. There was a great flag, six-feet square, green with a centred scene depicting Limerick Castle (the Attorney-General, F. E. Smith, was later to wave this about at the trial with considerable effect). And there were maps of Ireland which experts were to testify could only have been provided by German sources.

What folly was this? It is true that Casement himself was by nature impractical, was not in good health, and had possibly become completely reckless through loss of any real hope of success in his venture; it is true too that the 1914 war was fought in different circumstances and a different spirit from the second war, with the latter's hard-breathing attention to detail on the part of those who went on special missions behind the enemy lines; but it seems extraordinary that the Germans took so little trouble on behalf of Casement—unless it was the fact that they had simply decided to write him off, pushed him on to a U-boat and then left him to his own devices.

But there it was; Sir Roger Casement landed in his own Ireland—and on the west coast which he knew so well and for which he felt a special affection—and within less than twelve hours ignominiously caught by a couple of rural policemen. No heroics; just a couple of useless lies by a man in wet trousers, and then a meek surrender to bucolic authority; a futile attempt to destroy some of the evidence, which is foiled by a 12-year-old; Sir Roger goes quietly.

They took him from Ardfert to Tralee, and in Tralee he stayed the night. There, too, things went wrong from Casement's point of view. Tralee is a charming little town, with pleasant Georgian houses and that air of solid comfort and the good well-ordered life which one finds in so many Irish towns. Its police-station has a burnished, cleanly look. Its few cells, in one of which Casement was lodged, are spotless and by comparison with others which I have looked at in various parts of the world, not uncomfortable.

But astoundingly, as it now seems, no attempt was made to free Casement that night. A handful of determined men could have rushed the place and made off with him at any time. Monteith himself, the soldier-of-fortune, idolater of Casement, was in the town. The Irish Volunteers swarmed in the neighbourhood. Tralee was agog over news of strange events on the coast. The smell of coming Rebellion lay heavy in the air. But that night nothing at all happened.

Here is the testimony of Dr. Michael Shanahan, who still practises in Tralee, a handsome man with wavy white hair (November 12th, 1954): 'At 6 p.m. on the night of that Good Friday of 1916, the police sergeant came round to tell me that they had a commercial traveller of some kind over at the lock-up who had "got into trouble" and was in need of medical attention. I went along and found a clean-shaven man of distinguished appearance sitting over a smoky fire in the policemen's billiards room. He looked jittery and exhausted. When I went to examine him two policemen remained in the room. I ordered them outside and closed the door after them. The man then whispered to me that he was Casement, and expressed the hope that I was in sympathy with the Irish cause, which of course I said I was. Casement said he was exhausted "after twelve terrible nights in a U-boat". He did not definitely say that he wanted to be released but the impression I got was that I should tell the people outside that he was in the barracks and that he had no other purpose in his mind, only that he might be released which was quite an easy matter at that time. The barracks door was wide open and half a dozen men with revolvers could have walked in there and taken Sir Roger away.'

As Dr. Shanahan left the barracks, the Head Constable, Kearney, —'an astute man,' as Dr. Shanahan recalls—stepped up to him and showed him a newspaper cutting of Casement as he normally was, complete with beard. Kearney, narrowly watching the doctor, put a piece of paper across the beard in the photo and asked Shanahan whether the top part of the face did not remind him of the man in the lock-up. Loyally, Shanahan replied no. But, 'I could see that Kearney knew that the man he had inside was Sir Roger Casement or was really suspicious that he was Sir Roger Casement; but even so, the prisoner was under no heavy guard.'

Next Shanahan rushed about Tralee trying to incite the local Irish Volunteers into a rescue attempt, but without avail. To Shanahan's consternation, the local men shrugged off all his plans, saying merely that the man in jail was 'some Norwegian sailor'. 'In very plain language,' the doctor told the leaders of the Volunteers what he thought of their attitude, but they refused to budge. Some time later Shanahan was told that they knew perfectly well that it was Casement who was at the barracks, but that they did not want to risk doing anything which might set the Rising off at half-cock. Dr. Shanahan explains that the important Sinn Fein leader, Patrick Pearse, 'was in Tralee about three weeks before Good Friday. He met the leaders of the Volunteers in the town, including Austin Stack and his colleagues. The final warning he gave them was that not a shot should be fired before the Rebellion took place on Easter Monday. He told them that on no account should there be any shooting, so as not to give the enemy any foretaste of what was coming. Not only did Casement get in before he was expected, but the *Aud* was off the coast several days before her expected time of arrival.'

Austin Stack was the chief of the local Volunteers. He angered Monteith, because when Monteith and Bailey finally got to Tralee after leaving Casement at the Fort, and, still miserable in their wet clothes and ravenously hungry, asked a friendly news-agent to send for him, Stack sent back a leisurely message that he would be along 'in about an hour'. Monteith returned an urgent plea, whereupon Stack said he would come in half an hour. But before doing so, he sent along some strong-arm men to look Monteith and Bailey over to see if they appeared to be genuine. Later a motor car was produced and some attempt was made to seek Casement. The car halted for a puncture and was stopped several times by wary police patrols. Dr. Shanahan writes to me: 'You yourself have been out to McKenna's Fort and you can realise what a difficult place it is to find; so when Monteith came to Tralee on the morning of Good Friday and asked Stack to go and find Casement, Stack took the wrong road altogether and went on to Ballyheigue and missed Casement. Owing to that unfortunate mistake Casement was taken for a German spy, and information as to his whereabouts was given to the police in Ardfert before Mr. Stack could locate him.'

I would not have said that McKenna's Fort is so difficult to find, especially for someone who has lived all his life in the neighbourhood. It seems clear that for whatever reason, Stack was lukewarm about Casement. It is also the fact that no attempt was made to free Casement during the night he spent in the Tralee lock-up. It seems strange too that Monteith, who had shared the rigours of the U-boat journey with Casement, should not have made some attempt to free his friend. His personal loyalty, or so one would have thought, should have outbalanced the caution of the local men, who were acting on their strict orders from Dublin. (Monteith remained in Ireland for some months and eventually escaped to the U.S.A. Bailey, after hanging about for a day or so, was duly picked up by the police and stood trial with Casement. While he was in the Tralee lock-up Bailey asked that the District Inspector might visit him in his cell, and after asking for promises of 'special protection' against the wrath of the local populace, dramatically 'revealed' that the *Aud* was due with her cargo of German arms—only to have the wind taken out of his sails when the Inspector told him that the *Aud* had not only already turned up, but had scuppered herself and her cargo when intercepted by H.M.S. *Bluebell*.)

About 9 p.m. a Dominican priest, Father Ryan, came along to the police barracks in answer to a request by the prisoner for spiritual guidance (the R.I.C., considering that they strongly suspected Casement's identity, and realised the importance of their catch, were remarkably accommodating). Father Ryan too saw Casement in private and was also told of his identity. After a brief talk about such spiritual problems as were on his mind, Casement, according to next day's Dublin *Evening Mail*, told the Father that he wanted him to go to the Volunteers and urge them to keep quiet; to tell them that the Rebellion would be a hopeless failure because the help on which the Irish counted would not be forthcoming.

Father Ryan protested, according to the newspaper account, saying that he was a priest and not a political go-between. But Casement pleaded with him, saying, 'Do what I ask and you will bring God's blessing on the country and on everyone concerned.' Father Ryan, after giving the matter thought, decided that it would indeed be the best thing to convey the message to the Volunteers and thus perhaps to be the means by which bloodshed and suffering might be avoided. So, 'I saw the leader of the Volunteers in Tralee' [Stack, presumably] 'and gave him the message, and he informed the Head Constable of the steps he had taken and his reasons for doing so.'[1]

When the *Evening Mail* ran the story the next day, they got a telegram from Father Ryan which said that he had given no interview to 'any pressman anywhere'. The *Mail* published this telegram as requested, but thoughtfully pointed out that the Father might well have been unaware that he was talking to a newspaper reporter when he said what he was alleged to have said.

The last part of Father Ryan's statement is very surprising, and one supposes he must have been mistaken over it. Father Ryan, Stack and the police officers concerned are all dead, so we can only surmise. But although pretty well the whole of Ireland knew that a Rebellion was on the point of breaking out, for Stack, the leader of the Volunteers, to have gone to tell the Head Constable that he was trying to call off his men from participation in the Rising seems unlikely.

[1] Casement himself refers to that night in Tralee and to the Head Constable, in notes which he wrote for his Counsel, Serjeant A. M. Sullivan, K.C., after the first day of his trial at Bow Street, on May 16th. He wrote: 'The Chief Constable of Tralee was *v. friendly* to me. . . . It was he got me the priest, and I said a lot of things to him during the night. . . . Many of these things were in confidence, as at that time I was bent on taking the poison I had, and wanted this friendly man to tell my friends after—it was the following Wednesday evening, the 27th April, I first tried to rub the poison, curare, into a cut I made in my fingers at the Tower, and thought surely I would go off that night.'

Dr. Shanahan has views on the Ryan episode, and he writes to me: 'As a result of Sir Roger's statement to Father Ryan, one of the principal men in the Volunteers went to Dublin that night with the verbal statement "Germany sending arms, but will not send men". I was speaking to the man who went to Dublin with that message. His name is William Mullins, and he was one of the most active and responsible young men in the movement at the time. He told me that was the message he gave to Patrick Pearse on the Easter Saturday. There was no question whatever about calling off the Rebellion or anything else. The only statement Casement gave to Father Ryan was the one which was conveyed to Dublin by this man Mullins. The reason Casement came so early apparently was to deliver that message, and to tell the Volunteers that he was very much disappointed as Germany had promised men as well as guns, and we all know now that the arms they did send were obsolete and nearly useless.'

Mr. Mullins, incidentally, agrees with Dr. Shanahan that the reason no attempt was made to release Casement during the night in Tralee was because of the strict orders given by Patrick Pearse on his visit to Tralee not long before.

The next morning, Easter Saturday, was bright and sunny. The police did not even bother to take Casement to the railway station in a black maria, but marched him through the crowded streets under an escort of three men. 'His head was held high, but,' reflects Dr. Shanahan, 'he must have felt bitterly disappointed that none lifted a finger to help him.'

So Casement went striding off through the sunny streets of Tralee towards his death. Many of the townspeople going about their business and doing their last-minute Easter shopping, must have stared curiously at the tall man in the handcuffs. Members of the Volunteers who were about at the time, or who perhaps peered down through cracks in drawn shutters or glanced round the edges of window curtains, knew who he was. What, one wonders, went on in their minds?

While the train was standing in Killarney station, on the journey to Dublin, the local chief constable, checking up on the handcuffed V.I.P., who, he had been apprised, was passing through, looked into the carriage and casually mentioned to the sergeant in charge of Casement that two Volunteers had been drowned the night before when the car they were in had fallen into the sea. For some reason Casement jumped to the conclusion that this referred to Monteith and Bailey. He burst into tears and sobbingly told the sergeant: 'I am very sorry for those two. They were good Irishmen and it was on my account they ever came here.'

Then he pulled himself together and eagerly asked the sergeant if he thought that they would give him a comfortable bed that night, 'as I haven't slept properly for the last twelve.' But his spirits were dashed again when the sergeant handed him a newspaper containing the account of how the arms ship *Aud* had been intercepted.

Alerted by Washington, as a result of the Von Igel raid, of the actual date on which the *Aud* would be trying to land her Russian rifles, the Admiralty had seen to it that the waters off the western coast of Ireland were swarming with every available ship. The *Aud* in spite of all, did manage to enter Tralee Bay on the evening of Thursday, April 20th, but finding nobody waiting for delivery of her cargo (there was the same anxious but fruitless waiting as when Casement's U-boat arrived for the lights which were never flashed) she turned back. The next day she had put in again, only to be challenged by H.M.S. *Bluebell*, whereupon she had scuttled herself. So the fiasco was complete.

As he crossed the Irish Sea for the last time, one wonders if Casement was able to drive from his mind the gloomy thoughts which must for the most part have possessed it; if he pondered a little on the old days, when the younger Casement, full of energy and vitality, full of hope and spirit, returned so often to his Ireland, perhaps in the very cross-Channel packet in which he now found himself.

X

CASEMENT arrived at Euston Station at 6 a.m. on Easter Sunday, was met by Inspector Sandercock, and taken straight to Scotland Yard for his first interrogation at the hands of Basil Thomson,[1] Captain Reginald Hall, the brilliant chief of Naval Intelligence, and Superintendent Quinn, of the Yard.

Casement readily admitted that he had committed treason but said stoutly that he had not been afraid to do so, and was prepared to take the consequences. He told the authorities that he had buried fifty sovereigns on Banna Strand and drew a sketch map showing where. The police dug the sands and duly recovered the money. He mildly criticised the Germans who, he complained, had called him a dreamer and been prepared to make use of him only so long as it suited their book. He also averred that he had been an Irish Nationalist all his life, although not always an extremist.

It was during this first interrogation that the episode took place which started the train of events which has so embittered and bedevilled the whole Casement question. Basil Thomson describes it in one of his books *Queer People*. He says that while they were still questioning Casement, a policeman entered the room and asked Thomson if he could get from Casement the key to the trunks which had been found in Casement's Ebury Street lodgings and taken to Scotland Yard.

Thomson asked for the key, but Casement merely told him to break the locks since there was nothing in them but some clothes for which he would have no future use. When the trunks were opened they proved to contain, goes on Thomson, diaries and account books starting in 1903. 'It is enough to say of the diaries that they could not be printed in any age or in any language.'

[1] See Appendix I.

Later Casement's solicitor demanded the return of his effects. Most of them were given back—except the diaries, the Black Diaries, as they came to be called, which remained (and indeed remain to this day) in the custody of Scotland Yard.

After some hours Casement was taken to Brixton Jail, where he was enjoined not to reveal his identity to the warders. On Easter Tuesday he was removed to the Tower.

Years after Casement's execution his devoted cousin Gertrude Bannister wrote down an account of her experiences from the day she heard of Casement's capture. I propose to quote this moving narrative which has never before been published, in full; I shall not give it all at once but shall try to weave it in with my account of contemporary events. It begins:

'On Thursday, April 20th, I was staying in Frinton-on-Sea for my Easter holiday. I had had a very severe cold and was in bed. Two days previously I had been awakened by the shaking of the windows of my bedroom. I had learned that the Germans were bombarding Lowestoft from the sea. On the following Tuesday, being still ill, my sister went out for a walk and returned white-faced and scared. "There is bad news on the posters." "What is it?" "They say Roger has landed in Ireland and been captured."

'I got out of bed, packed at once and went to London with my sister. We stopped at the Wilton Hotel near Victoria Station. The same evening I went to see Mrs. A. S. Green at her house in Grosvenor Road, S.W., to ask her advice. We had few friends in London, none of them influential. Our first wish was to get into communication with Roger, and I thought Mrs. Green (who knew so many people in London) could advise.

'She was in despair at all the events; the Rebellion in Dublin she characterised as "madness"; the return of Roger to Ireland and his arrest she said was a calamity brought on by an insane desire of Roger's as well as the rest of the Irish Rebels to follow Wolf Tone—she saw no hope, could offer no advice. Later this first despair yielded to a more hopeful disposition, but at first she was unable to give any advice.

'In her study I wrote to the Home Secretary asking for an interview with Roger. She read and approved of the note, and then I left her. I took a tram down Vauxhall Bridge Road. Suddenly the tram stopped and all the people got out. I sat there quite unconscious of the fact until the conductor said, "Don't you want to get out? There's a Zeppelin over-head." I said, "Is there? I don't care—isn't the tram going on?" He looked at me as if he thought I was mad. The tram went to the end of the Vauxhall Bridge Road and I went back to the hotel and told my sister. We went down to the Home Office and asked to see the Home Secretary the next morning, and handed in the letter. Of course we were refused. We wrote a note asking for an interview and sent it in. Herbert Samuel was Home Secretary. A young upper clerk or lower secretary came out—he said the Home Secretary would not see us. He said in any case it would be useless as Roger was not in civil custody but in military. We then went back to the hotel and wrote to the Secretary for War (Mr. Tennant) and asked permission to visit Roger. We took it down. The Secretary of War refused to see us and sent a message that we should apply to the Home Office. We wrote again that we had already applied to the Home Office and they said Roger was in military custody. The secretary who came to the room where we were said that the War Office knew nothing about Roger at all, why not apply to Scotland Yard? We then sent a letter to Scotland Yard, to B. Thomson—a formal acknowledgment was the only result.

'Thus passed day after day of weary trudging from Public office to Public office, always refused with absolutely blank, stony indifference to our reiterated requests to be allowed to communicate with Roger. Then I wrote a short note, simply saying we were there in London, striving to see him, praying hourly for him and longing for a word. This note was enclosed in one written to the Governor of the Tower, begging him to give it to Roger or even to read it to him. He did neither. The most awful part of that time was the feeling (amounting to a certainty) that Roger was feeling in despair and imagining that he was being deserted by everyone.

'In the meantime Mrs. Green had introduced me to George Gavan Duffy, who was practising as a solicitor at 4 Raymond

Buildings, Gray's Inn. I went to ask him to undertake Roger's defence. He consented at once. I felt that it was the only possible way of getting at Roger. We knew that he was in the Tower and my sister and I went down and wandered round the Tower, trying to make our thoughts penetrate to Roger. Mr. Gavan Duffy applied as soon as ever I left him for permission to visit Roger and consult with him about his defence. Permission was refused.

'We heard rumours that he was to be shot at once. We re-doubled our efforts and wrote to the Prime Minister for per-mission to visit him—with no result.

'We went again to the Home Office and again were told that Roger was in military custody and that only the Secretary for War could give permission to see him. Then as a friend suggested that the Treasury were preparing the case against Roger, I went to the Treasury and sent in my card and asked to see Sir Charles Mathews. To my surprise he consented to see me. I asked him to let us, his cousins, visit Roger. I told him I had heard that Roger was to be shot at once in the Tower and begged for one inter-view. He said, "Your cousin is in military custody. The civil authorities have nothing to do with his arrest or detention. I have no influence. No civil authority has anything to do with the matter." He then went on to express much sympathy with me personally and to suggest I should leave the matter alone. I went back to the subject of an interview and told him of my visits to the War Office and my letters and told him that they denied they had any authority to grant an interview, and that only the Home Office or Treasury could do it. Sir Charles Mathews repeated that it was not so. I then said, "If Roger is entirely in military custody why has he been taken on two occasions to Scotland Yard and interrogated by Basil Thomson? And why are you engaged in drawing up a case against him?" His face changed and his manner became cold and harsh, and he asked me quite sharply how I knew he had been to Scotland Yard? I would not tell him. As a matter of fact the police had talked about it and it had been told to me. I saw that it was useless begging him to give me any help, so I left him, refusing to allow him to escort me or get me a lift or anything. I hated him!!'

Miss Bannister goes on: 'Then we again went forth every day to see anyone and everyone who might help or give us information. One man told me that Roger was really in the custody of the Life Guards—I thought it unlikely, but we set off again to Whitehall and went to the Life Guards and sent in our names. At last we saw a certain Major Arbuthnot who showed courtesy and sympathy. He said it was really the Governor of the Tower to whom application must be made, and when I told him I had written to the Governor and received no reply he said, "I will write personally." He then told us he had seen Roger. He said he needed clothes and suggested we should send in some.

'Mr. Gavan Duffy had at last received permission, the day before, to visit Roger and had gone down to the Tower. We went off and ordered clothes at a ready-made tailor's and then went back to see if Mr. Gavan Duffy had returned. He had and Mrs. Green was with him; he told us that he had seen Roger. He said he was not sure that it really was Roger (though he knew him well), that he was terribly changed, that his clothes were dirty, his face unshaven (he had shaved his beard off in Germany and it was half-grown) and his eyes red round the rims and bloodshot; his manner hesitating, and he was unable to remember names or words. His tie, bootlaces and braces had been taken away from him and his boots were hanging round his ankles; he was collarless and he had to hold up his trousers. I discovered afterwards that his cell in the Tower was verminous, and his poor arms, head and neck were all swollen with bites. Thus does England chivalrously treat her enemies. Mrs. Green, on hearing this horrible story from Mr. Gavan Duffy, wrote it out in detail and sent it to Mr. Asquith. Mr. Asquith made his secretary telephone at once to the Horse Guards, hence Major Arbuthnot's suggestion that we should send him clothes. We were with him apparently while Mr. Asquith's secretary telephoned. Mrs. Green had hinted that the letter might be sent in duplicate to the American papers if no notice was taken by the Prime Minister.'

An obscure paragraph in the London papers of Saturday, April 22nd had given little notice of the impending drama. 'Boat Laden with Arms', 'Mysterious Find on Irish Beach', were the headlines of one. 'A collapsible boat, containing a large quantity of arms and ammunition, was seized about four o'clock yesterday morning at Currahane Strand, Kerry, by the Ardfert police. A stranger of unknown nationality was arrested in the vicinity and is detained in custody. Where the boat came from or for whom the arms were intended is not known at present.'

Then came the truth—Casement! His capture, followed three days later by the rising in Dublin, caused terrific excitement. 'Farcical Invasion of Ireland. Notorious Traitor Captured,' was another London headline. The tight-lipped Admiralty statement said: 'April 24th, 10.25 p.m. During the period between p.m. April 20 and p.m. April 21, an attempt to land arms and ammunition in Ireland was made by a vessel under the guise of a neutral merchant ship, but in reality a German auxiliary, in conjunction with a German submarine. The auxiliary sank, and a number of prisoners were made, among them Sir Roger Casement.'

In London there was an all too human delight that Casement should have been delivered into the hands of those whom he had 'betrayed'. Casement, the one great British traitor of the first war —in contrast to the greater number of the second—Casement caught red-handed. Coming ashore from a Hun submarine!

None could know of the tangle of thoughts and motives which existed in Casement's disordered and despairing mind. On the face of it, and so far as the ordinary newspaper readers were concerned, Casement was simply the symbol of Judas. Rarely can a man have called down on his head such a storm of hatred and contempt as now burst over Roger Casement.

In the House of Commons, Mr. Pemberton Billing asked the Prime Minister, Mr. Asquith, if he could give assurances that 'this traitor will be shot forthwith' (loud laughter and cheers). It is arguable that had P.C. Riley's carbine gone off that day in McKenna's Fort, it might have been a great deal better for all concerned.

During the Rising, Dublin was the scene of bitter street fighting between the British Army and R.I.C. on one side and the Irish patriots on the other. Total casualties were 450 killed and 2,615 wounded. 3,430 men and 89 women were arrested, of whom 15 were executed and 160 given jail sentences.[1] 1,836 men and 5 women were interned in England.

A press report of the rising said, 'The rebel snipers showed ingenuity as well as persistence. They found excellent cover in the thickly built tenement districts where they lurked among the chimney-pots or fired from curtained windows; and in the solidly built warehouses and factory buildings which were proof against anything except artillery attacks. . . .'

In the popular mind the rising and Casement's advent and

[1] Of the 160 persons convicted by Courts Martial, apart from the 15 on whom the death sentence was carried out, 10 were sentenced to life imprisonment, one to twenty years, 33 to ten years, 3 to eight years, 1 to seven years, 18 to five years, 56 to three years, 2 to two years with hard labour, 17 to one year, and 4 to six months.

Those executed were the seven men who had signed a Declaration proclaiming the foundation of an Irish Republic: P. H. Pearse, Thomas McDonagh, Joseph Plunkett, Edmund Kent, Thomas J. Clarke, James Connolly and John McDermott. In addition, Edward Daly, William Pearse, Cornelius Colbert, J. J. Heuston, Michael O'Hanrahan, John McBride and Michael Mallin were shot as being prominently associated with the outbreak; and a fifteenth, Thomas Kent, was executed for the murder of a head constable of the R.I.C. at Fermoy. Ninety persons were in fact sentenced to death, but the sentences on the remaining 75 were commuted. The night before he was shot, P. H. Pearse wrote laconically in a farewell letter, 'The help I expected from Germany failed. The British sank the ships.'

The Dublin rising was officially declared crushed on May 1st. Sympathetic movements in various country districts collapsed about the same date. Damage in Dublin was estimated at £2,000,000. British casualties were 521, including 124 killed. Altogether 179 buildings were totally destroyed by fire, including twenty great business establishments and dozens of smaller shops and offices. Rebel forces were estimated at from two thousand to five thousand men.

capture were inextricably linked. Casement, so everyone took for granted, was not only a traitor but a murderous and callous inciter-to-rebellion into the bargain. In the public imagination the last act of the unspeakable renegade had been, like some premature Hitler, to try to pull down his own country with himself. None could guess (or would have believed it if they had been told) that the supreme irony of the Casement story was that the wretched man had purposed to halt the Rebellion, only to fail in that, too, as in so much else.

In 1916, while Casement waited in the Tower, what else was going on about the world? The Mesopotamian fortress of Kut-el-Amara had fallen to the Turks after 143 days of siege. Its commander, General Townsend, surrendered with 2,970 British and 6,000 Indian troops. Townsend was allowed to keep his sword.

At Verdun the French, under Pétain, were in the middle of their titanic struggle against an all-out German attempt to smash the fortress and achieve a break-through. Zeppelins still on occasion swam through the skies of Eastern England. They met with trifling success, but a Norfolk man was jailed for a month for nocturnally striking a match on a street 'just about the time that Zeppelins were in the vicinity'.

Parliament was violently arguing the question of conscription for married men, although it was not called that but 'compulsion'. Lloyd George was in full spate on the matter. Conscientious objectors were called 'pasty faces'. Eight of them, officials of the 'No Conscription Fellowship', were each fined £100 and costs at the Mansion House; and it was noted with amusement that a Pasty Face who was fined 40s. at Willesden for refusing to join the Army, ate a £1 note in his cell rather than use it to pay part of his fine. He expressed regret to the jailer that the balance of his money was in silver. 'But apparently the Pasty Face did not realise that he had defeated his own ends. For the note cannot now be presented and so the Treasury is 20s. to the good.'

The United States remained neutral. Not long before, there had been a formidable disagreement between the U.K. and the U.S.A.

over the Royal Navy's right to search neutral ships on the high seas. The British press was giving prominence to the diplomatic manœuvres of the Kaiser's Government in trying to interest the U.S.A. in acting as go-between in various peace overtures. 'A Trap!' warned Fleet Street.

The New York correspondent of a British newspaper cabled, under the headlines, 'U.S. Flouted Six Times. American Patience Nearing the End'. 'The Last Straw?'—'German submarine attacks on six vessels involving danger to American citizens are now occupying the Government's most serious attention, and the opinion is largely held in Administration circles that at least one of the six will prove to be the last straw which will break German-American diplomatic relations. . . . .'

But if the U.S. entry into the war was thought to be at hand, it was wishful thinking, as there was nearly another year to go before that happened. It is weird now to read the grave correspondence which was going on in the British newspapers as to whether American participation on the side of the Allies would add up to a good or bad thing. It was seriously advanced that once America became a belligerent, she would need all the armaments she was then selling to Britain and France for her own forces. America's fighting capabilities, scarcely tested in the push-over war against Spain in 1898, were an unknown quantity. And there were gloomy fears that once the U-boats got in among the Atlantic transports, American losses might prove prohibitive before ever her armies reached the fields of France and Flanders.

On May 4th three of the chief ring-leaders of the Dublin Rebellion were executed. They were Patrick Pearse, a barrister and schoolmaster of English descent; Thomas J. Clarke, an old-time dynamite man who had been released from jail and ran a newsvendor's shop, which was an intelligence centre for Sinn Fein; and Thomas MacDonagh, a postman-turned-poet. On the same day the papers reported the resignation of Augustine Birrell from his post as Secretary for Ireland. Birrell is described as 'stealing into the House at question time' (to announce his resignation) 'and dropping wearily into the gangway end seat of the bench immediately behind the Ministers, of whom, on his last appearance a week ago, he was himself one. . . .'

Miss Bannister continues her account of those days with her visit to the Tower: 'The next day but one after we had seen Major Arbuthnot, we had a permit from the Governor of the Tower to visit Roger. We went there and were shown into a guard-room and sat down there for an hour. Men kept coming into the room and looking at us and going out again. At last a soldier came and took us into a room with glass doors and a horsehair sofa and a table and some chairs. We waited some time and then Roger was brought in by two soldiers and Major Arbuthnot with them. They all stood by while we clung to Roger in silence, none of us able to speak. At last I turned and said, 'Couldn't you leave us alone?' Major Arbuthnot hesitated for a minute and then told the two soldiers to go outside and stand by the glass doors, from which we were all visible, and he went away.

'The interview was terrible. Roger thought he was to be shot and that was why we had been brought to say good-bye. We told him that we had been trying from the 25th April till that day May 5th, every day to see him. He had not been told this, in fact he had been deliberately told that none of us had made any effort to see him, as we were all "disgusted at his treachery". Damn all the people who told him those lies and tried to break his heart.

'He said he had come over in a submarine, had landed in Kerry and had been arrested as we knew. He said he had been taken to Dublin, to Arbour Hill Barracks, stripped naked and subjected to every indignity. That he had been taken over from Dunleary in the *Ulster* and that the steward had brought him cigarettes and whispered words of hope and encouragement. The only kind word he had had. He had then been taken to Brixton Prison and kept there for two nights. He had been taken to Scotland Yard and been interrogated by Basil Thomson and Captain Reginald Hall. A shorthand writer was there, taking down notes. All this time Roger had never had his clothes off, except for the search at A.H. He had been upset in landing at Currahane into the sea and had swum ashore. His boots were hard and his clothes sticky and dirty with the sea-water. He was collarless, unwashed, unshaven. Basil Thomson and Reginald Hall, these two high-minded, chivalrous English gentlemen, were dressed with all care and deliberately humiliated their prisoner by making him appear before them in a filthy condition. They tried to get out of Roger all his plans and hopes and the names of his friends in Ireland. He was unaware of the Rising, knew nothing of all that was happening in Ireland and knew nothing about the fate of his two companions in the submarine, the traitor Bailey and Robert Monteith. After he had told them of his own journey he refused any other information. They turned the young shorthand writer out of the room then. As he passed, he touched Roger lightly and whispered, "Greater love hath no man than this!" God reward you, kindly young shorthand writer!

'Then Captain R. Hall began to question Roger about Germany. Roger apparently admitted that the Germans had not carried out their promises—that they had let him down on several occasions. (Reginald Hall, who was the head of the Admiralty secret service spy system, knew really practically all that Roger could have told him—I found this out afterwards when I met Captain Spindler, the captain of the *Aud*, which brought over a cargo of arms from Germany to Ireland and was captured off Tralee by the *Bluebell*.) R. Hall tried on a time-honoured trick. He told Roger that Bailey and Monteith had both been captured (Bailey certainly was, and turned traitor to Roger—but Monteith never was). R. Hall told Roger he had interrogated Monteith and that Monteith had absolutely given Roger away, and he invited Roger to tell him everything from his own point of view as there was now no reason for sheltering Monteith. Roger refused to believe the story. Then Sir R. Hall told him that of course he being a gentleman or a man of honour or some such phrase would naturally not give his friends away but that Monteith had been "less scrupulous" and had told them all. Roger did not fall into the trap. After this long inquisition and torture he was taken to the Tower of London and there put in a cell to which daylight did not penetrate and which was lit by one dim electric lamp. Two soldiers were with him day and night. They were forbidden to speak to him. They belonged to a Welsh regiment. After days of this, one of his guards suddenly said, "I don't care whether it's orders or not. I'm going to speak to him. I want you to know, sir, that lots of us are very sorry about this and hope you will get off. We think you are a brave man."

'This young soldier never was on guard again, so it is to be presumed that the other gave him away. I was able to tell Roger that the story about Monteith being captured was untrue; that I knew for a fact that he was in hiding in Ireland. I was afraid to say more because I thought that probably what we were saying was overheard. I think it was, because Roger told me that he and Monteith had buried some papers, etc., at McKenna's Fort (Co. Kerry, near Ardfert) and that he could describe the place. I made a note of this—but when we sent a message, the place had been found, and the papers, etc., removed. They apparently went straight to the spot and dug them up. So I suppose word was sent over that day to get them. At the end of three-quarters of an hour Major Arbuthnot came in and said Roger must go and the soldiers took him away.

'We did not see him again until he went to Bow Street on May 15th for his preliminary trial before the magistrate. By that time he was shaved and clean-looking but was wearing the clothes we had sent in which were hopelessly bad. He was committed for trial on a charge of High Treason.

'He was then removed to Brixton Prison. Here conditions were much better. He was put into the Prison Hospital and given hospital diet and his friends were allowed to send him in occasional gifts. He was allowed to see visitors. The warders were decent and courteous. One of them told me that the Governor told them to try to imagine themselves in the position of the prisoners and as far as possible to treat them as they would wish they had been treated if they were there instead.

'Roger was constantly visited by my sister and myself and Mrs. Green, and he also saw Mr. Richard Morton (an old friend), Mr. Henry Nevinson, Robert Lynd, Sidney Parry, Professor Morgan, who afterwards helped in his defence, and one or two others. He was allowed to write and receive letters. The Governor visited him (as was his duty) but refrained from reproaching him with his "treachery" as the Governor of Pentonville did later.

'He asked me to procure him some insecticide as his head had become infested with lice in the Tower and caused him torture. Finally the doctor at Brixton did give him something and the torture ceased. It is things like that that make one despair entirely of the decency of *any* people when at war and really scared, as were the English. They lost any idea of what was human. Roger was an Irish Traitor to them and no beastliness was too bad for him.

'Roger remained in Brixton Prison from the time of his committal from the police court until his trial June 26–29. His health improved greatly under the changed conditions of his imprisonment. His solicitor, Mr. Gavan Duffy, saw him constantly and so did Mrs. Green and myself and my sister, but we always had two warders in the room. The question of Roger's defence was always before our minds. He himself wanted to conduct his own defence, but Mr. Gavan Duffy and Mrs. Green and other friends were much against this course. Mrs. Green attempted to get Sir John Simon to undertake it but he refused. Mr. Tim Healy was approached but returned the same answer.

'Mr. Bernard Shaw, with whom we had made friends and who was helpful and generous and sympathetic, wrote out a suggested defence of Roger which he sent to him in Brixton Prison; the gist of it was: "I am an Irishman. I deny England's right to rule our country and I submit that as an Irishman I owe no allegiance to England and I claim the right to go where I choose and appeal to whom I like for aid against England. I took the course I did with my eyes open and if England claims my life let her hang me, and be damned to her.' This appealed to Roger and he was ready to adopt this line and refuse all legal help. It came to our ears however that F. E. Smith planned a desperate attack on Roger personally if he could get him to go into the witness-box—he was anxious for this to happen. His friends felt, rightly or wrongly, that if Roger were put into the witness-box and subjected to F. E. Smith's insults and jibes, he might break down, as his health was so shattered by his experiences both before and after his arrest, that his nerves might give way. As it happened Roger's health and nervous system improved at Brixton and he would probably have been much more able to stand the strain than we feared. As it was, his friends, acting on Mr. Gavan Duffy's advice, consented to ask the latter's brother-in-law, Serjeant Sullivan, to undertake the defence. . . .

'We were able, while he was in Brixton, to get some of Roger's clothes that he had left with a friend two years before, so that he was decently and adequately clothed when he went to the Law Courts to await his trial. Professor J. H. Morgan, who had met Roger frequently at the house of a mutual friend in former days, offered to help in his defence. This was an entirely disinterested action—Professor Morgan alone among those who helped in Roger's defence neither asked nor received any fee . . . Professor Morgan kept to the constitutional side of the question, and only argued the legal points. The other counsel was Mr. Artemus Jones, an amiable and apparently capable young lawyer'.

In his Brixton cell Casement was in his usual ferment of writing activity. His mood was sometimes one of complete despair, in which he had no hope at all of escaping death, and indeed seemed to regard the prospect of execution not only as a welcome relief from the nightmare into which his life had been transformed, but as a deed—the last in which he could ever participate—which might at least do his cause some good. Sometimes he was inclined to let his case go by default and jettison all defence. He would, he said, simply make one last, great speech from the dock, then turn on his heel and go. As time went on he became outraged that his trial was to be in England and not Ireland, a fact which struck him as one more monstrous injustice.

In other moods he would work furiously on his own brief—he would not need the help of any lawyers!—in which he would put up the defence suggested by Shaw, that England possessed no jurisdiction over him in any case. As his health and nerves improved and he was able to cast off the exhaustion and misery in which he had been left by the last year in Germany and the horrors of the U-boat journey, something more like the will to live took the place of apathy and resignation. He began to interest himself increasingly in what the lawyers were brewing and at last, after hesitations, agreed to let Mr. Serjeant Sullivan go ahead with a surprise attempt to get the whole prosecution quashed on a legal technicality. One can hardly suppose that, in his heart of hearts, Casement ever imagined that he could get away with his life—unless the British Government decided it was more politic to adjudge him crazy and place him in Broadmoor—and in certain of his many moods there is no doubt that, as Mr. Sullivan states to-day, he was as a fakir longing for self-immolation. Yet hope springs eternal, and as he began to feel stronger and better, we may suppose that there were moments when the mercurial mind of this strange man may have, against all the odds, framed visions of a future in which Roger Casement might still somehow remain alive to carry on his fight for Ireland.

'Casement was certainly "mental",' says Serjeant Sullivan, chief Counsel for the Defence, whom, as described later, I interviewed at length in 1954. 'He was a megalomaniac who sincerely believed that all the world worshipped him as he deserved, and that whatever he did was right. Freddie Smith wanted me to make this defence, which he would have backed up, as the Government did not want to hang Casement in view of American feeling. Freddie made attempts to get me to use the "Black Diaries". It was in court that Travers Humphreys handed me the envelope, stating that Freddie had ordered him to put it in my hands. I refused to read them, as I knew all about them from Casement himself. But Casement would not accept my assurance that the Crown would not use them, and he instructed me to explain to the Jury that the filthy and disreputable practices and the rhapsodical glorification of them were inseparable from true genius; moreover, I was to cite a list of all truly great men to prove it. He was not a bit ashamed.'

Serjeant Sullivan continues: 'Through him I learned the story of the attack on Dublin. He clung to the idea that that was what he was really being charged with. His defence about that was that he tried to stop it, as he did. He was savage at the fellows who went on with it when John McNeill had countermanded it, and in truth it was for Easter Week in Dublin that he was hanged. . . .'

In London, Casement's loyal friends were rallying as best they might to his defence. On May 29th, from his Birmingham home, Mr. William Cadbury wrote a characteristically generous letter to Mr. Gavan Duffy:

'I understand from Mr. Morton' [Casement's great friend in Denham, whose identity he had vainly sought to assume at McKenna's Fort] 'that you are undertaking the defence of my friend Sir Roger Casement. I have had no communication from him since the war, and wish to make it quite clear that I have no sympathy whatever with his alleged actions in Germany. I however understand that he has no money himself, and has very few friends who are able to help with the cost of the trial, and I should wish him to have every proper opportunity of stating his case. I therefore send an anonymous contribution of £200 to be used if required, but I hope no political or other reason will prevent him from accepting from the Crown any contribution towards this defence as may be offered in the usual course. In the two years preceding the war I had ample evidence of the fact that he was at times exceedingly ill with the effects of malaria contracted in the carrying out of his duties for the Crown in Africa and America, and until sufficiently proved otherwise, I shall believe that the unwisdom of recent months has been largely caused by his serious state of health.

'In any case, I cannot forget the past years of his noble and unselfish life.'

A good letter, written by a man of faith and constancy. In fact Mr. Cadbury, as so many of his fellow Quakers would have done, rose to the challenge of the terrible misfortune in a manner which cannot fail to command our respect.

Here is the full record of how the money was subscribed for

Casement's defence (archives of the National Library of Ireland, Dublin:)[1]

Rex v. Casement

June 21st, 1916. Cash received on account of costs and expenses.

Mrs. Green	£200	0 0
Ditto	100	0 0
Mr. S. Parry	100	0 0
Miss Dobbs	10	0 0
Miss G. A. Bannister	100	0 0
Mr. W. Cadbury	200	0 0
Casement	25	0 0
Miss O'Farelly . . .	50	0 0
Mr. Robert Lynd . . .	4	4 0
Miss E. A. Bannister	50	0 0
Sir A. Conan Doyle . . .	700	0 0
Total £1,539		4 0

Outgoing Expenditure: June 21st, 1916

Estimated Expenses		
Counsel's fees and petty expenses		
(Police Court) . . . about	£165	0 0
Trial. Senior Counsel . . .	530	0 0
Junior Counsel . . .	325	0 0
	£1,020	0 0
Sundry expenses	50	0 0
(Estimated) £1,070		0 0

[1] On June 12th 1916, Bernstorff communicated with Berlin by means of a safe-hand, one Z. N. G. Olifiers, of 121 Keizergracht, Sloterdyk, nr. Amsterdam. In this he stated 'We have sent £1,000 to defend Casement, by Doyle, the American lawyer.' This money was undoubtedly spurned by counsel for the defence. In any case, the loyal friends of Casement had seen to it that the financial requirements were met.

About mid-May Casement wrote to Serjeant Sullivan from Brixton: '. . . the only way to defend me is to let me handle myself and let me justify my "treason" out of the pages of Irish history. . . .' (This is preceded and followed by many pages of suggestions as to how the cross-examination of the Irish prisoners of war from Limburg should be conducted.) Then he continues: 'Had I stayed on the ship, as was first intended, I should have had no chance to stop the rising—but I should in all probability have landed safely in Ireland—because they had *no suspicion* of the ship until they caught me and found the code . . . Tragedy on tragedy —the eternal doom of poor old Ireland, and now *you* know what I must feel and how it is I prefer to die. . . .'

On May 24th, Casement wrote some 'points for Counsel'. In these he said, 'I drew up two memoranda (March 7th and 8th) for the Germans, pointing out how the thing should be done, how I would go to Ireland at once, ahead in a submarine, to arrange all details. . . .'

There seems to be a marked confusion in Casement's mind about these points, and he sounds like a man trying to have it both ways. Either he thought it was the best plan to go ahead in a U-boat and 'arrange all details', or else he found it preferable to 'stay on the ship' (the arms ship *Aud*) 'as first intended'. And of course it is not possible to agree with him that had he travelled in the *Aud*, 'I should in all probability have landed safely in Ireland— because they had *no suspicion* of the ship until they caught me and found the code. . . .'

The fate of the *Aud* was certain long before the code was found at McKenna's Fort by the little boy. Casement did not know about the Admiralty intercepts of German messages concerning his own movements and those of the *Aud*. But when he was writing the memoranda to his Counsel in jail he knew well that the *Aud* had been intercepted by H.M.S. *Bluebell* and scuttled before the information in the code he had carried could have been acted on, all her officers and crew having been made prisoner in the process. That being so, why should Casement have thought that he could have escaped capture, along with Captain Karl

Spindler, master of the *Aud*, and the rest of the ship's complement?

Captain Karl Spindler, then aged thirty and standing nearly six feet, was a stiff-necked forerunner of the Nazi type of officer. His personal motto was 'What appears impossible can be made possible, if you have the will'. He lied copiously, arrogantly and indomitably under British interrogation, in spite of the efforts by Basil Thomson and other questioners to suggest to him that by not telling the truth he was being untrue to the code of the German corps of Naval Officers, and might in consequence not qualify for the usual treatment of captured officers.

In his book, *The Mystery of the Casement Ship* (Kribe-Verlag, Berlin, 1931), Spindler amply justifies the doubts concerning his veracity on the part of those who questioned him. 'In answer to their numerous questions, I told them fibs which our position necessitated. Among other things, I told them we had arms and ammunition on board for our troops in Africa[1] and heavy guns which, after breaking through the blockade, we intended to mount in order to start commerce-raiding.'

Casement, apparently suffering from foreboding concerning the defence to be offered on his behalf, wrote in Brixton: 'My objection to the line proposed is based on principle. It could be called "sentiment"... I owe it to Ireland, to the Irish in the U.S.A., who so loyally helped, to Germany and even to my own wretched self, to adopt the only course that is manly, straightforward and honourable. I think it is far better therefore ... to conduct my case myself.

'I should be in a less false position and could at least make my position clear—leave it on record—justify the cause of Ireland before the world and leave the British Government to do what it pleases. In any case, as G.B.S. says, I have nothing to lose—I've lost already—and the *only* thing to fight for now is the cause of others, not my life or fate at this trial.

'To go on as the case was presented to me yesterday leaves me

[1] The German forces still at that time operating in German East Africa.

in a state of complete breakdown. The Defence is one that seems to me . . . contrary to my past attitude and all my actions and leaves me without a leg to stand on before the only tribunal whose verdict I really seek.

'The Tribunal I am brought before here in London can give only one verdict—Judge, jury, prosecution are all one—and to take this case to them with any hope of acquittal or annulment on pleas of error or "technical" grounds is comparable to referring the Keeping of Lent to a jury of Butchers.

'I have passed a wholly wretched night and day . . . and to-day I see no right course but the one—to go my road alone. It will end just the same, in the same finding, but I shall have saved something from the wreck, and saved much good money too from being wasted on top of all that I have been the means of wasting already.

'R.C. 13.6.16.'

Casement, as the following memorandum shows, wished to call witnesses. None were in fact called on his behalf. But this is what he had in mind (Brixton, May 1916):

'Possible witnesses I may wish to call.

'Gerald Spicer, of the Foreign Office: To testify to [MS is here torn] . . . been given a C.M.G. in 1905 . . . having been consulted. Also that when I was to be knighted in 1911, I said I had not got the insignia of the C.M.G. (it was in the box, seals intact in which it came from the Chancery of the Order, in a trunk somewhere or other, I don't know where)—and I had to get the loan of the insignia from a branch of the Order in the Foreign Office. These things show how really, at heart, I did not want either decoration or knighthood. Mr. Hone, Correspondent of *The Times*, Dublin. He wrote a letter to the *New Statesman*, in February 1915 defending me, and pointing out that my revolutionary views were "no secret" in Dublin circles, and "The Foreign Office could have learned of them without difficulty". The Foreign Office knew them already! He might be got to *say* all this and produce the letter in question. Mr. Tilley, C.B. The Chief Clerk to the Foreign

Office. To produce the actual letter of mine to Lord Lansdowne in June 1905 wherein I so abruptly acknowledged the C.M.G. The Chancellor of the Order of St. Michael and St. George. To produce the letter in which I absolutely refused to go to Buckingham Palace in June or July 1905 in answer to the Royal Command to be invested with the C.M.G.

'I should not like these witnesses summoned too soon, or, if possible, told why I wanted them to give evidence until they were in the witness box. The letters required could then be got. If they knew beforehand the line I am taking, they *might*, I don't say they would, because they are gentlemen. . . .'

Casement, when writing down Spicer's name, must have thought back to a luncheon which they had in the fashionable and pleasant surroundings of the turn-of-the-century Carlton Hotel in London, when Casement was beginning his rise to fame, and perhaps to other occasions too when Spicer had been friendly. Indeed, apart from Sir William Tyrrell, Spicer is the only representative of the Foreign Office for whom Casement in his diaries and other writings has a good word to say.

All these jottings of Casement on the way in which his case 'ought' to be conducted, reveal the eternal breach between the romantics, as represented by Bernard Shaw and by Casement himself, and the hard-headed professionals, as represented by the able and dynamic Serjeant Sullivan. There was no doubt something to be said for the notion of dispensing entirely with legal counsel, and letting Casement have his hour of fireworks in the dock. That is to say, it was a good idea if Casement's life was to be written off in advance, and all he was supposed to do was strike a propaganda blow for the Irish cause. But so long as the professionals of the law, as exemplified by Serjeant Sullivan, were acting, it was their task to eschew romanticism and concentrate simply on finding ways in which their client's neck might be saved—by legal means. Nothing that Casement wrote in these (and many other) memoranda was of much relevance, so far as the legal conducting of his case was concerned. And he notably failed to touch on the one damning, inescapable fact, the fact which was to be produced in court by the prosecution and indeed made the whole of the prosecution case: Casement's attempts to suborn the Irish prisoners of war in Germany. So long as those attempts could not be gainsaid, Casement stood convicted of treason. There was not much use trying to gainsay them, and so Sullivan, as Casement's legal adviser, took the logical and professional course; he tried to show that the ancient law under which Casement was brought to trial could not apply where the treason had taken place outside the King's realm.

The idea of putting Casement himself into the box was not considered. Serjeant Sullivan tells me: 'It never occurred to me or anyone else to put Casement into the box to give evidence. I have often reviewed the case in retrospect, but I cannot see what evidence he could have given which would not have confirmed and enlarged the evidence against him, which was all true. . . .'

Over in the U.S.A. John Devoy was none too enthusiastic about the man who now faced an almost certain death sentence. He wrote, presumably after Casement's death: 'From our experience of his utter impracticability—he had been assuring us until we were sick, that there was "no hope for the Poor Old Woman" until the next war—we sent with the first note from home transmitted to Berlin a request that R.C. be asked to remain there, "to take care of Irish interests". We knew that he would meddle in his honest but visionary way to such an extent as to spoil things, but we did not dream that he would ruin everything as he has done. He took no notice whatever of decisions or instructions, but without quarrelling, pursued his own dreams. The last letter I got from him (last December) said the only hope now of making a demonstration that would impress the world was to send the "Brigade" to Egypt. To impress the world by sending sixty men to a place where they could do nothing! We had told him nearly a year before that we could not consent to this, but he took no notice.

'He was obsessed with the idea that he was a wonderful leader and that nothing could be done without him' [an echo there of Serjeant Sullivan's appraisal]. 'His letters always kept me awake on the night of the day I got them. . . . [He] says that . . . the Germans treated us shamefully, and that he had hard work to get the few arms that were on the ship, that they were no good, etc. Well, they were good enough for the Russians to over-run East Prussia with; and to drive the Austrians across the Carpathians. If our fellows had got them, they'd have been able to shoot a good many Englishmen with them. It is not true that the Germans treated us badly; they did everything we asked, but they were weary of Casement's impractical dreams and told us to deal directly with them *here*' [i.e. the U.S.A.]. 'He had no more to do with getting that shipload than the man in the moon. The request was made from Dublin, and we transmitted it from here. They replied in nine days and the message was sent to Dublin by the girl who had brought out the request.

'He [Casement] told Dublin that he wanted to be landed in Galway, to go to Dublin and lay the situation before them—that is, to tell them that Germany was not sincere, etc., and then if they decided to fight, *he would go out and die with them.* Every note he struck was one of despair. And he told everything to every fellow who ever called on him. Christensen, who "saved" him, is one of the worst crooks I ever met, and was in the pay of the English all along. He, Casement, was warned of that from Ireland, and the first thing he did was to tell the fellow himself, and to give him the name of the man who had warned him. Christensen was going over from here to testify against him, and incidentally to give away all our secrets that he had got from Roger, but *we kept him here.*

'. . . If that countermand had not been issued they could have taken Dublin, and the big force that was concentrated on Dublin would have had to be divided up. They would not have known where to send it for a while, and a lot of soldiers would have joined. . . .'

On May 16th, Casement appeared at Bow Street. According to one account, he 'showed signs of the most intense nervousness. To the general surprise, he was accompanied in the dock by the ex-soldier Daniel Bailey, formerly of the Royal Irish Rifles.

Bailey described the U-boat voyage in a statement read by Sir F. E. Smith.' Only cursory mention was made of Monteith and later the belief spread in London that he had been killed in the Dublin fighting. He lives happily in Illinois to-day.

As he sat in the dock, Casement was thus described: 'A tall slim figure, with nerves vibrant as violin strings and a classical head poised between slightly drooping shoulders—such was the first impression of Sir Roger Casement, Knight, as with long, slow strides he walked into the dock . . . charged with High Treason within and without the Realm of his King. . . . He wore a dark, striped tweed suit, a narrow double collar, a bluish tie and lace-up boots from which the laces had been removed by the police. . . . His hand, white and thin, almost womanish, quivered. . . . He stroked the veins which stood out like string at the back of his left hand. He extended his tapering, cigarette-stained fingers and slowly stroked his head. He rubbed his face upwards, scratched the back of his neck; he bit the nail of his right forefinger; he tapped on the seat; he pinched his cheeks and squeezed his eyes; he looked up at the ceiling and down at the floor; he felt in his breast-pocket and pulled nothing out; he repeatedly elevated his eyebrows, deepening the furrows on his forehead. . . .

'Whichever way he sat, whatever he did, he could find no ease. During the whole morning he was fidgeting, but singularly enough, the numerous notes he made and the comments he passed to his counsel were written quickly and were in a bold and apparently firm hand. . . . In the afternoon he was more settled. He had listened to the Attorney-General's dramatic and stirring indictment anxiously and gravely, but the witnesses evidently amused him. He frequently laughed. It was a silent laugh, a merry chuckle. His face was lit with smiles, especially when some of the witnesses—Irish soldiers who had been wounded prisoners in Germany—in rich Irish brogue told of the amazing inducements he held out to them in their camps if they would only join the Irish Brigade. . . . When the court adjourned, Bailey passed out heedless of everybody. But Casement strode slowly from the dock, smiled delightedly as he recognised two women friends, gracefully bowed to them and waved his hand, and so went to his cell.

'The court was packed, from the bench to the narrow public space at the back. On the right and left of the Magistrate, Sir John Dickinson, sat a military staff officer with a row of decorations, and a naval officer; Sir Charles Mathews, the Director of Public Prosecutions, and others. In the counsel's seats were Sir Frederick Smith, the Attorney-General, boyish and prim as ever, Mr. Bodkin, Mr. Travers Humphreys and the Treasury Solicitors. Only about fifty members of the public were in court. They included two women, a soldier or two, and a man with a coal-black skin.

'Two of the women were so determined to be in time'—presumably the devoted Bannister sisters—'that they arrived on the doorstep of the court at 1 a.m., prepared with cushions and books for a nine-hour wait. At 2 a.m. they were joined by a South African, and an hour later an Irishman came, "to see justice done to Ireland". By 5 a.m. there was a queue of about a dozen. The Attorney-General's opening statement occupied just an hour. It was admirably delivered in quiet, restrained tones, and the thrilling drama of history was intensified by the simplicity of its telling. During his statement the Attorney-General unfurled the flag of the Irish Brigade, which Casement had brought with him. It is a large flag, $6\frac{1}{2}$ feet square. . . .

'The quaintest feature of the day's procedure was that the somewhat notorious and indisputable fact that this country is at war with Germany was formally proved by Det.-Inspector Parker, of New Scotland Yard, who produced the *London Gazette* of Aug. 5th, 1914, containing the official declaration of war.'

Another workaday touch, according to *The Times*, was that 'Sir Roger Casement was described as of no fixed abode and having no fixed occupation'.

The Attorney-General pointed out that it was 'owing to the accident of their exchange' that the wounded Irish prisoners of war were present and ready to give evidence about what had occurred

238

in the camps.[1] Sir F. E. Smith, who spoke of 'Casement's considerable record of public usefulness', and read out to sharp effect Casement's sycophantic letter of acceptance of the proffered knighthood in 1911, went on to say that the vast majority of the prisoners of war treated Casement's rhetoric and persuasions with contempt.

Of the second day at Bow Street, a descriptive writer said, 'Whatever Casement's feelings may be, he certainly never misses a joke and he is always the first to laugh. . . . Weird, melodramatic and utterly ludicrous scenes were presented in yesterday's evidence. Most of the witnesses in this amazing story were Irish peasants from County Kerry. Their brogue was most pleasant to listen to, but difficult to understand. Mr. Bodkin frequently had trouble to catch the answer of the witnesses.

'In justice to Ireland, however, it must be said that the Irish witnesses occasionally experienced a difficulty in understanding Mr. Bodkin's English.'

Mr. Bodkin (to John McCarthy, the man who found the dinghy and who was described by the reporter as 'a sun-tanned, Irish peasant farmer'): How old is your daughter?

Witness: Phwat's that, sorr?

Bodkin (slowly and deliberately): How old is your daughter?

Witness: Oh, sure, sorr. About a hundred yards.

[1] What would have happened if the exchanges had not chanced to include any of the men involved in Casement's attempts at subornation? Perhaps the Crown would not have brought the prosecution until a later date, or else might have considered basing its charges on other facts. For it was the evidence of these men which was all important, in accordance with the case chosen by the Crown. Under the terms of the Geneva Convention, while an equal number of wounded prisoners of war may be exchanged by the belligerents, there is no compulsion on either side to send all the wounded home by a given date, nor to make any special selection of which prisoners they will return. Either the gratuitous provision of anti-Casement witnesses was due to carelessness on the part of the Germans, to indifference—or to sheer malice.

'Casement laughed as heartily as anyone else in the court.'

The charge against Casement (and Bailey), and the wording had importance, since it was contended by the defence, and by other law experts too, that Casement just might have got off on a technicality, was that 'they did, on November 1st, 1914, and on divers other occasions thereafter and between that day and April 21st, 1916, unlawfully, maliciously and traitorously commit High Treason within and without the realm of England, in contempt of our Sovereign Lord the King and his laws, to the evil example of others in the like case, contrary to the duty and allegiance of the said defendants'.

The procession of wounded and exchanged Irish prisoners of war went clumping into the witness-box. If anything had been needed to strengthen the general sentiment against the accused men, the impression made by these soldiers must have swayed the most scrupulous and dispassionate among the spectators. Brave, honest fellows these: one had lost an arm; another was temporarily blinded. They spoke out, in their bluff way, telling the story, deadly in its unadorned simplicity, of Casement's sorry attempts to suborn them in Germany. Daniel O'Brien, of the Leinster Fusiliers, described how on January 3rd, 1916, Casement, while trying to address the prisoners at Doerberitz, was hissed and booed by No. 6 Company 'from one end of the line to the other'. A sergeant-major of the 4th Dragoon Guards called out 'Traitor!' and, declared the witness, was sent to a punishment camp for his pains. (O'Brien himself was alleged to have had his rations reduced in consequence of his stout and outspoken rejection of Casement's blandishments. The Attorney-General stated that at Casement's suggestion, the Camp Commandant had ordered this.)

Next came James Wilson, a private in the 2nd Dublin Fusiliers, to say that Casement told his Limburg audience not to take any notice 'of their uncrowned king, Johnny Redmond'. How had that gone down? 'Oh, some of the soldiers laughed at him; others called him a renegade; and more said he was up the pole' (laughter in court).

Casement watched and listened to these Irish soldiers with an almost compassionate expression on his face. He often smiled as the familiar turns of phrase and cadence of voice reminded him of his native land. Sometimes, as a more than usually damaging point was brought out, he would gently shake his head, but seemingly in a spirit of sorrowful reproof.

One of the soldier witnesses was unaccountably a disappointment to the prosecution. His evidence appeared to add little to the case, and he was rather sharply told to stand down. The reason emerged later. As Serjeant Sullivan was leaving court at the interval, he saw the man approaching him, a wide smile on his face. 'He was a cripple and I cannot fail to remember him, for he added a shockingly fraudulent item to my reputation as a cross-examiner. The public in court grew amazed at the amount of evidence he contributed which was damaging to the prestige of the prosecution.' But to the Serjeant's acute embarrassment, 'This witness now waylaid me as I was leaving court and fell all over me. "How are you Serjeant?" he cried. "Tis grand to see you here, man! More power to you! An old towny man! Up Cork— ye're worth all of them!"'

'From which I inferred that he was more concerned with the triumph of a clansman than he was for the success of the prosecution!'

The finds at McKenna's Fort and down on the strand were duly listed, among them the sausage sandwich (renewed laughter) and the maps. Lieut.-Colonel Gordon, D.M.I., took the witness stand to point out that the maps could not have been made in the U.K. They used, he said, the meridian of Ferro, the most westerly of the Canaries. 'Ferro is the prime meridian used on the general maps of the German war staff. . . . There are also special patches of colour on the maps in the neighbourhood of garrisons. These are not shown on British maps.'

Here is the evidence of some more prisoners of war.

William Egan, of the Royal Irish Rifles:

Q—How did the men at Limburg behave?

A—They hissed and bullied Casement out of the place.

Q—What was he talking about?

A—He said he came to form an Irish Brigade and he wanted Irishmen to fight for Ireland.

Q—To fight against whom?

A—To fight against England.

Q—Where were the Irish to fight?

A—In Ireland.

Q—How?

A—If Germany were successful in winning the war, they would land a German army in Ireland. If not, all the Brigade would be sent to America, with £10 in their pockets and a situation guaranteed.

Q—How did he speak of the English?

A—He said England had been ruling Ireland and now was the opportunity to fight her.

Q—Did anyone set hands on him?

A—Yes, one of the Munsters.

Q—What did he do?

A—Shoved him out of the place.

Q—What did the Germans do?

A—They punished us.

Q—How?

A—We got less.

And then Michael O'Connor, a corporal in the Royal Irish Regiment, described how Casement 'stood on a railway signal' and declared that 'England is nearly bet' [sic]. Casement reminded the men that they 'need not go in hunger and in misery, but could quickly better themselves'. And so it went on.

Whether Casement in his trial received a scrupulously fair deal is a matter of opinion to-day. He was on trial for his life, in the middle of the war, in the middle of an outburst of tremendous feeling aroused by the Dublin Rising. In much of the popular press of the day, he was airily referred to as 'TRAITOR' in headlines and stories from the moment that his capture was announced. So for the month before his preliminary hearing the reading public grew accustomed to regarding him not merely as a man who was to appear on a treason charge, but as an already accepted traitor.

Some of the newspapers commented on the impartiality and scrupulous fairness which marked the trial, but one is perhaps reminded of the story about the Western sheriff who admonished the mob: 'Now, boys, let's give him a real nice trial before we hang him.' Indeed *The Times* itself, on the morning after Casement had been found guilty, pointed out that the trial could have had only one outcome.

To-day any British paper which wanted to avoid very serious trouble on contempt of court charges would not run the risk of calling an accused man a traitor before his trial had even begun. In the atmosphere of the London of May and June 1916 it must have been immensely difficult to secure a dispassionate approach and absolute impartiality on the part of the jurors. Indeed it seems surprising that it proved necessary to challenge only seventy-one of the prospective jurors before the chosen dozen were finally empanelled.

Some Irish chroniclers of Casement have said that the trial was pushed ahead with indecent haste; that Casement was more or less hustled to the gallows. It seems unlikely that a few weeks or even months would have made any difference to the outcome. As for the other complaint that it was somehow wrong or unethical for Sir F. E. Smith to be leading for the Crown, that eludes me entirely. It is held to have been somehow reprehensible because Smith had been closely associated with Carson and the Ulster Covenanters in the turbulent days of 1913–14, and so could scarcely have politically and emotionally been more opposed to all for which Casement stood.

The inference is that Smith's conduct of the case was thus rendered more vicious and merciless, and that he may have enjoyed some sort of indecorous personal satisfaction, in addition to his normal professional triumph; or that to confront Casement with a prosecutor who, it could be argued, had been prepared to do on behalf of Ulster something which might bear a far-fetched analogy to what Casement had been trying to do for Southern Ireland, was akin to rubbing salt into the wound and was in poor taste.

One supposes that the sight of Smith in court may have revived some unwelcome memories for Casement; that perhaps old resentments and antagonisms may fleetingly have flared within him. But since Casement was not to be put into the witness-box, a direct and melodramatic clash between the two was avoided. Besides, Smith was, after all, the Attorney-General. It was for him to lead for the Crown in such a case, as part of his duty. It is not as though he had been one of the judges—he was the prosecuting counsel. And carefully as one may search the record of the case, it is impossible to find anything to show that Smith behaved in any respect in an unfair or incorrect manner.

The Bow Street magistrate sent Casement for trial, and the date was set for June 26th. In his cell Casement fell to, with a resumption of his spate of letters and memos and 'points for counsel'. His friends continued to call upon him as often as the regulations allowed. Among them was Mrs. Cadbury. Here is an account of Mrs. Cadbury's painful encounter, in a private office of the Governor of the prison. This event has not previously been described in any publication.

'Roger, why did you do it? Why did you not come to Wast Hills instead?' 'How I wish that I had, Emmeline! But I had to go to Germany. I was sure that they would win, and I had at all costs to stop them from doing cruel things to the Irish. . . . Don't grieve for me, whatever you do.'

A pause. 'I always tried—others must try now—to get the Irish to look forward, not backwards. Not always to dwell in the past.' Suddenly Casement gave his charming and engaging smile. 'Don't look at my boots. They have been in an awful state since I tramped about in the sand that day, and they have taken my boot-laces away.'

They talked of his landing. 'I wanted to go to Carraroe' (this was the tiny place in Galway, in whose school Casement had interested himself). 'Emmeline, if only they had landed me at

Carraroe, things might have gone differently! They were waiting for me at Carraroe—armed men who would have protected me and hidden me. But the Germans chose instead to land me on an open beach at Tralee.'[1]

Then Casement remarked, 'What a lovely brooch you are wearing. May I see it?' and stretched out his hand. At this, the warder made a grumbling intervention. ' 'Ere, I don't think I ought to allow anything like that ' Then he shrugged, and good-naturedly added, 'Oh, all right.' .

Casement asked after the blue macaw from the Putumayo that he had given to the Cadburys at Wast Hills. His last words were, 'I've done my best. I shall always think of you there, and the cuckoos singing in the spring.'

'Always' for Casement at that point meant about seven weeks.

Now we turn again to Miss Bannister: 'June 26th. On the day of the trial Roger was brought to the Courts in a taxi with two warders. The usual crowds of sightseers bombarded the entrance with cameras, etc. Roger was taken in by a back entrance and escaped their curiosity. The Jury was called in and Mr. Gavan Duffy on behalf of Roger challenged some of them, and the Attorney-General others—but finally twelve were chosen and the rest dismissed. The Lord Chief Justice Reading presided, and with him were two other justices, Avory and Horridge.

'When my sister and I reached the courts, to which we were admitted as relatives, a lawyer friend told me that it was customary to allow the prisoners to see their friends in the interval for lunch. My sister and I therefore sent in a request to the warder in charge of the cells below the court. He said the Lord Chief Justice was the one to ask. I went up and found the Lord Chief Justice's secretary. He said the Home Secretary could give leave.

[1] The only other reference which I have come across to the suggestion that Casement wanted to be landed in Galway rather than Kerry was in the letter from Devoy already quoted. If he had named Galway as his landing-place, it must have been early on, while he was still in Germany. For reasons of their own, the Germans turned this down.

We thereupon took a taxi and went down to the Home Office and saw Sir Herbert Samuel's secretary. He went in with a note I had written and saw Sir Herbert and asked him to give us permission to see Roger.

'He sent out a message that he had no objection and that the Lord Chief Justice would no doubt accede. He also said that he would send a note to Lord Reading.

'We hurried back to the Courts and again saw Reading's secretary. We told him that Sir Herbert Samuel had said he had no objection to our seeing Roger in the lunch interval, and that the Lord Chief Justice might and probably would give us permission.

'While we spoke the secretary was nervously looking down at a piece of paper in his hand. I looked at it and saw it was *my note* to the Home Secretary, and on it written in red largely, "This request should by no means be granted." That was the sort of abominable trifle that was always happening.'

Miss Bannister goes on: 'Roger looked wonderfully tall and dignified and noble as he stood in the dock. He seemed to be looking away over the heads of the judges and advocates and sightseers, away to Ireland—probably his mind's eye was fixed on some well-known spot such as Fair Head—certainly he had no look of one who was conscious of his awful and sordid surroundings.

'A small band of his friends were in court—Mrs. Green (best and truest of friends), myself and my sister, Miss Ada McNeill, Miss Eva Gore Booth and Miss Roper, Mrs. Lynd, Mr. Henry Nevinson and perhaps a few more. Mrs. Gavan Duffy sat at the solicitors' table with her husband.

'There were crowds of reporters—two of them, I remember, Martin and Harold Begbie. Harold Begbie wrote rather a wonderful description of Roger the first day, but because it rather tended to excite sympathy for the prisoner he brought down on himself a reproof and was told not to indulge in any attempts to make Roger less black than he was painted' (From whom came these reproofs? Miss Bannister does not say).

246

'When the first day's trial was over Roger was hurried back to Brixton in his taxi. We hurried round to see Mr. Gavan Duffy and to hear how Roger felt. He said Roger was tired but un-daunted. I asked him if Roger had had any lunch in the lunch interval as one of the warders had said to me as we waited to see if he would come out: "He will be glad to get back; he is tired and *hungry!*" Mr. Gavan Duffy told me that the only lunch provided for Roger was thick slices of bread with cold mutton in between, and that it was so dry that Roger could not eat it. The next day I went and asked the warder in charge of the cells whether we could not send in lunch to Roger. He said: "Surely you can—it's always done." Another warder plucked him by the sleeve and said something in a low tone, so then the first said, "No, after all, you can't. He will be given something here."

'I told him of the mutton sandwiches of the day before and he looked embarrassed. I said, "Why is this prisoner to be treated differently from other prisoners? You said it was always done." The other warder said, "Look here, we have our orders, and if you want any information, apply to the Home Office."

'I went out of the Court while my sister remained, and I went again to the Home Office and asked to see Sir Ernley Blackwell. I waited about a quarter of an hour and then to my surprise (I was by now so used to being told I could *not* see this one or that one) I was shown into a room where Sir Ernley Blackwell was sitting at a table. A pale, narrow-faced, thin-lipped man with the sort of expression I knew by much bitter experience meant, "Get through with what you have to say quickly—I will consent to nothing you want. I care nothing at all about you or the suffering all this ghastly tragedy entails. All I want is to do and see that all legal forms are observed; all humanity and love and Christianity and joy and charity are put into the place where they belong, the place of the futilities of life."[1]

[1] One can readily make allowances for Miss Bannister's occasional hyperbole. She had gone through a time of stress, and even in the smaller matters, it is an enraging experience to be subjected to the red

'I told him I had come to ask permission to have luncheon sent in to Roger at the Courts. He said it was impossible.

' "It cannot be impossible. You mean that you will forbid it?"

' "I have no power to allow it."

' "You have. I have already inquired on that point from officials at the Courts."

' "I fear I cannot do it."

' "You mean you will not, although you could."

(*Long silence*)

' "Can you not imagine that this prisoner is going through a terrible strain and needs a little help—and even the knowledge that we are thinking of him and planning for him is likely to help?"

'A blank and stony stare met this.

' "I beg of you to be humane enough to grant this very simple request?"

' "I have no power."

' "But you have"—and so on. Finally—

' "I fear I cannot continue this interview."

' "But *I* fear I cannot leave until you accede to this simple request."

' He sat for a long time. He went out of the room. He returned. I was still there.

' "If I accede to your request it must be understood that this is the only matter in which a concession can be made."

' "I agree. Will you please telephone here and now to the Warder at the courts saying you permit this?"

' "It is unnecessary. You can say that I said so." '

Recalling the previous day's events, Miss Bannister said:

tape and slick 'buck-passing' of entrenched civil servants. In the case of the late Sir Ernley Blackwell, legal adviser to the Home Office, her strictures seem to have been thoroughly justified. As will be shown later, he saw fit to 'censor' the last letter written from his condemned cell by Casement to William Cadbury.

248

' "I should prefer that you telephoned now, in my presence, or else give me a note."

' "I will not give you a note."

'Then after a pause he took up the telephone and telephoned—there was no trick about it because I sent in a luncheon of roast chicken and a bottle of wine, and Roger was allowed to have it.

'A certain episode deserves recording. Henry Nevinson had to leave the court before the trial was ended. He was sitting in the body of the court and when he got up to go out, he strode across the courtroom to the dock, and before anyone could prevent him, stretched out his hand, grasped Roger's and said "Good-bye!" Only those who lived through that time and knew the insane and hysterical hatred of Roger that was worked up by the lower type of newspaper could appreciate the splendid bravery of Nevinson's action in thus publicly greeting his friend when such a gesture might have brought down on him a furious attack as a result. As it was, he was constantly attacked for his attitude to Roger and to Ireland, but nothing daunted, he went on his fearless way, the type of all that is finest and most chivalrous among English gentlemen. Would there were more like him.

'Roger had never met Eva Gore Booth, Countess Markievicz's sister, but there was a curious sort of affinity in their two characters. Both were mystics, Eva more so than Roger, both hated cruelty and deceit, both loved Ireland and idealised it—both worked in their several spheres to help the lot of the downtrodden —both incurred the enmity and cheap sneers of the worldly and materialistic.

'I asked Eva to go to Roger's trial. She said, "I don't think I could bear to go and look at him thus. It would seem like going to stare at his misfortune." I said, "Do you realise that the court will be full to overflowing with people hating Roger, looking for a sensation, anxious to be in at the death. Better that there should be some friends who can send him loving thoughts and try to sustain him." She had not thought of it in that way. While she sat in the gallery looking down at him, Roger suddenly raised his head and turned and looked full at her and smiled. Eva smiled back, and Roger waved his hand. It was as if a flash had passed between them, and from that moment those two people who had never met, never spoken to each other, formed a real friendship. On several occasions when I visited him in Pentonville Roger asked, "What does Eva say, or think, about this? What is Eva doing?" Always he spoke of her thus, simply by her Christian name, and until her death, she too thought and spoke of him as if he had been her intimate friend all her life.'

The Old Bailey trial began, as one British newspaper put it, in 'that atmosphere of serene and rigid impartiality which makes British justice the keystone of the Empire and the wonder of the world'. As was to be expected, the court was jammed. Up on the judges' bench sat Lord Reading, the Lord Chief Justice, who had preceded F. E. Smith as Attorney-General. He was flanked by Mr. Justice Avory and Mr. Justice Horridge. The latter, recalls the Dowager Countess of Birkenhead, who was present in court to hear her husband conduct the first great set-piece case of his new office, suffered from a nervous 'tic, and this on occasion made the judge appear to be grinning in a macabre way beneath his wig.

Said *The Times*: 'When Casement was brought into court between two warders one could feel very keenly that every eye was strained towards him. Those present knew of him as a man who had once striven in far lands to uphold his country's fame and humanity, and had been honoured by his Sovereign for having done so. They marvelled, therefore, what manner of man was he who, having earned such repute, now stood charged with an attempt to aid in the deliverance of his King and country into the hands of an enemy. The desire to gaze upon him was not, perhaps, unpardonable in the circumstances. Although the ordeal of such a scrutiny must be embarrassing at times to a prisoner in the dock, Casement was in no way disconcerted. His demeanour was generally nonchalant and a trifle languorous. . . . He affected an air of weariness during the reading of the indictment, and he took a merely detached heed of the process of challenging the jurors. . . .

It was clear that he had recovered from the ill-health from which he was said to be suffering a month or two ago. He ... seemed to be as vigorous as a man of his tall, lithe form and apparently nervous constitution could be expected to be.'

'Casement,' wrote another reporter, 'delicately fingered a white handkerchief peeping out of his left coat-sleeve. He was punctiliously dressed and groomed, a remarkable study in black and white. His black, wavy hair was parted at the side and brushed with care; his black moustache and pointed beard were well trimmed and curly; his black coat and vest with wide braid fitted his tall, slim figure like a glove; his black tie was arranged with mathematical niceness. A white wing collar, a white shirt and white vest-slip gave the necessary relief, and seemed to lighten his features, which are as clear-cut as a cameo. He smiled at friends and stood easily and with dignity as he heard the indictment against him read out. . . .'

The jury consisted of a shipping clerk, a schoolmaster and a warehouseman, all of Willesden; a clerk, a business agent, a tailor and a leather merchant, all from Hackney; a grocer's clerk and a bank clerk from Palmer's Green; a mechanical engineer from Wandsworth; a baker from Ealing, and a Chelsea coachman.

During the hour or so which was consumed in challenging seventy-one jurors, one man who came up as a prospective juror was named John Burns (namesake of a famous Labour party leader of the day). At this, Casement smiled cheerfully and observed in a stage aside to one of the warders at his elbow, 'But that's never the Right Honourable Gentleman!'

The presence in court of a member of the American bar, Mr. Michael Doyle, may well have caused some concern to the prosecution. Doyle was there to advise Sullivan, and Sullivan's two juniors, Artemus Jones and Professor J. H. Morgan, the expert on constitutional law.[1] Here is a note on that aspect of the affair, written for me by a man who had reason to be exceptionally well-informed about the events of the time, but who asks not to be quoted by name: 'H.M.G. was greatly concerned by reports

[1] See Appendix I.

251

that Casement's defence would be that he had become an American citizen, and therefore could not be tried for high treason. His lawyers obtained the extraordinary concession that he should be allowed to have an American lawyer from Philadelphia among his counsel at the Old Bailey.'

If Casement's counsel could have proved that he had indeed managed to change his nationality by naturalisation, there is no question but that the prosecution's case against him must have collapsed—always provided that the naturalisation had taken place before his activities in Germany. A foreigner, even a 'technical foreigner', cannot be tried for high treason against the British Crown. It may be recalled that in one of the treason trials in London which followed the 1939 war, all turned on whether the accused, William Joyce, retained his American nationality or had forfeited it.[1]

What gave H.M.G. in 1916 the notion that Casement might have become a U.S. citizen, I do not know. The few months which he had spent in that country in 1914 would have been inadequate for the purpose of acquiring citizenship, unless by special act of Congress, and there was certainly no question of that. In the event, the prosecution's apprehension proved baseless and Serjeant Sullivan relied instead on an early attempt to get the indictment quashed on the ground that there was no allegation of any overt act having been committed within the King's domains. The Lord Chief Justice ruled that such a motion should wait until the close of the prosecution's case, and Smith rose.

In his opening statement Smith referred to Casement—who lolled in the dock, studying his chief prosecutor with what seemed to the onlookers to be a rather dreamy interest—as 'an able and cultivated man, versed in affairs and experienced in political matters. He is not a life-long rebel against England and all that England stands for, as others well-known in history have been.' And the Attorney-General submitted that the prisoner, blinded by hatred of Britain, 'as malignant in quality as it was sudden in

[1] See Appendix I.

origin, played a desperate hazard. He has played it and lost it. Now the forfeit is claimed. ...'

Smith was, of course, wrong about the suddenness of the hatred. Having looked at the record, it is hard to quarrel with Casement's statement from his cell (to Mrs. Green and Mr. Lynd), 'I was always an Irish separatist at heart—and since 1905–1906, in deeper feeling than before.'

Smith again made play with Casement's famous knighthood acceptance letter. 'Such a man,' he remarked in dryly conversational tones, 'wrote in terms of gratitude, a little unusual perhaps in their warmth, and in the language almost of a courtier, and presented his "humble duty" to his King.' A pause. 'It will be my task to acquaint the Court with the way he carried out his "humble duty" ....'

Then Smith went into the question of Casement's pension (of £421 13s. 4d. a year) and of when he ceased to receive it. Claims for payment of pensions had at the time to be made by formal statutory declaration at each quarter. Casement had retired on August 1, 1913, and he made five formal applications for the pension, starting on October 2, 1913, and ending on October 7th, 1914. 'No payment has been made since that date,' added Smith.

Casement evidently thought that this was an erroneous statement and an important point. For as soon as he got back to his cell that night, he wrote this note to Gavan Duffy:

'Pension: the Crown state that "it was withdrawn on September 30th by order of the Treasury". This is a fearful blunder of theirs. The order for the stoppage of my pension, or "suspension" rather, was not made until February 1915, and *after* Sir E. Grey had received my letter of February 1, 1915, renouncing all my honours, dignities, etc., etc.

'Far from my pension having been "stopped", Sir E. Grey wrote to me officially on October 26, 1914, pointing out that I was "still liable under certain circumstances to be called upon to serve the Crown". The liability hinged on my being the drawer of a pension. That letter of Grey's is very significant. ... It asks me if I am the author of a letter that had been published in *The*

Irish Independent of October 5th counselling Irishmen *not* to enlist and that their sympathies "should rather be with Germany than Great Britain". This letter it was which was written from New York on the 15th (I think) September and signed *"Roger Casement"* (I only received this letter of Sir E. Grey's in Berlin, at the very end of February 1915—it had gone to the U.S.A. and finally reached me in Germany). At the date (October 26th) I was actually in *Kirkwall,* on the s.s. *Oskar II* en route for Christiania whither I arrived on October 29th—and that very day (three days after Sir E. Grey points out to me (in New York!) that I am "liable" to be called upon to serve the Crown) H. M. Minister and Envoy Extraordinary offers my man Adler Christensen £5,000 for my capture!'

Next Smith, in his opening speech, went into the description of events in the German prison camps, and again came the summary of the evidence to be given by the ten former Irish prisoners. Again too came the outline of what had taken place on Banna Strand, in Ardfert and Tralee. But all that the Crown was concerning itself with, in order to prove Casement's guilt of treason, were his activities in Limburg and the other camps. That was the vital point. His landing in Ireland was not linked by the prosecution with the events in Easter Week, and although Serjeant Sullivan may well be right when he says that Casement was really hanged for the Dublin Rebellion, that was not part of the Crown's case as it was presented, and its importance existed, if it existed, only in the minds of the Hackney leather merchant, the Willesden warehouseman, the Chelsea coachman and the others sitting in the jury box.

Said Smith in conclusion: 'Such, gentlemen, is in general outline the case which the Crown hopes to prove, and upon which the Crown relies. I have, I hope, outlined these facts without heart and without feeling. Neither, in my position, would be proper, and fortunately neither is required. Rhetoric would be misplaced, for the proven facts are more eloquent than words. . . .'

On Tuesday the 27th, matters rather dragged. There was an absence of anything at all sensational and nobody in court looked more bored than the accused himself. The various policemen told their stories. Twelve-year-old Martin Collins, who had found the code paper, told his. Mary Gorman told hers. Towards the end of the day Serjeant Sullivan made his big effort to get the indictment quashed on technical grounds. He and the three judges waded off into a morass of words, with Sullivan struggling with a six-hundred-year-old statute of Edward III, written in baffling Norman-French, in a vain attempt to win his all-important point. It has on occasion since been somewhat melodramatically suggested that Casement was 'hanged on a comma', of this Edward III statute.

The recording of the argument on the quashing of the indictment occupies sixty closely printed pages in the Notable British Trials series; and after that comes a nine-page follow-up, giving the judgement on why the motion must fail. So fail it did.

On the third day, Wednesday June 28th, after this argument was finally out of the way, Casement was allowed to make a preliminary statement—on which he could not be cross-examined, since he was not under oath. He made it, so he told the court, in order to try to put right some of the mis-statements which had thus far been made to his discredit. There were, said *The Times*, many more ladies present in court than on the two opening days. 'It may have been,' mused its reporter, 'that they had received a hint that the proceedings would be of greater interest; or it may have been that they had an intuition that a memorable trial could not approach its close without incidents which must evoke human feeling and afford matter for reminiscence. Such an intuition, if it existed, was well justified by events.'

Of his pension, Casement said that he had 'earned it by services rendered, and it was assigned by law. The knighthood it was not in my power to refuse.' He was brief and to the point, and made a by no means unfavourable impression. His four main points were: (1)—that he had never at any time advised Irishmen to fight on the side of the Turks against the Russians, nor to fight alongside the German Army on the Western Front. (2)—that he had never asked an Irishman to fight for Germany. (3)—as to the 'horrible insinuation' that he got the Irish prisoners' rations reduced because they would not join the Irish Brigade, that was 'an abominable falsehood'. It was all due, he told the court, to the British blockade, and the Irish rations were in consequence reduced just like those of everyone living inside Germany. (4)—the 'widespread imputation of German gold'—he wished to nail the lie. 'I have never sold myself to any man or any government to use me. . . . I never accepted a single penny-piece of foreign money. . . . I refute so obvious a slander. . . . Money was offered to me in Germany more than once, and offered liberally and unconditionally, but I rejected every suggestion of the kind, and I left Germany a poorer man than when I entered it. . . .'

Casement also took the opportunity of saying how deeply he had been touched by the generosity and loyalty of those English friends of his who had 'given me proof of their abiding friendship during these last dark weeks of strain and trial'.

'I trust, gentlemen of the jury, that I have made that statement clearly and emphatically enough for all men, even my most bitter enemies, to comprehend that a man who in all the newspapers is said to be just another Irish traitor, may be a gentleman.

'There is another matter I wish to touch on. The Attorney-General of England thought it consistent with the tradition of which he is the public representative, to make a veiled allusion in his opening address to the rising in Ireland, of which he brought forward no evidence in this case from first to last, and to which, therefore, you and I, gentlemen, as laymen, would have supposed that he would have scrupulously refrained from referring. Since the rising has been mentioned, however, I must state categorically that the rebellion was not made in Germany, and that not one penny of German gold went to finance it.'

Then came Sullivan. *The Times* said that 'Mr. Sullivan's speech was delivered to a court which had become crowded to its utmost capacity. For the first time the scene was that of a state trial, and as the prisoner's counsel unfolded his defence a great silence fell on all present. He, as he said of his client, came from another land, "where people think differently, and perhaps to some extent speak differently and act differently". That no doubt accounted for much of the influence of the oratory with which he held his hearers spell-bound. His eloquence was of a kind not often heard in English courts of law. His political views, where it was necessary to his case to express them, were not those, broad as they are in many respects, to which an English audience is accustomed to listen. . . .'

The black-bearded Serjeant was quickly into his stride. 'I shall say much perhaps that will strike a jarring note in your minds. I only ask you to believe that I am trying to do my duty. I appreciate how difficult it is that you should be put into the position—I doubt my power to do it—to understand what goes on in the mind of an Irishman. I am conscious of a strange atmosphere as I stand here. You have to try the man for his intentions; you have to judge of his motives; and there is no task so difficult as judging of the motives or intentions of a man who is not of your race and is not one of yourselves. Now, the intention of the prisoner is the whole substance of the offence of treason. It is his view of his own acts which must justify him or condemn him. Unless he intends treachery to the King, the fact that others may use with advantage that which he does, against his intentions, perhaps to the public detriment of the realm, does not make him guilty of treason. The essence of treason is the evil mind which plans it.'

Sullivan hammered away at the proposition that Casement had never asked any of the men in the prison camps to do anything but join up to fight for Ireland, in Ireland, with Ireland—and after the (European) war was over. Ireland was the crucial thing. Germany mattered not. It might be that by an accident of circumstance Casement had been acting as a would-be recruiting-sergeant in Germany in time of war; but that, maintained Sullivan in effect, was beside the point. Casement's blandishments had nothing to do with Germany or German intentions. It was strictly an Irish plan for which he sought to engage the men, and Ireland his sole and total concern.

' . . . Oh, says the Attorney-General, the German Government was interested in his succeeding. But what cared Casement? *He* was not a German. It was nothing to *him* what were the calculations of any German as to what would be the result of anything he did. . . .'

Of the rations reduction charge: 'If you are dealing with a people in the condition of the Germans, the first who will feel the pinch of hunger if supplies run short in Germany, you may be perfectly sure, will be the soldiers who fought against the Germans. Are you to believe that when rations are reduced . . . that this man was a party in starving them (the prisoners of war) in order to vindicate his own conceit and self-sufficiency?'

Then Sullivan went back to the state of affairs which existed in Ireland just before the war, and of which he had sought to gain some corroboration when he had cross-examined the R.I.C. witnesses, and he reminded the jury that people in Southern Ireland, hearing rumours of the Ulstermen illegally arming and illegally drilling, might have felt that they were being abandoned to their fate by the forces of law and order, by the police and the British Army, by the government in far-off Whitehall and by Parliament itself. So 'what are you to do when, after years of labour, your representatives may have won something that you yearn for, for many a long day, won it under the constitution, had it guaranteed by the King and the Commons, and you are informed that you should not possess it because those that dislike you were arming to resist the King and Commons and to blow the statute off the book with gun-powder? The civil police could not protect you, and the military force would perhaps prove inadequate for your support. You may lie down under it, but if you are men—to arms! When all else fails—defend yourself! . . . That is the case I present to you on behalf of Sir Roger Casement. That is the explanation of all which he has done. . . . If you are indeed to scrutinise the intention of Sir Roger Casement in what he did abroad, not by what was passing in his mind or what he intended, but the profit the German politicians might calculate that they might ultimately get out of it, you might go back and find that German calculations do not all come right; for you might well think that the enterprising commercial country that filled Ulster with Mausers in 1914 expected a better dividend than she got. . . .'

Sullivan was going on to expand this line, speaking of 'Ireland becoming the foundation of two hells when the war ended, because the Ulstermen had not surrendered their illegal arms, and there were not wanting men who, distrusting the truce proclaimed in Ireland, seeing that one man would observe that his neighbour had not given up his rifle, another that another had got a new gun—he would arm himself; and one by one in small quantities you have the danger of the arms still coming in, and people fearing that the truce was not real, and that at any moment there might break out——'

The Lord Chief Justice (who has been fidgeting slightly): Where is the evidence of this?

Mr. Sullivan: The evidence of the sergeant (Sergeant Herne of the R.I.C.) and Robinson (John Robinson, of the R.A.M.C., one of the prisoners of war who gave evidence).

Lord Chief Justice: Of what you are now saying?

Attorney-General (who has also been showing signs of impatience): I was most loth to intervene, but I have heard a great many statements which are wholly uncorroborated.

Lord Chief Justice: You have the right to intervene.

Attorney-General: Statements as to the importation of rifles into the North of Ireland.

Lord Chief Justice (to Sullivan): We have allowed you very great latitude. I confess for myself I have found it rather difficult not to intervene on several occasions, and I intervene at this moment, because I think you are stating matter which is not in evidence, or which I have no recollection of being stated in evidence. . . .

Mr. Sullivan: I am exceedingly sorry your lordship did not intervene sooner . . . I am exceedingly sorry I have gone outside what I ought. . . .

Then Sullivan quoted some of the R.I.C. evidence and tried to go on with his speech, but the thread was broken. More, he was beginning to show startling signs of strain. He faltered and repeated himself. Said *The Times*: 'A little after four o'clock it became evident that Mr. Sullivan was beginning to suffer from the strain which his heavy work on behalf of his client had imposed. He paused frequently in his speech and displayed symptoms of nervous exhaustion. At length he exclaimed in faltering accents, "My lords, I regret to say that I have completely broken down." He then sank to his seat and rested his head on his hands. The Lord Chief Justice, who had already shown his consideration for Mr. Sullivan in the discharge of his heavy task, at once adjourned the court.'[1]

Casement watched the collapse of his chief counsel with a quizzical smile.

Thursday the 29th of June was the fourth and last day of the trial of Roger Casement. Up to the Old Bailey he came once again in his taxi, accompanied by the two warders. That his chief counsel should have crumpled under pressure and at the climax of the main defence speech must have seemed to Casement's friends and followers the final malevolent stroke of a fate which had been hovering over Casement ever since his last respectable exploit, that of the Putumayo. Since then nothing had seemed to go right for him.

Scenting the kill, public and privileged elbowed their way into the Old Bailey. The courtroom was suffocatingly hot, and as the hours passed some of those present tried to fan themselves surreptitiously with whatever was handy.

Up on the bench they sat there in a row, Reading and Horridge and Avory, and looked down gravely at Artemus Jones, as he rose and observed, 'My lords, I regret to say that my learned leader is in a condition this morning which does not permit of his appearance in court. I have just seen him. He is in consultation with his medical adviser, and the effect of the advice is that he must not go on. In these circumstances, will your lordship grant

[1] In a letter to me, dated October 25th, 1955, Serjeant Sullivan writes: 'Three days and nights of worrying caused me to break down and fall senseless while addressing the jury. I had used up every red corpuscle in my body.'

me the indulgence of allowing me to conclude his speech and deal with the points he has not quite covered?'

The Lord Chief Justice: 'Yes, certainly. I am sorry Mr. Sullivan is not able to be here; it was obvious that he was labouring under a strain yesterday afternoon. Will you kindly proceed with his address.'

No doubt Artemus Jones did his best that day; but in contrast to the day before, there was a constant dislocation of the defence address, with interruptions now from the Bench and now from the Attorney-General. Artemus Jones found it heavy going, and where Sullivan, himself Irish, had contrived brilliantly to suggest the 'Irishness' of the defence, while yet more or less maintaining the niceties of English court etiquette, Jones was reduced, when he took up the burden, to the somewhat pedestrian reading aloud of another's brief.

He scarcely rose to the occasion. Jones approached his peroration thus, '. . . I am not going to address you upon the terrible responsibility that rests upon you in considering this case. It is, as I have said before, a matter of life and death; and it would ill become me to dwell upon that aspect of the matter as far as you are concerned. I spoke just now of the responsibility which devolves upon counsel who are pleading for the life of a fellow-creature. That responsibility is small compared with your own responsibility. . . . The law demands, as the Attorney-General said, a forfeit; but that is not all the law demands. That man has a right to demand from you the same care and scrutiny in weighing the evidence as any one of you would expect to get, were you standing in the dock. It is said that life is a comedy to those who look on, and a tragedy to those who feel. This trial may mean a tragedy to the prisoner, on account of the terrible responsibility which rests upon your shoulders. . . . I am not going to address any appeal to you based upon sympathy or upon any emotional plea in the way of mercy. . . .'

Then came the Attorney-General for the Crown. Said he, in summary: the defence case is that the prisoner did not attempt to seduce Irish soldiers from their allegiance to their King in order that they might assist Germany; that he did not attempt to seduce these soldiers from their allegiance that they might fight against England; but that he was so struck, his mind was so affected, by the growing lawlessness in Ireland, by the constantly increasing military accession of equipment and strength of the Volunteers in the North of Ireland, that with the object of establishing an equipoise, to become effective after the war, between the strengh of the Volunteers in the North of Ireland and the strength of those opposed to this view in the other parts of Ireland, he made attempts to procure men under oath of military allegiance to pledge themselves that at the end of the war they would go to Ireland, not for the purpose of assisting Germany, not for the purpose of fighting England, but for the purpose of holding themselves as a balance against the military power of the Volunteers of the North of Ireland which, in the view of the prisoner, had attained excessive proportions.

'. . . Consider the two alternatives: That as presented to you by the Crown that this man, as you knew well, was long in the service of this country, and a man who well understood public affairs, that this man on the outbreak of war . . . went to the country of our principal enemy, that he found there captured soldiers of the King, that he set himself then and there to seduce these men from their allegiance, with the object of using them in violation of their military duty and at the risk of their lives. . . . That is the charge made by the Crown. The answer is that they were not to be used to assist Germany in any way, but they were only to be used at the conclusion of the war for matters concerned with the internal politics of Ireland. Those are the two cases. . . .

'. . . If the nature of the activities which were contemplated for these men were of the character which it is now suggested to you on behalf of the prisoner they were, here again I pause to express my surprise that the German Government, in return for prospective services after the war, were found advancing or promising them £10 or £20 pocket money at the end of the war and a passage to America. It may be so—but it would surprise me if it were so. . . .

'. . . Is there one witness to whom it was suggested that all they had to do was to come and be ready in order to watch the Volunteers in the North of Ireland? Can any man who has listened to that evidence as to what the prisoner actually said, doubt that it is an invented story that he was concerned to obtain the services of these men remotely in the future, in order that they might deal with the situation as it emerged in Ireland after the war? . . . He was not asking anything of the kind. What he was asking them was this: if Germany gains a naval success, in other words, if Germany acquires the facility for landing troops in Ireland, are you prepared to go and fight in Ireland against England?'

The Attorney-General made some telling points over the code of which Casement had vainly tried to disembarrass himself that day in McKenna's Fort. '. . . Look at this code, gentlemen. "Railway communications have been stopped." "Our men are at——" ' It would be very interesting to the German Government, on the theory of the defence, to know that railway communications had been stopped. What had they got to do with it? "Further ammunition is needed." Does that throw light on the cargo of the *Aud*? Why does Germany send some ammunition, in addition to which it is contemplated that further ammunition may be required? The mere message that further ammunition may be required, the mere language in which the message is couched, presupposes and renders necessary the conclusion that some ammunition has already been given. Why is the prisoner arranging that Germany shall send ammunition to Ireland, not at the end of the war, but during the war, and at the very moment of the bitterest struggles of the war? Is it being done so that at the end of the war some steps may be taken to meet the Ulster Volunteers? . . .

'The prisoner, who is only concerned with the Volunteers in the North after the war, leaves Germany in the middle of the war with a code in which he and the Germans, acting in concert, have carefully prepared themselves with secret messages by which he in Ireland can send them a plan for hostile landings in the middle of this war, and then we are told a fairy-tale about what is going

263

to be done after the war with the Volunteers in the North of Ireland. . . .

'This code, on the submission of the Crown, shows that the prisoner Casement, who went under circumstances unexplained to us, and which I cannot explain, to the enemy country while hostilities were in progress, who was allowed his freedom in that country while hostilities were in progress, who left that country for Ireland while hostilities were in progress, had agreed with the Germans to send them messages arranging for a landing, asking for another ship, and asking for explosives, cannon and ammunition. Gentlemen, if you can reconcile those facts with the submissions which have been made to you on behalf of the defence—do so. But if those facts taken together—his journey to Germany, his speeches when in Germany, the inducement he held out to these soldiers, the freedom which he there enjoyed, the course which he pursued in Ireland, the messages which he contemplated as likely to take place between himself and the Germans—satisfy you of his guilt, then you must give expression of that view in your verdict.'

The Lord Chief Justice summed up fairly crisply, including in his remarks a warm tribute to Serjeant Sullivan, not only for his skill but also his courage. He also warned the jury to banish from their minds everything which they might have read or heard outside the court—which, one imagines, was a good deal easier said than done. And speaking of the introduction by Sullivan of Irish politics into the defence he had elected to make, the Lord Chief Justice urged the jury to consider the case calmly and dispassionately, 'for justice is ever in jeopardy when passion is aroused'.

It was 2.53 when the jury retired. They were back at 3.48. The King's Coroner called the roll—names such as Wheeler, Watts, Scoble, Scantlebury and Saunders.

After the verdict, the King's Coroner asked Casement if he had anything to say. Here then was Casement's big moment—his last. His chance to stand as a latter-day Robert Emmett and speak for Ireland. He had been brooding on this speech for weeks, drafting and re-drafting. It was too much to hope that he would have cut it as ruthlessly as was required. Nobody likes pruning their own material, and least of all Casement. And nobody, knowing that they are making nearly their last appearance in the living world of men and women, is anxious to curtail it. He knew that, barring the brief appearance for the appeal, his remaining days and nights on earth would be bounded by the squalid confines of his prison cell. So this was his moment of glory and farewell. He must make the most of it.

The speech had to be memorable not only for putting Ireland's point of view but that of Casement too. Very few men could have risen in unmitigated triumph to such an occasion. Few could have compressed into fifteen or twenty minutes all that needed to be said—or that they considered needed to be said. In point of fact Casement continued for close on an hour. This was too long at the end of a hot day in a close and crowded court. Drama was dissipated, the keen edge of tension blunted. It would probably have been better if Casement had flung away his manuscript and let them have it in hot eloquence, just as it came to mind. But he chose to read it, and not many people are proof against the lulling effect of watching a man turn page after page of a written speech.

But Casement, as he said himself, was addressing a far vaster audience than the comparatively few who listened to him in the Old Bailey. He spoke to the world, and some of what he said was good.

'When this statute' [under the terms of which he had been tried] 'was passed in 1351, what was the state of men's minds on the question of a far higher allegiance—that of man to God and His Kingdom? The law of that day did not permit a man to forsake his church or deny his God save at the cost of his life! The "heretic" then had the same doom as the "traitor". To-day a man may forswear God and His heavenly kingdom without fear or penalty, all earlier statutes having gone the way of Nero's edicts against the Christians, but that Constitutional phantom, "The King", can still dig up from the dungeons and torture chambers of the Dark Ages a law that takes a man's life and limbs for an exercise of conscience. To-day it can still deprive an Irishman of life and honour, not for adhering to the King's enemies, but for adhering to his own people.'

Looking over at F. E. Smith, Casement, with a significant stressing of his words, said: 'The difference between us was that the Unionist champions chose a path they felt would lead to the woolsack; while I went a road I knew must lead to the dock. And the event proves that both were right. The difference between us was that my "treason" was based on a ruthless sincerity that forced me to attempt in time and season to carry out in action what I said in word—whereas their treason lay in verbal incitements that they knew need never be made good with their bodies. And so I am prouder to stand here to-day in the traitor's dock to answer this impeachment than to fill the place of my right honourable accuser![1]

'Judicial assassination to-day,' cried Casement ringingly, 'is reserved only for one race of the King's subjects, for Irishmen, for those who cannot forget their allegiance to the realm of Ireland. In Ireland alone in this twentieth century is loyalty held to be a crime. If we are to be indicted as criminals, to be shot as murderers, to be imprisoned as convicts, because our offence is that we love Ireland more than we value our lives, then I know not what virtue resides in any offer of self-government held out to brave men on such terms. . . .

'I for one was determined that Ireland was much more to me than "Empire" and that if charity begins at home so must loyalty. Since arms were so necessary to make our organisation a reality and to give to the minds of Irishmen menaced with the most outrageous threats a sense of security it was our bounden duty to get arms before all else. I decided with that end in view to go to America to appeal to Irishmen there for help in an hour of great national trial. . . .

'If true religion rests on love, it is equally true that loyalty rests

[1] At this, Sir F. E. Smith (recalls the Dowager Countess of Birkenhead), smiled ironically and murmured in an audible aside, 'Change places with him? Nothing doing!'

on love. The law I am being charged under has no parentage in love, and claims the allegiance of to-day on the ignorance and blindness of the past. I am being tried, in truth, not by my peers of the live present, but by the peers of the dead past; not by the civilisation of the twentieth century but by the brutality of the fourteenth; even by a statute framed in the language of an enemy land—so antiquated is the law which must be sought to-day to slay an Irishman whose offence it is that he puts Ireland first. . . .'

Casement contended that when he was in America he felt that his first duty was to keep Irishmen at home. 'If small nationalities were to be pawns in the game of embattled giants, I saw no reason why Ireland should shed her blood in any cause but her own. If that be treason beyond the seas I am not ashamed to avow it or to answer for it here with my life. . . . We have been told that if Irishmen go by the thousand to die not for Ireland, but for Flanders, for Belgium, for a patch of sand on the deserts of Mesopotamia or a rocky trench on the heights of Gallipoli, they are winning self-government for Ireland. But if they dare to lay down their lives on their native soil, if they dare to dream even that freedom can be won only at home by men resolved to fight for it there, then they are traitors. . . .'

Finally he reminded the jurymen, 'How would you feel, or rather how would all men here feel, if an Englishman had landed here in England, and the Crown for its own purposes had conveyed him secretly from England to Ireland under a false name, committed him to prison under a false name, and brought him before a tribunal in Ireland under a statute which they knew involved a trial before an Irish jury? How would you feel yourselves as Englishmen if that man was to be submitted to trial by jury in a land inflamed against him and believing him to be a criminal, when his only crime was that he cared more for England than for Ireland?'

Said *The Times* next day, 'He leaned across the rail and read a statement which, although mainly concerned with abstract doctrines, was listened to with great attention. He challenged the jurisdiction of an English court to try an Irishman, and he referred with considerable grace of diction to those political ideals which had already received a place in the oratory of his counsel. In all, he seemed to seek for remembrance among that band of dreamers and patriot threnodists who have figured so conspicuously in the recent misfortunes of Ireland.'

The Dowager Lady Birkenhead recalls that Casement's 'long, thin nervous forefinger stabbed constantly at the air as he spoke. His white face and dark, deepset eyes resembled an Italian's. As he spoke, it was as if we were listening to a voice from the grave.'

During Casement's hour-long discourse the attendants waiting with the black caps in their hands grew weary, and so when at last Casement was done and it was the moment to place the caps on the heads of their lordships, the task was performed with maladress. The black caps were thus set somewhat askew upon the wigs and beneath this inappropriately rakish headgear Horridge with his nervous 'tic still appeared to be surveying the proceedings with a smile.

Next day the headlines were uncompromising: 'PALTRY TRAITOR MEETS HIS JUST DESERTS. DEATH FOR SIR ROGER CASEMENT. THE DIARIES OF A DEGENERATE.' The account in one paper said, 'Casement, glorying in his guilt, withstood the shock of sentence like a sphinx. When the Lord Chief Justice had put on the black cap, and the court, crowded with men and women well-known in the diplomatic and political world, was solemnly silent, Casement rested his arms squarely on the dock rail and, leaning forward, stared impudently at the Bench. . . . He listened to the sentence of death with callous, brutal indifference. . . . He had entered the dock on the jury's return with a smile on his face, and he waved twice to women friends. . . . Before sentence was passed, Casement read a long and very silly and fatuous statement. . . .'

Then came what was, as far as can be ascertained, the first allusion in print to Casement's perversions: 'It is common knowledge that Sir Roger Casement is a man with no sense of honour or decency. His written diaries are the monuments of a foul private life. He is a moral degenerate.'

That and nothing more was dropped suddenly into the middle

of the descriptive story. 'Common knowledge'? Since, according to Basil Thomson, the diaries were first found by the London police in April, their contents must have been 'leaked', if they really were common knowledge, either by a police, an intelligence or a political source in the two months which had since elapsed. And was this 'leak' deliberate or inadvertent?

This is Miss Bannister's account: 'The trial ended as it was bound to end, in a verdict of Guilty and in Roger being condemned to death. To hear the Jew Isaacs pronouncing those dread words and ending up with "May the Lord have mercy on your soul"—was so awful and revolting to me that I murmured "And may He have mercy on yours". A reporter saw my lips move and said in his report, "A woman attempted to address the court but was promptly suppressed" which was, of course, a lie.

'Roger's speech from the dock was a wonderful piece of oratory, beautifully worded and perfectly delivered. His voice was calm and his manner simple and direct. F. E. Smith was referred to in an allusion to the Ulster leaders' playing with treason "but the difference is that in the case of my accusers their treason leads to the Woolsack, mine to the dock". A prophecy which was fulfilled when years later the same F. E. Smith became Lord Chancellor of England. Smith, to show his contempt of Roger, got up and ostentatiously lounged from the court with his hands in his pockets and a most unpleasant sneer on his face.

'After the trial Roger was not taken back to Brixton but was taken to Pentonville and put in the condemned cell. He was dressed in a blue convict's dress and given a dreadful cap—"A felon's cap's the brightest crown an Irish head can wear" he quoted to me the first time I was allowed to visit him and saw him thus clothed.

'Visits were not allowed frequently. No one of course ever saw him alone except Father Carey, Canon Ring and the Catholic Chaplain Father McCarroll. He was allowed to read letters but not allowed to keep them. By some manner of means he managed to keep one or two. One a long letter from C—— (a man who knew him and was constantly at Mr. Francis Joseph Biggar's, at

Ardrigh, Belfast) was written on foolscap and only on one side of the paper. On the other side Roger wrote a long letter to me, which was smuggled out of the prison and never went through the hands of the authorities.

'At the interviews in Pentonville he was brought into a long room with a long table in it—a warder sat on each side of him and another warder always stood just inside the door. There was a big window behind Roger's back, of ground glass, and outside that one could see a warder's figure, pacing up and down. I saw him in all five times. Mrs. J. R. Green saw him twice. Mr. Gavan Duffy of course saw him, and also Mr. J. H. Morgan, as they decided to appeal against the sentence.

'At our interviews the feeling of the warders being there and the horrible gloom of the place seemed to put a blight over everything, and one felt unable to speak freely. One day he said to me, "I wish you would write to some people for me; I will tell you what to say, and explain to them exactly my views on the justice of my action." I had an envelope in my hand and I took a pencil and began to jot down a few words—the warder at the door at once went out and came back in a few seconds, and said to me, "Come to the Governor's room and bring that paper." I went, feeling sick with apprehension. The Governor said, "Give me that paper." I handed it up. He said, "You are not to take down any notes of what the prisoner says to you—you are to confine yourself entirely to personal and family matters—if you do anything against regulations, you will not be admitted. In fact, I think I shall not admit you again." I said, "I am sure you could not inflict such a cruel punishment on us for doing something which we did not know was forbidden." After a few minutes he gave in and let me go. This incident added to the nervousness and misery of the interviews. On going out that day, the Governor again sent for me and gave me a long lecture about the wickedness of the Irish in rebelling against the English in the middle of a war. Roger should have known better than to encourage such infamy. Why didn't the Irish wait till England's hands were free?—was the burden of his remarks.

'I said, "Because there are only 4,000,000 in Ireland and over 40,000,000 in England, and unless England had something to occupy her troops, we in Ireland should have had less chance of gaining anything than we have now".'

While still at Brixton, Casement wrote the following letter to the Scotland Yard man who had accepted custody of him from the R.I.C. when he arrived in London from Ireland:

'Brixton, 17th May, 1916.

'Dear Superintendent Sandercock:

'Before I have the misfortune (as I will term it in truth) to be taken out of your custody on my journeys to and from this prison to Bow Street I want to thank you very warmly and most sincerely for your unfailing courtesy, manliness and kindness to me. From the time you took me in custody at Euston on Easter Sunday and again took me to the Tower on Easter Tuesday you showed me the best side of an Englishman's character—his native good heart. Whatever you may think of my attitude towards your Government and the Realm I would only ask you to keep one thing in that good heart of yours—and that is that a man may fight a country and its policy and yet not hate any individual of that country.

'Robert Louis Stevenson once said "An Irishman's hatred of England is natural, right and sincere—it is against a Rule and Government and not based on any personal end. It is impersonal and may be most unselfish."

'I hope my feeling is something of that kind—at any rate I feel for you (and for so many others who have had charge of me ever since my arrest) that you have treated me in a wholly chivalrous and high-minded way, and I can only tell you that I thank you from the bottom of my heart.

'I hope your life may be happy and prosperous and that you will gain speedy promotion and so be able, often again, to help some other man in great trouble.

'Yours faithfully,'

So Casement was taken off to Pentonville, there to await the end and brood sadly on the hopeless gesture of an appeal. On July 15th, he wrote to Mrs. Green: 'I have decided to go to the Appeal Court, not that I have the remotest expectation of the appeal proving successful—but I am advised that I *should* go—and I shall see you and the others, I hope, again—and I shall only be a spectator this time—sitting in a reserved box and looking on at the actors with a quite detached and even cynical smile—especially the wigs. . . .'

Mrs. Green also received a letter from Mr. Cadbury, dated June 30th: 'The trial has ended as one can only see it must end, but I feel R's words were heartfelt and sincere, if I may say so to you, more so than the defence set up, and appealing more to the little spark of humanity and chivalry that even we English may possess. The point of an Irish trial for an Irishman is the practical suggestion.

'The other side, his work of twenty years for Africa and the people of the Upper Amazon, must not be forgotten, though he was too proud to claim any credit for that.

'To him death may be the greatest glory, self-sacrifice the greatest gift to the country he loved. Life is not always gain.

'Tell me if in any way I can help you. There are many who cannot forget his courageous Congo Report—I can't believe that *all* the Bishops wish to see him pay the ultimate penalty. In any case, you know how Emmeline and I feel without too many words.'

And Mrs. Green replied: 'When I got your letter I wrote at once to Miss Bannister, to send you her petition, which I think is very good, and with which you would, I believe, agree. I wrote with it to about twenty influential people, but so far all for different reasons have refused to sign. It is a *private* memorial and we only ask personally for names to be sent in privately. Bernard Shaw wrote one for his clientèle, and Conan Doyle for his, in the same way. I do not know if there has been any response. We only want to create the impression of a feeling in the public. The upper classes are intensely hostile, the lower classes uninformed and silent. The clergy outdoing the laymen in "imperialism" . . . . All effort seems to fall back from a wall of passion or of indifference. The war has formed all minds into a single groove.

'I saw our friend under the new, terrible conditions—calm, serene, saying that he has now no nerves and is perfect master of himself. "All is good now," he repeated three times. "I know that it is all good."

'I intend to go back to London for some days, so that I can see him twice, once in each week. No one but Miss Bannister and myself are allowed.'

E. D. Morel decided that it was not for him to visit Casement in jail. Certainly he was under heavy attack at the time for his pacifist activities, and if word had got round that he had been seeing Casement, no doubt life would have been rendered even more difficult for him. However, as one who wrote for the newspapers one of the most glowing of all the eulogies at the time of Casement's greatest pre-war fame—he termed him then 'the Bayard of the Consular Service'—the decision to neglect his old friend and comrade-in-arms cannot have been an easy one to take.

Morel wrote a letter to Mrs. Green in which he said that he hoped he would not be thought of as 'a moral coward' for not going to Pentonville. He complained that the 'atmosphere has been poisoned by vague charges made in the Press, and the ridiculous assertion that the Congo campaign was fought in the interests of Germany. Trevelyan and Ponsonby, whom I have consulted, feel equally certain that if I made this application, the worst construction would be placed upon it.'

In reply Mrs. Green wrote back a characteristically generous and friendly letter from her Wexford home: '. . . It would have been small comfort to you to have a visit—three warders—a distance of about the length of a good-sized room, every word called out audibly. Alas, what commission of a farewell is thus possible! It is just a desolation, except for his gentle dignity, his serenity, his confidence in his friends and absence of distrust. He told me he thought you were *quite right* to have accepted the decision of your colleagues, that there was no question about it. He says that he sleeps, that he has no nerves, that he is master of himself, that he feels now that all is good. I think he meant me to understand an entire resignation and spiritual consolation. The priest is full of sympathy and ardour. We can but lift up our hearts and renew our faith. . . .'

While Casement awaited the final formalities, in the world outside the jailhouse there rose a growing furore. Immense indignation had been aroused—and not in Ireland and the U.S.A. alone—by the post-rising executions in Dublin, and there was an angry clamour of 'No more noose!' Asquith went across the Irish Sea to see for himself, and while there made the humanitarian gesture of visiting the hospital where some of the Irish patriot wounded were lodged, and chatting with them in the ward. John Redmond was busy pointing out to Whitehall that Sir John Maxwell, the British C.-in-C. in Ireland, was vastly overdoing matters.

But the sentiments expressed in the general humanitarian outcry often stopped abruptly short when it came to Casement. 'No more noose' most emphatically failed to apply in his case. He still, in the popular imagination, remained Judas. The boys over in Dublin, after all, had come out fighting with guns in their hands; misguided, if you like—but honest patriots, trying to strike a blow for their country in open battle and against a hugely superior force. One could not help admiring their spirit. But Casement— that was different.

Quite different views prevailed in many of the big cities across the Atlantic. Always ultra-sensitive to the 'Irish Vote', the politicians—and this was a presidential election year—gave attentive ear to what the Irish of New York, Boston, Philadelphia and Chicago had to say about Casement. Indignation meetings were being held and many petitions for reprieve were getting large support. And whatever may have been his private view of Casement's usefulness as a free agent, hard-boiled John Devoy was not slow in recognising his nuisance value once he was in a British jail.

For that matter there were a number of reprieve petitions in England too—excellent petitions, signed, despite Mrs. Green's forebodings, by men and women of high esteem and honour, not harum-scarum nobodies and cranks. To The Right Honourable Herbert Louis Samuel, M.P., Secretary of State for the Home Department, from your most obedient, humble servants. . . . To The Right Honourable H. H. Asquith, K.C., M.P., Prime Minister . . . from your most obedient, humble servants. . . . In they came. One would give much to know what went on in the minds of Asquith and Samuel concerning the propriety of the course taken, but Asquith is long dead, and Lord Samuel tells me that he does not feel free to discuss any matter with which he was concerned as Home Secretary.

The Conan Doyle petition bore the signatures of forty distinguished men and women, among them John Drinkwater, Arnold Bennett, C. P. Scott, famous Editor of *The Manchester Guardian*, Israel Zangwill, John Galsworthy and the Bishop of Winchester. Sir Arthur Conan Doyle, in this petition directed to Asquith, reminded the Prime Minister of the 'violent change' which had taken place in Casement's attitude towards Britain, and 'without going so far as to urge complete mental irresponsibility', stressed that Casement's experiences during the two tropical investigations must have put him under a great physical and nervous strain. The petition further pointed out that the execution of Casement would probably suit the German book; and finally reminded Asquith of the object lesson provided by the United States after the Civil War, when the leaders of the Confederacy were entirely in the power of the North, many of them being officers and officials who had sworn allegiance to the laws of the United States and had afterwards taken up arms and inflicted enormous losses upon her. 'None the less, not one of these men was executed, and this policy of mercy was attended by such happy results that a breach which seemed irreparable has now been happily healed over.'

In Washington, the British Ambassador, Sir Cecil Spring Rice, had his ear to the ground and kept Whitehall well supplied with memoranda, the burden of which was that if the execution of Casement were to take place, it might well have unfortunate consequences. The trouble, he pointed out, was that while many Americans, including some of the Irish moderates, had been prepared to condone as a harsh necessity of war and just retribution the quick executions in Dublin in the immediate wake of the rising, the notion of a laborious trial and the prospect of the hanging of Casement stuck in their gorges. 'All here are agreed,' wrote Spring Rice to Sir Edward Grey, 'that it will be dangerous to make Casement a martyr.' He followed that with another letter a few days later: 'The great bulk of American public opinion, while it might excuse executions in hot blood, would very greatly regret an execution some time after the event. This is the view of impartial friends of ours here who have nothing to do with the Irish movement. It is far better to make Casement ridiculous than a martyr. The universal impression here seems to be that he acted like a madman. There is no doubt whatever that the Germans here look forward with great interest to his execution, of which they will take full advantage. It is quite true that if he is spared, the fact that he is not executed will be used against us. But if he is executed, his execution would be an even more formidable weapon.'

This was the petition drawn up by Bernard Shaw (original draft in the archives of the National Library of Ireland, Dublin, with corrections in his own handwriting): 'We the undersigned beg leave to place before you certain considerations affecting the case of Roger David Casement, now under sentence of death for High Treason. Our object is to show reason why the sentence of the court should not be executed.

'We will not occupy your time with matters as well known to you as to ourselves, and on which your judgment cannot be challenged such, for example, as the conspicuous public services of the condemned man and so forth. We address ourselves solely to points on which you may desire information as to the state of public opinion.

'We assume that the penalty for High Treason is peculiar in

criminal law inasmuch as it depends for its sanction, not on the general principle of the sacredness of the law, but on its effect on the public peace. The conclusion is arrived at in every case by balancing the deterrent effect of carrying out the sentence against the conciliatory effect of remitting it. Recent events in South Africa have accustomed the public to this view. We therefore need trouble you with no apology for treating the decision as one of expediency only.

'In our opinion Casement had not, up to the time of his trial, any serious hold on the Irish people. His Nationalist writings were circulated in America, not Ireland. His political projects, being those of an educated diplomatist, were too technical to be understood by such groups as the Republican Brotherhood and the irreconcilable section of Sinn Fein. We are confident that if, during your recent visit to Ireland you had inquired what Casement was driving at, you would not have received a single well-informed reply. You certainly did not find him a national hero there.

'There is, however, one infallible way by which that can be done; and that is to hang him. His trial and sentence have already raised his status in Nationalist Ireland; but it lacks the final consecration of death. We urge you very strongly not to effect that consecration. In the position of Mr. Arthur Lynch and General de Wet' [leaders in the Boer South African rebellion in 1914, whose lives were subsequently spared—the incident referred to at the start of the petition] 'Casement will be harmless, disabled by his own failure. On a British scaffold he will do endless mischief. The contrast between ruthless severity in his case, and conspicuous lenience—not to mention impunity—in others, will provide an overwhelming argument and illustration to the propagandists of hatred and revenge, whilst the halo which surrounds the national martyr will make a national faith of his belief, and a gospel of his writing.

'As against this, nothing can be claimed but that other rebels may be intimidated. But the likelihood is all the other way. The Irish movement is not a solid phalanx of irreconcilables. The

Casementites and Fenians were a negligible minority of it until the Rebellion. If, though still a minority, they are no longer negligible, it is precisely because of the policy of intimidation, of "giving Ireland a lesson", attempted by General Maxwell. The swing of the pendulum, not only in Ireland but in the neutral countries which are interested in Ireland, was immediate and unmistakable. But it has not been decisive. The Nationalist movement is still reasonable, and a friendly settlement is easy, provided no more executions take place. Even the crude notion that England owes Ireland a life for Mr. Skeffington's had better be respected [Skeffington's was one of the post-rebellion executions which raised the biggest outcry both in Ireland and the U.S.A.].

'You will observe that in thus putting the case before you, we have deprived ourselves of the support of those who see in the specific proposals of Casement a real hope for Irish independence, and who must, therefore, within the limits imposed by common humanity, desire the strenuous impulse which would be given to his authority and influence by his death as an Irish patriot in an English prison. But you will hardly attach the less weight on that account to our urgent representation, which is prompted by a sincere desire for an unembittered settlement of the question which has occupied so large a share of the labours of your administration.'

Many would agree that that document ranks among the most sagacious pieces of writing that Shaw produced. Everything which he said has, of course, turned out to be true. It is a pity that there must have been so many closed minds in the Asquith Cabinet.

But there was a third, and most sinister, factor at play in the Casement affair. Governments can make mistakes. Popular fury in wartime we can understand, even while deploring it. We now come to the Black Diaries.

For the last forty years, the British Government of 1916 has stood accused of having clandestinely used Casement's Black Diaries—those discovered in his trunks at Ebury Street by the police after his arrest and which contained a voluminous and detailed record of homosexual behaviour—to smear Casement personally during the all-important period while his appeal was pending and when the petitions might have otherwise carried the day and saved his life.

Did they do it? Mr. Denis Gwynn, author of *The Life and Death of Roger Casement* (Jonathan Cape, 1930) relates that when he was working at the Ministry of Information in 1917, the late G. H. Mair, whom he describes as one of the principal officers of the Ministry, made no secret among his friends that it was he who had been responsible the year before for having the diaries photographed for distribution. Mair said that he had read the diaries and referred to a certain incident in London which was described in them. Mair, 'who was closely in touch with several Liberal Cabinet Ministers,' also told Gwynn that the Cabinet had seriously considered whether they should drop the treason charge against Casement and make him the centre of another Wilde case, 'in order to discredit him finally in Ireland'.

Mr. Gwynn further states that photographs of selected passages from the diaries were shown in the London clubs, handed round in the House of Commons (including the Press Gallery), shown to important newspapermen—especially Americans—who were thought to be possible Casement sympathisers, and sent over to the U.S.A. to be used to put the quietus on any of Casement's friends there who might be disposed to be troublesome. In America (adds Mr. Gwynn) one of the men who was shown the documents was John Quinn, a leading New York lawyer and an influential leader among the Irish-American community who had known Casement quite well. He was apparently appalled when he clapped eyes on the diary photos and could not deny that the writing was that of Casement.

Mr. Alfred Noyes, the distinguished poet, worked for a time during the 1914 war in the Foreign Office News Department. He was sitting in his office of that department one day, either in August or September 1916, when the Foreign Office Librarian, the late Sir Stephen Gaselee, came in and placed in his hands what Noyes describes as '200 pages of concentrated erotica' purporting to be photographs of typewritten copies of the diaries of Casement. Horror-stricken, Mr. Noyes glanced briefly at the unlooked-for exhibit before handing it back to Gaselee.

Mr. Noyes also states as a fact in his book, *Two Worlds for Memory* (Sheed & Ward, 1953) that John Redmond, Bernard Shaw and Michael Collins were among prominent Irishmen who were shown the photographed diary and who accepted it as genuine. But who was it who was showing these unpleasant documents to these Irishmen? And for what purpose?

The clerics, naturally, were especially susceptible to the impact of these unsavoury revelations. One glimpse of the diary, an assurance that it was in Casement's handwriting—and Casement's was a highly individual hand, easily recognised—and the thing was done. In this connexion the late Dean Inge wrote, on December 24th, 1953, to Mr. Alfred Noyes, 'I feel sure that Casement was a man of infamous character. The King' [George V] 'showed my friend Bishop Henson the Diary, which of course the Irish say was forged.' It will be recalled that it was Canon Henson, as he was then, who had preached a vigorous sermon in Westminster Abbey in the wake of Casement's Putumayo findings. He had obviously been greatly moved by the Putumayo business, and must have been a warm supporter and admirer of Casement. Can it be—and here, of course, we enter the realm of speculation—that Henson may have wished to plead for clemency on behalf of Casement, may have sought an audience of the Sovereign himself in order to do so, only to have his pleas blasted by terrible proof of his hero's moral degradation?

During Casement's trial it is certain that the Government prosecutors approached the defence with the suggestion that if the defence would agree to the diaries being produced in evidence, the prosecution would co-operate in a defence attempt to obtain a verdict of guilty but insane. This proposal the defence, through Serjeant Sullivan, refused.

According to allegations which have been repeatedly made during the past four decades, the British Government had thus decided on a master-stroke of perfidy. To ensure that the petitions for mercy should come to nothing, and that decent men every-where should shrink in horror at the very name of Casement, His Majesty's Government—so it is alleged—deliberately made copies of the diaries and showed them, through its appointed agents, where they would have the most effect on both sides of the Atlantic.

All's fair in war, of course. The Government had small cause to look with compunction upon a man who, in two years, had changed rôles from lionised Foreign Office official to a furtive creature attempting to suborn men in enemy prison camps into treasonable paths. And the execration in which Casement was held by the public and much of the press of the time probably caused the Liberal Government to feel that it was justified in going to extremes.

And yet there is something frightful about the idea of British Government agents peddling these photographs with this in mind. If a man is under sentence of death, even for the crime of Treason, can anyone be justified, while the man waits to die, in blackening his character into the bargain?

However, that is the allegation which has repeatedly been made. It seems beyond doubt that many patriotic Irishmen were shown photographed copies of the diary at that time, which they identi-fied to their consternation and horror as being in Casement's hand-writing, and as being concerned largely with homosexual adven-tures. To this a curious rebuttal has occasionally been made. The friends of Casement maintain that while in the Putumayo jungles, Casement discovered that Normand was not only persecuting and brutalising the natives, but was indulging in sodomy at their expense. Casement managed to possess himself of Normand's diary, and for some reason copied it all out, and sent it, together with the original, to the Foreign Office.

The contention is that, not content with blackening the charac-ter of a man awaiting the noose, the Government was doing so on the basis of a document which they knew to have nothing what-ever to do with their victim, but which they had produced from their files for their own purposes.

It is a case of no holds barred—if we are to believe that story; and the story has been put forward often enough, notably in *The Forged Casement Diaries*, by the late William Moloney (Talbot Press of Dublin, 1936) and *The Life and Times of Roger Casement*, by Herbert Mackey, F.R.C.S. (C. J. Fallon Ltd., Dublin 1954). Various efforts down the years to try to clear matters up and to obtain from the Home Office some sort of clarifying statement have met with nothing but evasions. This, needless to say, has played into the hands of the fanatical pro-Casement faction, who say that it proves British duplicity.

Mr. Gwynn sent a letter to the then Home Secretary, the late J. R. Clynes, in 1930, asking if he might be allowed to see the diaries, which are understood to be housed in Scotland Yard's 'Black Museum'. He got back this note: 'I have carefully considered your letter of the 21st June about Casement's diaries. On inquiry I find that it was decided long ago not to make any official statement as to the existence or non-existence of these diaries. I have carefully considered whether it is still necessary to maintain that rule, and there seem to me to be very good reasons why in the public interest it is desirable not to break the official silence.'

Gwynn had asked in his letter about Basil Thomson's detailed account in his book of the episode of the request for the key to Casement's trunk and Thomson's outright description of the diaries themselves. About this Clynes said, 'You mention that reference to these diaries has been made by Sir Basil Thomson, but any such statements were completely unauthorised.'

My own efforts with the Home Office did not even get as far as those of Professor Gwynn. I wrote to Major Lloyd George, the Home Secretary, on March 25th, 1955, saying that I did not want to read the diaries, but asking whether he would at least confirm their existence. I pointed out in the letter that 'so long as Her Majesty's Government maintain silence on this not unimportant subject, so will this country continue to appear in an equivocal light in regard to the handling of the Casement affair'.

I received a formal acknowledgment, and then on April 2nd,

282

a brief note saying that the Home Secretary was unable to supply me with any information on the matter.

Mr. G. de C. Parmiter, in his book *Roger Casement* (Arthur Barker, 1936), also went through the motions of trying to get some sort of statement out of the stonewalling Home Office. He, too, wrote to the Home Secretary of that day, the late Lord (then Sir John) Simon, but fared no better than anyone else.

Perhaps the most astonishing performance on the part of the Home Office took place in 1925, when a respected Fleet Street crime reporter was preparing to publish a book about Casement.

He was summoned to the Home Office, and the late Sir William Joynson-Hicks, then Home Secretary, threatened him with prosecution if he persisted. Publication of that book was dropped in face of the threats.

Present at the interview between the Home Secretary and the Fleet Street man was Sir Ernley Blackwell. Sir Ernley may well have had excellent grounds for feeling that anything to do with the Casement affair should be hushed up.

While all the covering up persists, so will rumours and accusations tend to flourish. Was there an official conspiracy to denigrate Casement in 1916?[1] While bureaucratic secrecy remains, the British Government can only continue to come badly out of things. And while successive Home Secretaries shrug and say that it is not in the public interest to admit whether certain documents of historical importance exist or not, the Irish or some of them feel that they have the right to say that the English played a bad rôle in the Casement story.

As the result of my own researches I have come to the firm conclusion that there is not the slightest doubt that Casement was a confirmed and habitual homosexual.

I base that finding on two main considerations: (1)—Serjeant A. M. Sullivan, Q.C., with whom I have spoken at length, told me that his client Casement not only admitted to him that he was a homosexual—but 'gloried in it, saying that many of the great men of history had been of that persuasion. He was proud of it.

[1] See Appendix III.

If the matter had come up in court, he wished me to impress on the jury the fact that it was a rather distinguished thing to be.' (2)—There was a *second* group of Casement homosexual diaries and account books. This fact has until now been a secret. Casement's *pied-à-terre* in Northern Ireland was the home of Francis J. Biggar, just outside Belfast. Biggar, an antiquarian, was a close friend, and when Casement left for the U.S.A., he asked Biggar to hold on his behalf a tin trunk containing his papers.

After Casement's execution Biggar opened the trunk. What he discovered inside gave him a staggering shock for he, presumably, like so many of Casement's intimate friends, had not the slightest inkling of his sex inclinations. There lay a voluminous diary, full of homosexual notations and reminiscences; and there was also a large quantity of letters from various young men, the contents of which left no doubt as to the nature of their relations with Casement. Biggar then did what Casement ought to have done, not only with these but with the sorry records which he left behind in Ebury Street—burned them.

My source for this is the following: not long before his death, the late Senator Biggar, a nephew of F. J. Biggar, and a highly respected member of the Irish Dail (as well as being Professor of Pathology at Trinity College, Dublin) was dining at his club. There he fell into conversation with a well-known resident of Cork. He told this gentleman that the episode, related to him by his uncle, had always deeply worried him. But he had no doubt that it clinched the story of the London diaries of the same nature.

I regret the use of the rather clumsy phrase 'well-known resident of Cork'; but I gave him my assurance, when we talked together in Cork, in November 1954, that I would not disclose his identity. I can only say that he is a most respected citizen, well-known in many parts of Ireland; and—I would say—neutral in his feelings about Casement. He has no doubts about the genuineness of the story.

But although I feel certain that Casement was homosexual, I do not see how this fact has any direct relevance to his public life and achievements. From first to last his career was startlingly unlikely. He drifted into the British Foreign Service as a totally unknown 'extra'—and then scored two resounding triumphs with his Congo and Putumayo reports. Then—from the English official viewpoint—he played a squalid game for the Germans in war-time, was captured, tried and hanged.

There are two ways of looking at Casement's history, as indeed there are at least two ways of looking at nearly everything in history. The English regard Casement as the worst sort of renegade and traitor; a man who, only lately a respected official in the employ of the Crown, actively tried to seduce men wearing British uniform into a seditious organisation. The Irish—or some of them—say that he was a great and high-minded patriot, who was driven by his anguished conscience into yet one more fine act of selfless valour on behalf of the downtrodden, just as he had done in Africa and South America.

These are both tenable points of view. But the question of his homosexuality is not involved. I suppose that at this point I should make clear that I share with other 'normal' persons a lack of understanding of what makes perverts behave in the way that they do—a lack of understanding, based partly on instinct and partly on tradition, which can very easily turn into revulsion and loathing. But because I do not understand this particular form of sexual gratification I do not necessarily condemn out of hand all of its practitioners as monsters. And so, although I am certain that Roger Casement was a pervert, it makes as little difference to me, in assessing his place in history, as if he had possessed a club-foot.

But *in*directly, the matter of Casement's homosexuality has proved of first-rate importance. It is this side of the question which must concern us. I submit that we must in particular consider (1)—the rather unorthodox offer by Sir F. E. Smith, the Attorney-General, leading for the Crown in Casement's prosecution, to co-operate with Serjeant Sullivan in the production of the Black Diaries as evidence, on the understanding that both prosecution and defence would then jointly try to persuade the court to agree to a verdict of guilty but insane; (2)—the repeated allegations that photographed copies of the Black Diaries were used by agents of the British Government in 1916 to prevent sympathy for Casement from taking a practical form, between the date of his being found guilty and the day of his hanging; (3)—the persistence of successive British ministers, notably those in the Home Office, in evading periodic attempts to discover the exact truth about Casement's Black Diaries.

As regards the suggestions of insanity, I consider that these can be set aside. Casement was clearly highly-strung, subject to bouts of intense melancholy, fits of weeping, and, as his prolonged correspondence with the Foreign Office tends to show, the victim of a persecution mania. But I think he was sane, in the legal sense, and it is perhaps astonishing that the Attorney-General should have felt that the diaries might afford sufficient grounds for an insanity plea.

But although I, writing in 1955, can see no relevance in the fact that Casement was a self-confessed pervert—and I imagine that I am not alone in this—we have to cast our minds back to the state of opinion which existed in this country nearly forty years ago.

Victorian *mores* still had loud echoes in the England of 1916; and although there was a fierce public outcry against Casement the traitor, there would have been an even wilder outburst if it had become widely known that he was also a pervert. Execration of him in that case would have reached a pitch not at all hard to imagine when the obvious analogy of the Wilde case is considered.

Less than twenty years earlier, English public opinion, not content with seeing Wilde put in prison on a charge of homosexuality, had for some time felt it logical to try also to annihilate him as a writer. If Wilde's plays were to be performed at all, then the author's name must nowhere appear on programme or poster. His sons were forced to change their family name. The story is a sadly familiar one—but who nowadays sees the slightest relevance between the fact of Wilde's homosexuality and the esteem in which he is everywhere held as a brilliant author?

After nearly forty years, those who knew Casement well or who came in contact with him at significant times during his life are, unfortunately, a fast-dwindling band. A key figure among the survivors is Serjeant Alexander Martin Sullivan, with whom I had a considerable conversation at his home in Greenmount Road, Terenure, Dublin, on November 16th, 1954. (A curious point is that none of the authors of the earlier books on Casement saw fit, so Serjeant Sullivan tells me, to seek him out for source material on their works.)

At ninety-three Sullivan is a spry and lively figure, slim and full of vitality and interest in things. His eyes are giving him trouble nowadays and the famous black 'Captain Kettle' beard, pictured by Sir John Lavery, in his painting of the Casement trial which hangs in the King's Inn at Dublin, has gone white. But with the utmost courtesy and alertness Sullivan answered my questions in the drawing-room of the modest red-brick villa where he now lives.

Said he: 'Freddie Smith did his best to get me to plead guilty but insane, but I refused to have anything to do with the diaries. I refused even to look at them. Smith wrote to me and wired me to try to persuade me to go over and inspect the diaries. These, you see, could not be given in evidence against Casement unless the defence put them in, and Freddie Smith was savage that I wouldn't go anywhere near the diaries, much less use them.

'It would only have dirtied the man (Casement) and no tribunal could have said that it was evidence of insanity. A perverted diary would not in itself prove insanity. But I could not persuade Casement himself that these documents would never appear in evidence. As for Moloney's thesis' [that the diaries belonged in reality to Normand and had merely been copied out by Casement in the course of his duties] 'that is the most arrant nonsense. There is no doubt whatever about the genuineness of the perverted diaries.

'But of course His Majesty's Government were unsure about executing Casement. They were clutching at straws to save him. They were angling for America, and they knew that the execution would be seized on for glorifying him in America. F. E. Smith was searching desperately for an excuse to thwart the public of their victim.

'I took the personal responsibility for refusing to introduce the diaries into evidence. I did not give Casement any option in the matter. I knew it might save his life, but I finally decided that death was better than besmirching and dishonour. The judges would have been bound to say that there was no legal evidence of insanity. It might have yielded the excuse of commuting his sentence. I feel sure that the prosecution would have done its honest best—but what of the judges ? I am certain to-day that I did the right thing.'

Sullivan considers that his erstwhile client was 'a megalomaniac, a man with a fantastic estimate of his own importance'. And he adds musingly, 'Casement ought to have been a "con" man. You would believe anything he told you. He never consciously told a lie. He had all the instincts of a gentleman. He would tell you the most appalling falsehoods, and not only believe them himself—but make you believe them, too.'

Of the suggestions that the British Government deliberately set out to smear Casement with copies of his perverted diaries, Sullivan comments: 'Gavan Duffy, my brother-in-law, told me that the diaries had been shown to certain American correspondents in London, before the trial. The Irish-Americans were savage with Maxwell' (Sir John Maxwell, C.-in-C., British forces in Ireland) 'for his brutality in shooting all those fellows. The British Government of the day wasn't very particular about what they were prepared to do to damp down the pro-Irish and anti-British sentiment in America. I believe it' [the dissemination of the diaries] 'was done at some time or other before the U.S.A. entered the war. What people do in war is unpredictable. Perfectly decent men will do perfectly shocking things in the prevailing hysteria.'

Since the copies of the diaries were apparently circulated among the Cabinet, it seems not impossible that it should have been felt fitting to convey a copy to the Sovereign, since, although of so reprehensible a nature, it was being regarded as a vital document in a Crown case. And since the charge was High Treason, the Sovereign would have every reason to take a deep and even personal interest in all aspects, however distasteful, of so unusual and grave a case.

Of course I have tried to get into touch with as many of those surviving who might be thought to have played some part—under orders, no doubt—in the circulation of the copied diaries. Few survive nowadays, and those who do display marked reluctance, understandable in the circumstances, to say much about the matter. They tend either to plead imperfect memory or to say that the fact that they formerly held official positions makes it impossible for them to speak.

But we have at least one living witness, and an important one. In his book *The Forged Casement Diaries*, William Moloney states that Mr. Ben S. Allen, then a member of the London bureau of the Associated Press of America, was called in by the then Captain (later Admiral) Hall, Chief of Naval Intelligence, and shown the Casement diaries. 'In July 1916,' wrote Moloney, 'Admiral Sir Reginald Hall, at his regular Wednesday afternoon interviews with Ben S. Allen, of the Associated Press, repeatedly showed Casement's diaries to Allen. . . . Allen says, "I read it over rather perfunctorily until my eye caught passages tending to confirm the gossip I had already heard concerning the document." But he further writes that he was shown "typewritten excerpts designed to illustrate . . . the ravings of a victim of perversion". And he comments, "My own theory is that it was a diary copied by Sir Roger Casement during the Putumayo investigations." '

Allen asked leave to visit Casement in jail, in order to confront him with the document, adds Moloney in his book, but permission for this visit was not forthcoming.

Mr. Allen is nowadays living in retirement in California. I wrote to him to ask him if he would be kind enough to comment on the above passages in the Moloney book, to which he replied (January 30th, 1955, from Palo Alto, California): 'The incident of the efforts of Admiral Hall to prevail upon me to accept certain pages of the so-called Casement Diary is exactly as recorded by Moloney in *The Forged Casement Diaries* . . . Of course the motive is clear, as the United States Senate was on the point of considering a resolution asking clemency for the convicted man. That resolution would have passed, and since England at that time was so eagerly cultivating the support of the U.S.A. the pressure to grant at least a reprieve would have proven irresistible.'

I had also asked Mr. Allen to give me a categorical yes or no on the accuracy of the description of his dealings with Admiral Hall over the Casement diaries, as described in the Moloney book. 'My answer to your question,' he writes, 'is an outright, unqualified YES.'

I have received the following letter from a former member of the Dail. He has an unimpeachable record for disinterestedness and honesty.

'Of his sodomy I think there is no doubt. . . . When ————— was the Dominions Secretary some years ago, he studied the subject of the diaries at my request, and gave me a written assurance that the diaries were authentic. The uses to which they were put by the British Government during World War I is, of course, a different issue. But it enrages me that in Ireland and the U.S.A. the diary is now frequently referred to as an ignoble forgery. It has been the policy of successive British Governments to ignore these attacks. I believe they are wrong. . . Who made the decision to show round photographs of the diaries in America in order to kill the agitation for a reprieve, I don't know, but it was neither a creditable nor a fortunate decision.'

The reason why successive British Governments of all parties have seen fit to evade this particular issue is all too obvious. It is purely a matter of expediency and politics, but honesty is so often the best policy. It was put to me like this by an extremely shrewd observer and practitioner of politics:

'This is what any Home Secretary would say, if he were asked anything about this: "Why should I help you in this matter? It would only mean more trouble with the Irish. All over the world we are having our troubles. But Ireland, the storm-centre for so many hundreds of years, is calm. We enjoy good relations with her. Your book might stir up sharp reactions. Will it help *me* to be the

Home Secretary who took on himself the responsibility of reversing the policy laid down by his predecessors, Tory and Labour, over the last forty years?" '

Casement's big mistake was in committing his sex experiences to paper and keeping the record. In that way he got found out, which was unnecessary. Any man with an ounce of normal prudence would have destroyed them at some point, especially when he began to place himself in jeopardy with Britain. It is the same old Casement who landed in Kerry complete with German code and sleeping car ticket. Casement seemed doomed to scatter a trail of incriminating evidence, from improper diaries to foreign rail tickets.

Assuming that Casement was a homosexual and that the British authorities did gain possession of his diaries and that these were genuine, the big question is—was His Majesty's Government justified, even in time of war, in making any use of them, either in court proceedings—as was clearly attempted—or for the purpose of character assassination, as was also evidently attempted and with success?

I have discussed the matter with various men of affairs, whose opinion I value. They are no more cynical than most, but a great deal better informed. They accept that the diaries existed, were genuine, and that they were used for smear purposes. And they consider that, since what was then the greatest war in history was in full flood, it was justifiable to do so.

I leave the reader to form his own conclusions.

Casement's appeal was heard on July 17th, by Justices Darling, Bray, Lawrence, Scrutton and Aitken. It turned out that Darling and Aitken had spent many a weary hour beforehand at the Public Record Office in Chancery Lane, studying the original of the Norman-French statute of Edward III through microscopes. They had peered painstakingly at the unfamiliar script, striving to arrive at its exact intent and meaning, and looking to see if perhaps the form in which it had been couched would after all allow a nimble mind like Sullivan's to plead with justification that his man should get off. The microscope was used especially to determine whether a mark on the yellowing parchment was what is nowadays technically known as a 'break'—was a crease in the fabric, or was in fact a comma. It might have made all the difference to Casement, but the justices satisfied themselves that it did not.

It offends one's sense of the fitness of things that in England an appeal can so rarely, if ever, produce the high drama which ought to brood upon the scene when what is virtually the last attempt to save the life of a human being is taking place. The legal discussions, and in this instance they were of an especially baffling nature for the layman, seem remote from matters of life or death. There is not the intimate unity of a normal court of law, in which all those taking part are together in a fairly small space and all constantly visible as the story runs its course. At the appeal, as Casement himself said, the accused, the man whose life is at stake, does not really participate but is a spectator only. The lawyers are there, as in a vacuum, pursuing their abstract arguments; the voices drone on. The accused can barely be glimpsed from the public gallery. The matter comes to resemble a game of chess which necessitates constant recourse to a quantity of immensely venerable books of rules. At the end of the second day the appeal was dismissed.

Miss Bannister, not unexpectedly, found the proceedings unsatisfactory and, being so emotionally involved, in the upshot she naturally found the dry sentences in which small points were discussed 'too niggling'. They 'did not drive home the thing that really mattered'. Her account goes on:

'The appeal was dismissed and the execution was fixed for August 3rd. This gave us a fortnight for trying to get petitions signed for a reprieve. We were at once up against a campaign of lying and intrigue. . . . They said Roger had always been in the pay of Germany since Congo days—that he was immoral—that he had never been known to take any interest in Irish affairs until 1913, etc. Also the story that Roger was a moral pervert was spread throughout all the London clubs. F. E. Smith and Basil Thomson sent for various men who could be trusted to do their dirty work and showed them Roger's supposed diary and asked them to spread the stories. Roger had been visited constantly both in Brixton and Pentonville by Father Carey and had given deep thought to the question of becoming a Catholic. He would not act on an emotional instinct but wanted to be rationally convinced of the truths of the Catholic religion. When he had definitely made up his mind, the Cardinal (Bourne) was approached. I was told by a priest and by Mr. Gavan Duffy that the Cardinal tried to insist on Roger signing a sort of recantation in his belief in Irish freedom and a confession of abhorrence at his own action.

'On my third visit to him he said, "I want to be a Catholic, but they are trying to make me betray my soul." I was entirely in the dark as to what he meant, and did not dare to question him because of the warders. Afterwards, when I told the chaplain of this, he said it was "the paper they tried to make him sign". Finally, on the day before he died, he made his confession, was reconciled to the Church (he had been baptised a Catholic in infancy but had never practised) and received Holy Communion. Father McCarroll said that when he approached the altar he put off his shoes (as a sign of humility) and as he raised his head to receive the Host his face was transfigured—he remained a long time in prayer at the altar rails.

'On Thursday the 27th July I went to see him alone. He had had an interview with the Governor which had upset him, the Governor having told him that he felt it right to tell him how abhorrent his action had been. Also he had tried to get his oldest friend, Herbert Ward, to send him a message (he had asked one of his counsel to try) and he had had a rebuff. He was for the first time broken and sorrowful. We both tried to keep cheerful on the surface. Then he said, "What will you do, Gee, when it is all over?" I cried, "Don't, don't, I can't think of that." He said, "Go back to Ireland, and don't let me lie here in this dreadful place—take my body back with you and let it lie in the old churchyard in Murlough Bay." I said, "I will," and then I broke down, I couldn't help it, it was the only time I was in tears when I was with him. He too wept, and said, "I don't want to die and leave you and the rest of you dear ones, but I must." With a superhuman effort I stopped and said, "It won't be, we are working, all of us, to prevent it—there are petitions." But he broke in "No, Gee, don't delude yourself—they want my death, nothing else will do. And after all, it's a glorious death, to die for Ireland—and I could not stand long years in a place like this—it would destroy my reason."

'The warders broke off the interview and marched him out. I stood up and stretched out my hands to him; he turned at the door and said, "Good-bye, God bless you"—I went out and in the corridor outside I simply abandoned myself to my grief. I couldn't help it. I cried loud and uncontrolledly. A warder took me across the courtyard and put me into the little waiting-room at the gate where the warder with the keys was. He got up to open the outer gate, and I said, "Stop, I can't go yet." I was shaking so I could hardly stand and the sobs were rending me. "You can't wait," he said. "You must go." "I can't go like this," I said, "into the public street. Do ask the policeman outside to get me a taxi." "No," he said. "Pull yourself together, and go now." And he opened the gate and pushed me out and locked it with a clang behind me.

'I wanted to shriek and beat on the gate with my hands. My lips kept saying, "Let him out. Let him out." I staggered down the road, crying out loud and people gazed at me. I got home somehow. Now, writing it down, I cry and cry and want to scream out, but what's the good. I can't see now to write any more to-day—He was there waiting for death, such a death. I was outside and I wanted to die.'

Of course the devoted women maintained their wretched struggle on Casement's behalf to the very end. Hope must have vanished, but they refused to give up. I am not sure whether Miss Bannister actually obtained a personal interview with Asquith towards the very end (on or about August 1st) or whether a letter went to him by special messenger. In any case she got this reply on the evening of August 2nd (the execution was fixed for the following morning). It was written in longhand and said:

> '10 Downing Street,
> Whitehall, S.W.
> 2 August, 1916.

Dear Madam,

It is with sincere pain (and only in compliance with your request) that I inform you that, after very full consideration, the Cabinet to-day came to the conclusion that there were not sufficient grounds for a reprieve.

I need not assure you that I wish it had been possible for them to arrive at a different decision.

> Yours very faithfully,
> H. H. Asquith.

I am returning the documents.'

In jail Casement's thoughts had turned, as reported by Miss Bannister, towards making his peace with God. He had been having talks with the sympathetic Irish Roman Catholic priests who ministered to the prisoners, and had become increasingly attracted to the idea of turning Roman Catholic before his death. William Cadbury, with whom I discussed the point, thinks that the main reason for his conversion was that he wanted to identify himself with Ireland—'to be as close to Ireland and to her heart as possible'. And since Ireland is overwhelmingly Roman Catholic so in his last days 'Casement no doubt felt it more fitting to become a Catholic too. And he preferred to have Catholic priests about him at the end, rather than others.'

It is also claimed that Casement had asked Father Crotty, back in the prisoner of war camp days, to instruct him with a view to becoming a Catholic, because he had been so impressed with Father Crotty's soothing and encouraging influence among the men at Limburg. Whatever the motive and however complete the act of faith, Casement was received into the Roman Catholic Church, and it is only Miss Bannister, so far as I know, who has produced the rather chilling story of the attempt to get him to sign some sort of document as a quid pro quo.

The day after the execution we have the Rev. Thomas Carey, one of the priests who ministered to Casement in the last days at Pentonville, and who performed the burial rites when he was hanged, writing this letter, possibly to Sidney Parry, as it was found among Miss Bannister's papers, and she subsequently married Parry:

'Catholic Church,
Eden Grove, Holloway,
London, N.
5 August, 1916

Dear Sir—I know you will be glad to learn that your friend Roger Casement was reconciled to the Church and made his first Confession on last Wednesday evening and made his first and last Communion on the morning of his execution on last Thursday. He died with all the faith and piety of an Irish peasant woman, and had, as far as I could judge, all the dispositions, faith, hope, charity and contrition, resignation to God's will, etc., etc., to meet his Creator, I gave him the Holy Father's Blessing, with Plenary Indulgence attached shortly before his execution and for an hour before he followed me in fervent and earnest prayer. He marched to the scaffold with the dignity of a prince and towered straight over all of us on the scaffold. He feared not death and he prayed with me to the last. It was an edifying Catholic death and it is wonderful how he grasped the Catholic faith at the end. I have no doubt that he has gone to Heaven. He sobbed like a child after his confession and his contrition for any sins he may have committed was intense. From the way he spoke repeatedly of you, I know you will be glad of all this. Don't think I exaggerate in the least—I was deeply touched by his death and I had got to love him during the month he was under my care. I am going away for a month for a rest—I need it much. So do not be surprised if there should be a delay in replying to any questions you may ask. If you should be in town I shall gladly answer any questions I am allowed. I am hard pressed at present.

Yours sincerely,
Thomas Carey.

P.S.—Hundreds of Masses were offered for him on the morning of his execution, the Cardinal and about fifty priests who were
in Retreat offered them for him. I can only say that the fruit of all
appeared to me abundant at his death.—TC.'

On August 3rd, 1916, at six minutes past nine in the morning,
Casement was hanged. A couple of hundred people gathered in
the roadway outside the jail—women workers from nearby offices,
labourers and so on—and when the bell began to toll, they raised
a thin cheer before dispersing.

One newspaper account said that 'The convict showed no sign
of nervousness. He rose early, and seeing the glory of the morning
remarked, "What a beautiful day!" Then he ate a fairly good
breakfast and spent the remainder of his time with the priests. . . .
Ellis, the executioner, pinioned him in his cell, and, headed by the
clergy, a procession was formed and moved to the execution
shed. Casement listened to the words of the litany for the dying
and made the responses, "Into Thy hands, O Lord, I commend
my spirit," and "Lord Jesus, receive my soul."

'Ellis quickly adjusted a strap round the convict's ankles, put
the noose round his neck, and pulled the lever releasing the trap
door. Death was instantaneous.'

The newspaper account concluded: 'Dr. Mander, the M.O. of
the prison, said that he saw no sign of insanity during the time
Casement was in the prison.'

The *Manchester Guardian* commented editorially on the morning of the execution: 'It must, we fear, be assumed that the
Government have decided that Roger Casement shall be executed
to-day. By doing so they will have missed a rare opportunity of
showing that wisdom of magnanimity which distinguishes the
statesman from the politician. Of a man discredited otherwise
before the world they will have made a martyr to live long in the
traditions of Irishmen at home and abroad. They will have set at
naught the very unusual request of the Senate of the United
States, disregarding utterly the sentiments of a nation on whose
goodwill much depends. It was open to them to pay some regard
to this man's notable services to this country and to humanity in

the past. It was incumbent on them to consider the future. They have had eyes and ears for nothing but the hot resentment of the present, that clamour for blood which rises so vehemently in times of excitement from normally placable and kindly men. It is strange that everyone can appreciate the blended wisdom and nobility of General Botha's treatment of de Wet, everyone can understand the stupidity of the execution of Italian rebels by Austria, everyone is proud of acts of clemency in our past history, and feels the awkwardness of apologising for severity and ruthlessness, yet so few can apply the lesson here and now. For no serious object of policy our Government have decided to make our uphill task still harder, to diminish our authority among the nations, and weaken the sympathy for our cause in quarters where it is most needed.'

The Times said the day after the execution: 'We have absolutely refused in these past weeks—in spite of some very curious pressures—to have the Casement case re-tried in these columns. Newspapers have many and great responsibilities these days, but the function of a final court of appeal is not one of them. . . . On the other hand, we cannot help protesting against certain other attempts which have been made to use the Press for the purpose of raising issues which are utterly damaging to Casement's character but which have no connexion whatever with the charges on which he was tried. These issues should either have been raised in a public and straightforward manner, or they should have been left severely alone. The colour of his proved crime is deep enough by itself. It would have been fortunate for everyone concerned, and the simplest act of justice, if he had been shot out of hand on the Kerry coast. But if there was ever any virtue in the pomp and circumstance of a great state trial, it can only be weakened by inspired innuendoes which, whatever their substance, are now irrelevant, improper, and un-English.'

It is hard to believe that the *Times* editorial can have referred to anything save the hawking about of the Casement diaries, and the whispering campaign about them which by now was in full swing in London and elsewhere. It would be interesting to know whom the writer had in mind when he spoke of 'inspired innuen-does'. Who were the inspirers?

On the same day the Government issued a final statement about Casement. It said that conclusive evidence had come into the hands of the Government since the trial to the effect that Case-ment had entered into an agreement with the Germans which explicitly provided that the Irish Brigade might be employed in Egypt against Britain. The statement went on: 'A suggestion that Casement was out of his mind is without foundation. Materials bearing on his mental condition were placed at the disposal of his Counsel, who did not raise the plea of insanity. . . .'

That, or so one supposes, can only refer to the Attorney-General's unsuccessful attempt to induce Sullivan to put the diaries into evidence while the trial was going on.

From Dublin the *Times* correspondent telegraphed: 'It is pro-bable that the execution of Roger Casement will be violently denounced in Ireland. The appeal for his reprieve has been largely signed, and it was supported by Cardinal Logue and other Roman Catholic prelates. Most of the signatories had no sympathy with Casement's crime. Their position was that enough blood had been shed in the rebellion and that the pardon of Casement would have had a good effect on public opinion in Ireland. . . . It is quite certain, however, that if Casement had been reprieved, the Nationalist press would have hastened to compare that clemency with the severity of the executions in Dublin and would have raised a new campaign against Sir John Maxwell. Nothing that the Government could have done with Casement would have satisfied the whole of Ireland.'

What is the final judgment on Casement's complex and volatile character? Most of the appraisals of his personality which I have come across in the course of examining the formidable mass of documentary records about and by him which are available in this country and in Ireland are unanimous concerning his personal charm, kindness, selflessness and chivalry (the last an especially favoured adjective). The famous novelist Joseph Conrad, who knew Casement in the early African days, described him as 'a limpid personality' and said that as he strode off into the tropical jungle, a walking-stick his only weapon, 'there was a touch of the Conquistadore about him'.

He has further been described as 'a true knight', a 'Don Quixote, setting forth to do battle against the forces of intolerance', and 'a gentleman, first, last and all the time'. There is no question but that Casement could and did inspire a warmth of friendship which often touched the level of hero-worship. The sincerity of those friends who stood by him until the end and refused, before and after his execution, to believe the proffered evidence of homosexuality, cannot for a moment excite anything but admiration.

There are plenty of photographs of him, and these show, especially in his thirties and forties, a man of striking, not to say commanding, appearance and vivid good looks. He had a long, lean head, with well-chiselled cheeks; thick, curly hair, parted on the left; a good nose, and a well-tended moustache and beard, which he was well able to carry off. His most striking features were his eyes—deep-set, even sunken, beneath thick eyebrows and a splendid forehead. They have an expression, in nearly all the photographs which I have studied, of gentleness and friendliness that could most easily be captivating.

Herbert Ward, in his *Voice of the Congo* (Heinemann, 1910), says: 'Imagine a tall, handsome man, of fine bearing; thin, mere muscle and bone, a sun-tanned face, blue eyes and black curly hair. A pure Irishman he is, with a captivating voice and a singular charm of manner. A man of distinction and great refinement, high-minded and courteous, impulsive, poetical. Quixotic perhaps, some would say, and with a certain truth, for few men have shown themselves so regardless of personal advancement.'

E. D. Morel, writing in the London *Daily News*, of July 20th, 1912, had this: 'Tall, muscular, lithe, with a swing of the torso and limbs; chest thrown out, neck held high, suggestive of one who has lived long years in the vast open spaces. Jet black hair and beard covering cheeks hollowed out by tropical inroads, and a chin prominent, narrow and square. Strongly-marked features. A dark, penetrating eye, a little sunken in the socket. A long, lean, swarthy Vandyck type of face, graven with power and withal great gentleness. An extraordinarily handsome and arresting face. There you have only a bald outline. There is in the whole carriage and play of the man a something which would stamp him as distinctive and apart in any assembly; a something which speaks of pure metal and a soul almost primitive both in simplicity and strength, set in the frame of an athlete and seen through the outward trappings of a grave courtesy and perfect ease of manner. I have never known such personal magnetism emanate from any man. It is felt by all. Alike by the cultured statesman and cynical diplomatist of the West, and by the naked savage. It is not the physical gifts which are the primary cause, rather the mental unuttered conviction that is instantly formed that this man is the soul of honour, and has imbibed from his solitary communion with Nature an unerring faculty of distinguishing truth from falsehood.'

Although Casement was a clandestine pervert, he certainly looked anything but degenerate, and there was nothing effeminate about his manner or speech. Nor was there any vaunting of his secret passion, the Christensen affair excepted. Some years after Casement's death, Count Richard Koudenhove-Kalergi wrote this estimate of him for the late Prince Blücher: 'All I can say from personal experience and a long friendship is that I always found him most sympathetic, clever and fascinating; and that I have met very few men during my whole life who had such an exceptional personality. He was perfectly honest and true—from *his* point of view—without a trace of showing off or posing. He possessed an absolutely genuine but somewhat exaggerated idealism; nothing whatever would stop him assisting the weaker against the stronger, because he simply could not help it.'

Mr. G. Winthrop Young, the famous alpinist, who met Casement in the early years of this century, tells me, 'Casement was a word-spinner, a charmer. With his lovely, soft, beguiling voice, he would spin you castles in the air—celestial, rose-tinted, shimmering castles. And while he was speaking, you felt that little else mattered. But he was humourless—had absolutely no sense of fun.'

Casement enjoyed the close friendship of a number of women, but Miss Gertrude Bannister (later Mrs. Sidney Parry) and Mrs. Green were outstanding. These two devoted ladies never once failed him and it is impossible not to admire their loyalty and bitter-end attachment to him and his interests. Casement wrote to them both, sometimes twice daily, for years on end, and in those letters he poured out his fears and hopes, his fitfully glimpsed triumphs, and—more often—his frustrations and disappointments.

To such friends as Miss Bannister and Mrs. Green, the whispered suggestion of Casement's moral delinquency came as a frightful shock—a slander to be instantly and scornfully dismissed. One can only sympathise with them and applaud their devotion. There was no evident reason why these ladies should for a moment have harboured suspicions about the Hyde side of Casement's life.

Both are now dead; and so, to try to get the generous view typical of the ladies who knew Casement well and admitted him to close friendship, let us consider what Mrs. William A. Cadbury has to say about him (Wast Hills, Birmingham, January 1954): 'He was so gay, so sensitive, so light-hearted. And above all, so kind. He lived for and by kindness, and he said that he could never understand anyone else not being actuated by it. And once he said to me, "I wish that it were possible to hear nothing but the truth for one whole month—oh, what a different world it would be!"'

About the allegations of Casement's moral failings: 'He was such a high-minded, pure and gentle soul. There was never a coarse word or deed in all the years that we knew him. I am sure that if there had been anything remotely like that, we should have sensed it. He used to go for walks with me and the children, telling them fairy-stories in his wonderful brogue. He seemed like a good uncle.

'He was such a good man. I was with him a great deal when he was staying at Wast Hills, and William away working in Birmingham. He never, by the slightest hint of word or deed, suggested anything than the soul of honour and of proper conduct.'

Mrs. Cadbury recalls that John Harris, a Baptist missionary, later knighted for his work as an official of the Anti-Slavery Society, told her, soon after Casement's conviction, that he had been called in 'by the Home Office' and shown the diaries. 'It was in his own dear hand-writing,' Harris told Mrs. Cadbury. 'There can be no doubt of that. It was a most terrible shock.'

Had a breakdown in health, induced, as has so often been suggested, by his long sojourns in the tropics, any bearing on the tragic decisions taken in the last years of Casement's life? In talking to Casement's surviving friends, one often encounters, after the vehement denials of possible moral divagations, the inclination to suggest that just possibly his mentality had been warped as the result of the experiences to which he had been subjected in the Congo and the Putumayo and that he was 'broken in health and in mind'.

It is true that ill-health was finally accepted as the reason for his retirement from the Foreign Service. And it seems clear that in the 1913–14 period he was intermittently suffering from some sort of fever, which may well have been malaria. Kidney stone, appendicitis, and arthritis were also suggested, but these are maladies which can be encountered in those who have got no nearer the tropics than the cinema at the corner of the road. In spite of the talk of nervous exhaustion, we find Sir Lauder Brinton noting, 'Sleeps well. Slight headaches.' That is scarcely the description of a man on the edge of a nervous breakdown. There is no reason to think that Brinton's findings were other than disinterested.

However, Sir R. H. Bruce Lockhart, in his remarkable book, *Memoirs of a British Agent* (Putnam, 1932) says concerning the after-effects of malaria: 'It had left me with an impaired will-power and an unhealthy morbidness. If a certain amount of morbidity in the thoughts of a young man is normal, the lack of will-power, which is a characteristic reaction of tropical fevers, is serious and not easily remedied. I had no ambitions of any kind. . . .'

One of the men who knew Casement well was Bulmer Hobson.

He had been in the Irish Independence movement from his early days, and had ample opportunities for sizing up Casement. Hobson was a member of the Irish Republican Brotherhood, forerunner of Sinn Fein, and the fiery editor of *Irish Freedom*. To-day he lives in a charming cottage perched on the extreme western edge of Galway, a few miles past the village of Roundstone. The Hobson of to-day is a plump, greying man, red-faced and genial. He told me (Errisbeg West, November 14th, 1954): 'Casement was a highly sensitive man, and these horrors which he exposed made a great impression on him. He did not like to talk of the Congo or of the Putumayo.

'After the Putumayo ordeal, Casement developed terrible arthritis. And he was also psychologically shocked by the things which he had seen. He was a tremendously emotional man.

'There was never the slightest sign of perversion. No one who knew him ever believed a word of that. There was nothing of the sort. I knew him intimately for eleven years. We went for long walks together, talked and ate. He stayed with me. He had made up his mind that marriage could not fit in with an isolated, strange career such as he led. Many women fell in love with him, thanks to his fine appearance and great charm—but he did not respond. He felt that he could not ask any woman to share such a life as he led where, for months on end, he was off in the jungle, where no woman could possibly accompany him.'

There followed from Mr. Hobson the familiar and obviously sincere tributes—to Casement's generosity, his friendliness and his sensitiveness.

It is undeniable that many people who encountered Casement felt all of this about him: his greatness, his charm, his beguiling quality. Above all—that he was a rare individual.

Three groups of people seem signally not to have felt thus: the Irish-Americans; the Irish prisoners in Germany; the Germans. How is one to account for this?

I, who should have been able only with difficulty to read much of what he wrote, have with regret to place on record the fact that the greatness, the extraordinary qualities, the shining virtues which were evidently felt by those who met him in person, do not emerge in his writings.

And of his writings there are vast troves. The man was a fountain of written words. His output was prodigious. Letters—eleven, twelve, twenty pages—were a commonplace. He poured them out to friends and acquaintances, to anybody and everybody. He sent them to whatever allies offered themselves in the latest crusade. He slung them at the Foreign Office, whipped them off to the Press. And there was the constant flow to his relatives. In the Putumayo he not only kept voluminous official diaries, in addition to writing to all the friends and family with whom he normally corresponded, but he also kept the Black Diaries going as a side-line. There were draft reports, memoranda, drafts of speeches, articles for the newspapers, and a spate of patriotic poems, which I confess I have no more than dipped into, since they strike me as painfully mediocre. In jail he wrote the most considerable briefs for his Counsel, whether expected or not, and maintained a correspondence, to the limit of what was allowed, with the outside world. For sheer writing fecundity, the man was a marvel.

But the style is irritating and immensely redundant. If Casement can make seven words do the work of one—be sure that he will. He has the tiresome habit of underlining many words. He sprinkles his letters with masses of notes of exclamation. He dotes on the interpolated 'God willing!' which is often shortened to 'D.V!' There is a sort of verbal posturing running through all. He is forever playing everything to the top of its bent, and indeed beyond. Huge enthusiasm is there, of course, but it seems all too seldom to be tempered by cool sagacity; and I can find very little originality of phrase, or arresting revelation of a mind to match the great esteem which he so often evoked. He was, I regret to say, verbose and boring. He was also embarrassingly vain. 'They cheered and cheered and cheered me!' 'They are praising me to the skies.' 'I had to appeal for silence to speak before they would stop cheering me.'

There are frequent relapses into the facetious ('Au reservoir', he writes at the end of one letter), and Gertrude Bannister, whom he normally addresses as 'Dear Gee', or 'Dear Wee Gee', was once greeted as 'Ye Geelets' and assured that 'All goeth exceeding well'. Sometimes there is a 'dear cheeyild' thrown in, and once the hope that 'this will amoose yer'. He bombarded Mrs. Green with a succession of droll openings—'Dear Woman of Three Cows', 'Dear Woman of the Ships', and so on. He signed his letters to Miss Bannister 'Scrodgie' and occasionally 'The O'Scrodge'. (In the period when all was well between Morel and Casement, Morel signed his letters 'Bulldog' and Casement responded with 'Tiger'.)

There is almost never a leavening of real humour in all of this vast correspondence; virtually never a whiff of wit. There is a great deal of self-pity, occasional signs of instability, and a general desire to see things bettered in various places and directions. I suppose that a later generation of Americans might have described Casement as 'a starry-eyed do-gooder'.

As has been shown, Casement was openly in much of his correspondence before 1914 hoping and working for the defeat of England and the victory of Germany in the war which he was sure was coming. The Foreign Office, for at least a decade, appears not to have known of their representative's moral delinquency, which is perhaps excusable, for it was well hidden; but that the Foreign Office should have remained in ignorance of his anti-British and pro-German sentiments, and of the fact that, under various *noms-de-guerre*, he was writing anti-British articles, seems strange.

After this prolonged ignoring of their man's treasonable intentions by one British Government department, another, the Home Office, seems to have acted with exceptional harshness over small details once the man was dead.

At the inquest in Pentonville, Gavan Duffy announced that he had applied to the Home Office on behalf of Miss Bannister for permission to have the body. 'I think,' he roundly declared, 'that it is a monstrous act of indecency that they have refused the request.'

This was but the first of a long series of such requests. Sir

Ernley Blackwell, of whose methods and manner we have already seen something, turned down the request on the ground that the law required that the bodies of all men executed within a prison be buried within the prison precincts. Duffy asked to know what law was being referred to? Blackwell rejoined that he was referring to Section No. 6 of the Capital Punishment Amendment Act of 1868. Gavan Duffy in his turn replied that the Act of 1868 applies to the corpses of murderers only.

But his renewed pleas that a grievous wrong had been done in withholding the remains of Casement from his family went unrewarded. So did those of the late Brigadier-General J. H. Morgan, Sullivan's adviser at the trial. Here is the telling letter which the then Mr. Morgan sent to Herbert Samuel, the Home Secretary.

'1 Mitre Court Buildings,
Temple, E.C.
4 August, 1916

Dear Mr. Samuel: The day before yesterday I called at the House of Commons to see you in order to support the request of Miss Gertrude Bannister that the body of Roger Casement might be handed over to her for private burial. I did this because I was deeply moved by the distress of a noble woman whose unflinching devotion to her cousin through the long-drawn agony of his trial was such as to provoke my profound admiration and regret. I did not—indeed as counsel, I could not—support the movement for reprieve. But he has paid the full penalty—he has not only died a felon's death on the scaffold, but before dying he was publicly degraded of all his honours, a step for which I believe there is no precedent in any treason case in the last 300 years. The law has therefore exacted its uttermost.

'Under these circumstances it is surely not asking too much to ask that the pitiful request of his relatives be granted. Roger Casement is now beyond the reach of human vengeance; it cannot matter to him whether his body remains in a felon's grave in Pentonville or not. But it matters a great deal to this unhappy lady, sorrowing under a sorrow almost too grievous for any man or woman to bear. I cannot conceive any petition which it would be easier for the authorities to grant and harder for any humane person to refuse. It is not for me to urge any question of policy, though I can imagine few things more likely to exasperate Irish opinion than an implacable severity which wounds the living while it is quite powerless to harm the dead. Moreover there is a very strong opinion abroad—*The Times* gives expression to it this morning—that someone in authority "inspired" a campaign of malignant and studied calumny against the prisoner which was not only not necessary to the course of justice but calculated to pervert it. It is surely highly undesirable that any impression of ruthlessness should get abroad?

'But be that as it may, I do beg of you on grounds of humanity to reconsider your decision. Miss Bannister is, I understand, prepared to give every guarantee as to privacy.'

This letter from the man who was later to be an adviser to Mr. Churchill must have been difficult to sweep aside on any grounds, legalistic, practical, or even humanitarian. Yet Mr. Samuel, who was later to go on to triumphs in Palestine and India, saw fit, on behalf of a Liberal government, not to grant the 'pitiful request'.

Over small points as well as large the Home Office was not, in August 1916, magnanimous. On August 16th, William Cadbury received this letter from Sir Ernley Blackwell:

'Home Office, Whitehall, Aug. 16, 1916

To W. A. Cadbury, Esq.

Sir: With reference to your letter of 7th instant, I am directed by the Secretary of State to transmit to you herewith a copy of portions of the letter addressed to you by Roger Casement on the 26th July last, and to say that he cannot send you the remainder of the letter, which is purely propagandist in character and contains statements which contravene Regulation 27 of the Defence of the Realm Regulations.

I am, Sir,
Your obedient servant,
E. Blackwell.'

What was left of Casement's letter read:

'My dear William:

Mrs. Green told me of your and Emmeline's letters. I thank you both (Deletions by order of Sir E. Blackwell).

I thank you and Emmeline from the bottom of my heart—you have been like a brother and sister to me. Farewell, dear gentle hearts (Deletions by order of Sir E. Blackwell).

Please help the schoolchildren at Carraroe, for my poor sake. I failed in that trust, alas!—but hope still to make it good through others' help. My dear love and affection to you, dear, honest, faithful and affectionate friend—to you and to Emmeline—and my love to tender-hearted John and the children. And so farewell.

I have been very sad the last few days, sad with myself, but am better to-day.

Good-bye,

Roger.'

One wonders if it is possible that the matter cut from this letter can have contained anything of moment which Casement did not cover in his final speech in open court.

'Purely propagandist in character.' I have greatly regretted since I started to write this book, the fact that so many of the protagonists in the Casement story are now dead. I especially regret the death of Sir Ernley Blackwell. I should have so much enjoyed putting a few questions to this outstandingly conscientious official.

At intervals during the past quarter of a century discreet requests have been made by the authorities in Eire for the return of Casement's remains to Ireland. One of the last such requests was made in the autumn of 1953, when Mr. De Valera came to London. The request met with no success.

In May 1935 the late Mr. J. W. Dulanty, then Ireland's popular High Commissioner in London, wrote to Mrs. Parry (the former Miss Bannister) at Cushenden, telling her that there was a rumour going round in London that Pentonville was to be razed, and that he had taken the opportunity of discussing with Sir John Gilmour, then the Home Secretary, and Mr. J. H. Thomas, then

Dominions Secretary, the possibility of Casement's remains being transferred to Dublin. Dulanty reported in this letter that Gilmour had told him that he thought that no British Government had the power—apart from any question of inclination—to accede to such a request. Mr. Dulanty added in his letter that Gilmour might be leaving the Home Office soon, and that if a rumour as to his successor were true, a more sympathetic reception might be forthcoming from the new incumbent. At that time Dulanty officially advised the Irish President to make no further move about the return of Casement's remains until it was seen whether there would in fact be changes at the Home and Dominions Offices. Whether the eventual changes were the ones which Dulanty expected, the newcomers apparently proved no more tractable in the matter than had their predecessors.

The repeated Irish pleas for the return of Casement's remains— and it would be the most symbolic of gestures, since his body was dropped into quicklime almost as soon as the inquest was finished— are based, of course, on emotion. England's refusals are based on 'policy' and the dry letter of the law. One can see both sides of the question—hear the arguments almost before they are uttered. The bureaucratic dread of 'creating a precedent' looms large. If you were to allow the corpse of a single convicted felon to be transferred out of Pentonville, especially a felon convicted of high treason, the worst crime known to British law, what can you say to the distraught mother or wife of the next man to be hanged there for the lesser crime of murder?

Yet Casement's is a story so wildly different from those of other men hanged in Pentonville, that one wonders if it should not now be allowed to end differently too. The body of no other traitor has ever been officially claimed from Britain by a friendly government; claimed not once, but repeatedly. It is perhaps worth recalling that Major André, the English officer during the American war of the revolution, who was hanged by the Americans as a spy, lies now in an honoured tomb in Westminster Abbey.

Nearly forty years have passed since Casement expiated his crime. Perhaps it is time to declare a statute of limitations on the crimes committed by the dead. All passion is long spent. Soon the last men who knew Casement will be gone and the story of Casement will be itself only a yellowing page in history. Can we not agree to end it all on a note of magnanimity?

While he lived, Casement's story was one of almost constant frustration and failure. After the Putumayo very little went right for him. The British, the Germans, the Irish-Americans—none of them thought very much of Casement. In Ireland itself he was barely known. His thoughts, as he mounted the scaffold, must have been dark.

And yet he did not die altogether in vain. In his own strange, confused and characteristically inefficient way, he was a patriot. He did his best for Ireland.

Only five years after he was hanged, Ireland in 1921 gained the independence which she had fought for and longed for so ardently through several centuries. Roger Casement longed for it too. And in his own strange fumbling fashion, he did his best to get it.

Let him have the credit for having played his part in the attaining of his country's freedom.

APPENDIX I

BARRINGTON, Sir (Bernard) Eric, was born in 1847 and educated at Eton. He entered the Foreign Office in 1867, and was Private Secretary to Lord Salisbury from 1887–92 and from 1895–1900. He served Lord Lansdowne in the same capacity from 1900–05. In 1906 he became Assistant Under Secretary of State for Foreign Affairs, before retiring in 1907. He died in 1918.

DEVOY, John, was the acknowledged leader of all the Irish revolutionary associations in the U.S.A.; he edited the *Gaelic-American* during the 1914–18 war. He was the chief link in the U.S. for communication between the Germans and Sinn Fein, and Bernstorff regarded him as Germany's 'best confidential agent' in America.

DILKE, Sir Charles, born 1843. Entered the House of Commons with advanced radical views in 1868, promptly attacked the Civil List. Became Under Secretary for Foreign Affairs in a Gladstone government, 1880–82. A notorious divorce action caused his temporary retirement from politics but he re-entered the House of Commons in 1892, and was outstanding in the movement for such innovations as the municipal enfranchisement of women.

GUINESS, The Rev. Dr. H. Grattan, was the founder and Director of the 'Regions Beyond Missionary Society' with headquarters at Harley House, Bow Road, London.

HOBSON, Bulmer, was born in Holywood, Co. Down, about eighty-five years ago. He became a publisher in Dublin, and was associated with the Irish revolutionary movement from his early years. In 1910 was editor of *Irish Freedom*, an extreme Nationalist publication, and Dublin Correspondent of Devoy's *Gaelic-American*. Later became successively member of the Provisional Committee, General Secretary and Quarter-Master of the Irish Volunteers, and vice-president of Fianna Eireann. He opposed the 1916 rising, sharing Casement's opinion that it was doomed to fail, and was kidnapped by order of the Military Council. After the civil war he held the post of head of the Stamp Duty Office. He now lives in retirement in Galway.

HORGAN, John J., is a distinguished solicitor, who has for several decades past been a Coroner in Cork. In that capacity he performed the inquests on the corpses of victims recovered after the *Lusitania* was torpedoed and sunk by a U-boat off the Old Head of Kinsale, in May 1915.

JOYCE, William, was born in New York in 1906 (his father was a naturalised American citizen). In his youth the family moved to the U.K. and William Joyce applied for a British Passport, declaring in his application that he was a British subject. The passport was issued and he subsequently renewed it twice. During the 1939–45 war Joyce was known to millions of people in Britain as 'Lord Haw-Haw', as a result of his pro-Nazi broadcasts from Germany, in which he adopted a languid, stage-Englishman's accent. He was tried for treason in 1945; the defence contended that he was a U.S. citizen. But owing to his British passport Sir Hartley Shawcross, prosecuting, said 'Joyce left the country wrapped up in the Union Jack and must take the logical consequences'. He was found guilty and hanged.

MACDONALD, Major-General Sir Hector Archibald, K.C.B., D.S.O., G.O.C. Ceylon, from 1901. Born 1853, enlisted 92nd (afterwards Gordon Highlanders) in 1870. He was present at the Battle of Kandahar where he was awarded a medal and three clasps and was promoted 2nd Lieut. Fought in the Afghan War; accompanied Sir F. Roberts on march to Kabul; fought at Majuba Hill, 1881; capture of Tokar, 1891 and many other campaigns. Became Colonel 1898. Was successively Honorary A.D.C. to Queen Victoria and to Edward VII. He received the formal thanks of Parliament after the Boer War, where he had commanded the Highland Brigade from 1899–1901. He was recalled to London in the spring of 1903, and while on his way back to Ceylon, where he knew a court martial awaited him on charges of homosexuality, committed suicide in Paris.

MOREL, Edmund D., M.P. (Lab., Dundee) from 1922; Secretary and part-founder Union of Democratic Control, Editor *Foreign Affairs*.

Born 1873, son of Edmond Morel-de-Ville, married, four sons, one daughter. Educated Eastbourne. Editor *West African Mail* for a decade. Wrote pamphlets and books attacking misrule in Africa, among them *Red Rubber, The Black Man's Burden, Leopold's Rule in the Congo*. Founder Congo Reform Association, 1904, visited U.S.A. to inaugurate similar movement. Member of the West African Lands Committee (Colonial Office) 1912–14. Came under bitter attack during 1914–18 war as a pacifist and pro-German by opponents of the Union of Democratic Control. Died 1924.

MORGAN, Brigadier-General John Hartman, K.C., M.A., D.L. Born 1876, Staff *Daily Chronicle* 1901–3, *Manchester Guardian* 1904–5; Home Office Commissioner with B.E.F. 1914–15 (Mentioned in Despatches); AAG Military Section Paris Peace Conference, 1919; Inter-Allied Military Commission of Control in Germany 1919–23; Reader in Constitutional Law to the Inns of Court, 1926–36; Advised Churchill on Constitutional Law during the 1939–45 war; was Hon. Adviser to the U.S. War Crimes Commission at Nuremberg, 1947; participated in the trial of William Joyce. Legal Editor of the *Encyclopedia Britannica*, and Emeritus Professor of Constitutional Law in the University of London at the time of his death in 1955.

PEACE, Charles. At the close of the last century his name was synonymous with callous brutality. He was born in Sheffield in 1832, he received his first sentence for burglary at the age of 19, and thereafter, while posing as a picture-framer and gilder by day, pursued persistent campaigns of burglary after nightfall. In 1876 he murdered a policeman but escaped. Later that year he shot dead Arthur Dyson, the husband of a woman on whom he was pressing his attentions. He changed his name, went to Peckham and was arrested in October 1878, after he had fired several revolver shots during an attempted house-breaking at Blackheath. While he was serving sentence at Pentonville for attempted murder, the authorities realised that he was the man who had killed Dyson. He was transferred to Sheffield for trial, found guilty, and hanged at Leeds on February 25th, 1879.

STANLEY, Sir Henry Morton, was born John Rowlands at Denbigh, North Wales, in 1841. He emigrated to New Orleans at 17, and there gratefully assumed the name of the man who gave him his first job;

he served in the American Civil War, entered journalism, and became war correspondent for the *New York Herald*. In 1871, having tracked down and greeted Doctor Livingstone, the missing explorer, at Ujiji on Lake Tanganyika, he was himself attracted to explore Africa and later was knighted for his work in this field. He was M.P. for North Lambeth from 1895-1900. He died in 1904.

THOMSON, Sir Basil, born 1861, son of an Archbishop of York. Educated Eton and New College, married, two sons and a daughter. While in the Colonial Service he acted as Prime Minister of Tonga. He was successively Governor of Dartmoor, Assistant Commissioner of Police, 1913-19, Director of Intelligence, 1919-21. His seventeen books included *The Diversions of a Prime Minister*. He died in 1939.

In 1925 Thomson and a woman with whom he had been sitting were arrested in Hyde Park. He was found guilty of committing an act in violation of public decency and was fined £5 and £5 costs, also forfeiting his original recognisances of £5. This finding was upheld on appeal. Thomson's defence was that he had gone to the Park to find a certain Communist speaker, and to gain firsthand material for a book he was writing, called *The Police and the Public*. Character witnesses included Vice-Admiral Sir William Hall, M.P. and Mr. Reginald McKenna, a former Home Secretary. The Magistrate rendered his verdict 'with regret'.

TYRRELL, 1st Baron (cr. 1929) of Avon, P.C., G.C.B., G.C.M.G., K.C.V.O., President of the Board of Film Censors from 1935. Born 1866, son of a Judge of the High Courts of Judicature, N.W. Frontier of India; married and had one daughter. Educated Balliol; entered Foreign Office 1889; secretary to the Imperial Defence Committee, 1903-4; Senior Clerk in the Foreign Office 1905-15 and Private Secretary to Sir Edward Grey, 1907-15. Permanent Under Secretary at the Foreign Office 1925-28; Ambassador to France, 1928-34. Died in 1947.

Casement held Tyrrell in high regard till the end; thus when he was brought to London after his arrest on the Irish coast in 1916, the first thing he asked on arriving at Scotland Yard was whether he might see Tyrrell. Sir Basil Thomson refused the request.

APPENDIX II

Suggestions concerning the treatment of the Irish Brigade. See pages 183-4.

Having dealt with the question of the band, a flag, and new quarters, the agent goes on:

'Until recruitment has been completed, postal deliveries must either be stopped with regard to *all* prisoners in the camp, or else a very strict censorship must be introduced. At present, letters—allegedly with the help of the French working in the parcels delivery office—are hidden in newspapers and smuggled. As they contain mendacious information, they make propaganda among the Irish almost impossible.

'The greatest influence over an Irishman is exercised by his priest. Father Crotty, who has been sent from Rome, desires, if the Brigade develops satisfactorily, to be appointed its military chaplain. He is a staunch Irish patriot and would, as would also his superior authorities in Rome, welcome the creation of the Irish Brigade with the greatest pleasure imaginable. But in conformity with his pastoral status, he cannot at present make propaganda for it. Once it is formed, he will be most useful. Father Nicholson, the other priest, makes open propaganda.

'An important side would be, in due course, to bring in a few suitable Irish officers from America.

'When the right moment comes, the news of the formation of the Irish Brigade, and the text of the agreement concerning the Brigade between Sir Roger Casement and the German Government, should be published simultaneously by newspapers throughout America. The Irish newspapers should carry inflammatory articles, and photographs of the Irish Brigade in their new uniforms, with the Irish flag flying, and Sir Roger Casement standing in front. The impression in America would be tremendous, let alone Ireland

'Considerable sums of money will no doubt be raised in the U.S.A. on behalf of the Irish Brigade. John Devoy, Robert E. Ford, John F. Kelly and others will see to the widest possible circulation of propaganda concerning the Brigade, including in Ireland itself. John Devoy, the leader of the group around the *Gaelic-American*, is the most embittered, mortal enemy of England.

'Robert E. Ford is the publisher of the *Irish World*, the most influential, the most anti-English and pro-German Irish organ in America. His father, Patrick Ford, was the bugbear of the English Parliament; both Tories and Liberals hated and feared him. He collected 4 million marks in the U.S.A. and Canada and sent the money to Ireland in order to maintain there a party free from any English influence. Robert E. Ford will support any attempt to liberate Ireland from the English yoke.

'John E. Kelly, a highly educated and distinguished Irishman married to a German, is the author of many anti-English and pro-German articles in the American newspapers. He is a born leader and willing to help in word and deed. His sister, Dr. Gertrude B. Kelly, the President of the United Irishwomen of America, is very anti-English. She is intelligent and energetic, has connexions with many influential people in New York and throughout America and also enjoys a high reputation in Ireland.

'Dr. Edward A. Rumely is of German origin, rich and independent, acquainted with the most distinguished people in America, and has a talent for publicity. At present he has special copies of the *Irish-American*, whose co-publisher he is, printed and distributed among the Catholic clergy in America, Canada and Ireland; among teachers and professors in Catholic schools, influential Catholic politicians and all Catholic newspapers. The latter, especially the weeklies—some of which are widely distributed and read—are not to be under-estimated for propaganda purposes. They represent a large, ready-made propaganda machine which can, at little cost, be made useful to the Irish-Catholics and thereby to the cause of friendly Germany. There are many Germans among the Catholic priests who are directors of such newspapers or who write for them, such as the Rev. Peter E. Dietz, who is now well-known everywhere, and others. Here there is a wide field of action which can be made very useful through Rumely's intervention.

'The above mentioned people are all known to me personally; I have discussed with them the problem of Irish-German relations and I am confident of their fullest support; further connexions can be developed through them.

'Pressure should be brought to bear on American newspapers by

317

unions of Germans and Irish in every town, and systematic boycotts of all newspapers save the friendly ones, which would then receive all the benefits, such as advertising, etc.

'It might also be considered whether the activity of the Press could not be backed by a lecture tour, undertaken by Irish speakers of ability (entrance free) throughout the U.S.A. Seamus McManus, at present one of the outstanding Irish authors and a fiery Anglophobe, with whom I had a conversation in January, would either undertake the tour in person or else recommend someone suitable to do so.

'The English should be prevented from buying up the *Irish World*, Robert Ford's newspaper. Financial backing for its present ownership might be considered.

'Shipment of newspapers to Ireland, financial support for Irish Nationalist editors, and the shipment of arms and the sending of officers (from America) might also be considered.

'BOEHM,
'*First Lieutenant.*'

Soon afterwards Boehm was promoted to Captain—but then his luck turned. In October 1916, Bernstorff sent a petulant message to Berlin asking that 'Reserve Captain Boehm may be directed by his superiors to send no further letters to Irishmen here. His letters only endanger their undertakings, especially as they are sometimes addressed to the wrong people.'

Finally Boehm was captured by the Royal Navy while cruising about off Falmouth, on some mission of his own in the spring of 1917, and interned for the rest of the war.

APPENDIX III
[See page 283]

In his biography of Admiral Sir Reginald Hall (*The Eyes of the Navy*, Methuen, 1955) Admiral Sir William James, who worked with Hall in the Admiralty's famous 'Room 40', where the intercepted German naval and political wireless messages were decyphered and decoded in the 1914 war, states that he has no doubt that Hall was responsible for circulating the extracts from the diary, after having received it from Basil Thomson. This statement, after four decades of speculation, is ostensibly based on the fact that Hall did not dispute the allegations contained in *The Forged Casement Diaries* by the late W. J. Moloney (Talbot Press, Dublin, 1937). This book was mainly pro-Casement propaganda and it is not, to me, at all surprising that Hall preferred not to answer the allegations contained in it. Since Admiral James admired the late Admiral Hall it seemed to me that, since he made an allegation which does not especially redound to the credit of his old chief, he must have had something more to go on. Accordingly I wrote to him asking for more information. Sir William's replies were courteous and helpful, and there is now left in my mind no doubt but that he had strong grounds for making his statement. Sir William felt obliged to 'pin' the allegation on the Moloney book. In fact he was and is quite certain, from other sources, that it was Hall who took the decision. In defence of his old chief, Sir William makes the point that during total war even decent civilised men will do things from which in peace time they would shrink. Casement, Hall felt, had tried to create an Irish bloodbath, had tried to bring about sabotage in the U.S.A., had tried to induce Irish soldiers to fight alongside the Turks; therefore he should not escape hanging. Hall was a tough courageous man who never flinched from shouldering the most terrifying responsibilities if he was sure that in so doing he could aid the war effort. Therefore, to have decided to circulate the Casement diaries on his own responsibility is entirely in character. A lesser man would never have done it.

We are left to wonder what was the Cabinet reaction to this startling decision. Admiral James says in his book that he thinks that one reason why Hall received no honour when peace came was because in circulating the diaries, Hall was thought to have gone too far.

It should be noted that Admiral Hall's son, Commander R. A. Hall, R.N. (retd.), tells me that the allegation in Admiral James's book concerning his father and the Casement diaries came as a shock to him.

Following publication of Admiral James's book, there took place a correspondence about the diaries and their use, in the *New Statesman and Nation*. Mr. Bulmer Hobson, as was to be expected, rallied loyally to the memory of his old friend, and produced the familiar arguments on the other side; that the diary was not Casement's but Normand's; that the diary was copied and circulated although the British Government knew that Casement was not the author, and so on.

Neither Mr. Hobson, nor Mr. Gerald Hamilton, who also did his best to defend Casement, appears to have the slightest knowledge of what might be described as the reporter's approach to such matters. Mr. Hamilton talks airily of the diary being 'found on Casement when he landed from the German submarine at Tralee', and Mr. Hobson himself seems to be under the impression that the dirty diaries dealt only with the Putumayo, or at most, the Putumayo and the Congo.

What gives them these notions? Have they ever tried to visualise what these diaries and account books look like physically? Has it ever occurred to them that they may cover a period of far more than a decade? That they may cover episodes taking place not only in the Putumayo and Congo—but also in London, Denham, Belfast, Dublin, Las Palmas, Pará, Lisbon, on the high seas, on the Amazon; in fact, wherever Casement went in the period from the turn of the century until just before the 1914 war? How could Casement have come ashore from the U-boat with all that on him? He would have needed an extra man to carry it all.

In the correspondence to which I allude, it was variously stated that copies of the diaries were shown to President Wilson, Pope Pius and the then U.S. Ambassador to Britain, Walter Hines Page. I note this as a matter of interest—I did not myself know that these public figures were among the scrutineers.

Finally, Mr. Hobson alleges that Sir F. E. Smith had the photographs 'ready in his pocket', during Casement's trial, 'and when the court adjourned, he was running about in the corridors, thrusting them into the unwilling hands of people attending the trial.'

This I find an unconvincing picture.

INDEX

Gordon, Lt.-Col., 241
Gorman, Mary, 203, 205, 255
Gosselin, Sir Martin, 26
Graeff, Gen. de, 155, 180
Graham, Cunninghame, 42
Grantully Castle, 110
Green, Mrs. Alice S. A., 10, 49–51, 55, 58, 69, 70, 71, 72, 83, 85, 95, 96, 108, 110, 111, 112, 114, 121, 125, 126, 129, 132, 134, 135, 136, 137, 153, 215, 216, 218, 225, 230, 246, 253, 270, 272, 273, 274, 275, 302, 306
Green, J. R., 50
Gregory, J. D., 158
Grey, Sir Edward, 66, 67, 68, 69, 72, 83, 87, 96, 97–8, 99, 103, 104, 108, 137, 143, 165, 169, 170, 174, 177, 253–4, 276
Griffiths, Arthur, 58 n.
Guiness, the Rev. D. H. Grattan, 42, 45, 56, 65, 312
Gwynn, Denis, 47, 279, 282

Haldane, Viscount, 108
Hall, Captain R. (later Admiral Sir Reginald), 214, 223, 224, 289–90, 319, 320
Hall, Vice-Admiral Sir William, M.P., 315
Hamburg-Amerika Line, 124, 125, 126
Hamilton, Duke and Duchess of, 100
Hamilton, Gerald, 320
Harris, John, 68, 303
Haugwitz, Graf von, 198
Hayes, Dr. R. J., 10
Healy, Tim, 226
Henson, Rev. (later Bishop) Hensley, 104–5, 280
Herne, Sgt., 205, 206, 259
Heuston, J. J., 220 n.
Heydell, Capt., 198
Hindenburg, General, 152
Hobson, Bulmer, 11, 30 n., 57, 58, 64, 86 n., 117, 120, 126, 127, 129, 303–4, 312–13, 320

Home Rule, 103, 115, 116, 118
Hone, Mr., 233
Horgan, John J., 11, 124, 125, 313
Horridge, Mr. Justice, 245, 250, 260
Horst, Baron von, 124, 125, 126
Howth incident, 132, 133
Hoy, T. G., 168, 169
Humphreys, Travers, 228, 238

Igel, W. von, 194, 200, 213
Inge, Dean, 280
International Association of the Congo, 15
Iquitos, 81, 84, 85, 88, 96, 100, 101, 102
I.R.A. (Dublin), 188
'Ireland and the German Menace' (Casement), 114
Irish-American, The, 317
Irish Brigades: Boer, 75; Limburg, etc., 149, 150, 156, 162, 165, 166, 170, 178, 180, 182, 183, 184, 187, 189, 190, 238, 241–2, 299, 316–18. *See* Limburg
Irish Freedom, 114–15, 304, 312
Irish Independent, 136, 254
Irish Republican Brotherhood, 117, 304
Irish Review, 114, 127
Irish Volunteers, 117, 121, 132, 134, 136, 208, 209, 210, 212, 312
Irish World, 317, 318

Jagow, Herr von, 149, 156, 159
James, Admiral Sir W., 319–20
Jameson, Dr., 21
Jephson, Anne, 13
Jimenez, 86, 102
Joll, James, 10
Jones, Artemus, 227, 251, 260, 261
Joyce, William, 313, 314
Joynson-Hicks, Sir William, 283

Kearney, H. Const., 208
Keating, John P., 191
Kelly, Bryan, 166
Kelly, Dr. Gertrude, 317

Morel-de-Ville, Edmond, 314
Morgan, Professor J. H., 108, 225, 227, 251–2, 270, 307, 314
Morning Post, 78
Morton, Richard, 41, 47, 65, 82, 205, 225, 229
Mosley, Sir O. and Lady C., 106 n.
Muhlig, Dr., 183 n.
Muller, Walter, 144, 145
Mullins, William, 212
Mystery of the Casement Ship (Spindler), 232

Nadolny, Capt., 181, 187, 190, 194, 195
National African Company, 18
National Liberal Federation, 122
National Library of Ireland (Dublin), 230, 276
Nevinson, H. W., 109, 225, 246
New Statesman and Nation, 233, 320
New York, 129, 130 *seqq.*
New York Herald, 315
Nicholson, the Rev. J. T., 151, 161, 166, 170, 179, 180, 181, 316
Nicolson, Arthur, 136
Nightingale, Florence, 50
Nile, 69
Nisco, Baron, 52, 53
'No Conscription Fellowship', 221
Noegerrath, Herr, 195
Norbury, Lord, 65
Normand, Armando, 86, 86 n. 87, 89, 92, 93, 281, 320
Northbourne, Lord, 59
Northcliffe, Lord, 106, 107
Noyes, Alfred, 11, 279–80

Oberndorff, Herr von, 141, 151, 167, 167 n.
O'Brien, Daniel, 240
O'Connor, Michael, 242
O'Connor, T. P., 129
O'Farelly, Miss, 230
O'Gorman, Father, 151, 155
O'Hanrahan, M., 220 n.

O'Hegerty, P. S., 57, 86 n.
Old Bailey, 250 *seqq.*
O'Leary, Jeremiah, 191
Olifiers, Z. N. G., 230 n.
Oppenheim, Professor, 182 n.
O'Rell, Max, 70

Page, Walter Hines, 320
Paget, Sir Arthur, 118 n.
Papen, F. von, 149
Pará, 74, 75, 76, 77 *seqq.*, 83
Parker, Det. Insp., 238
Parminter, 81, 114
Parmiter, G. de C., 283
Parnell, C. S., 116
Parry, Sidney, 225, 230, 296, 302, 309
Peace, Charles, 71, 314
Pearse, Patrick, 121, 209, 212, 220 n., 222
Pearse, William, 220 n.
'*Peasant, The*', 70
Pentonville, 64, 226, 269 *seqq.*, 293, 296, 306, 307, 310
Percy, Lord, 41
Peruvian-Amazon Co. (prev. Arana), 89, 90, 95, 98
Pétain, 221
Phipps, Sir Constantine, 52, 53, 54, 55, 56, 62 n.
Pius XI, Pope, 320
Pless, Princess of, 153, 160, 186
Plunkett, Count, 184
Plunkett, Joseph, 114, 184, 184 n., 195, 220 n.
Police and the Public, The (Thomson), 315
Ponsonby, Arthur, 273
Public Record Office (London), 10, 291
Pulteney, Major, 22
Purser, Sara, 112
Putumayo (region and report), 80 *seqq.*, 87 *seqq.*, 102–5, 107, 129, 151, 245, 280, 285–9, 303, 304, 311, 320

Quinn, John, 130, 134, 279
Quinn, Superintendent, 214

United States of America, 31, 45, 78, 81, 95, 103, 119–20, 124, 125, 126, 127, 130 *seqq.*, 148–50, 157, 173, 174, 177, 179, 186, 187, 188, 191, 192 *seqq.*, 221–2, 252, 274, 275, 276, 288, 310

Valera, Eamonn de, 309
Vansittart, A. G., 73, 75
Victor Napoleon, Prince, 29

Walther, Oberleut., 198
Wangermée, E., 34, 39
Ward, Herbert, 106, 293, 300
Ward, Humphry, 50
Washington, 103, 192, 193, 213, 275
Wedel, Count G. von, 151, 154, 156, 157, 162, 163 n., 165, 166, 167, 168, 169, 177, 178, 180, 182, 184, 187, 194, 196
Weldon, Bishop, 95
West African Lands Committee, 314
West African Mail, 33, 314
Wet, Gen. C. de, 140, 277, 298
Wiegand, K. von, 175
Wilhelm, Kaiser, 149, 169
Wilson, James, 240
Wilson, President, 135, 320
Winchester, Bishop of, 275
Woledge, M. G., 10

Young, G. Winthrop, 301

Zangwill, Israel, 275
Zegarra, Alfred, 94
Zimmermann, 146, 164, 182, 187, 194